SCARLETT'S STORY

Other Books in this Series
The Amethyst Necklace (2020)

Scarlett's Story

Susan Griffin

First Published in Great Britain 2021 by Tanzanite Press.

ISBN: 978-1-8382742-1-4

Cover Art by: Berni Stevens Book Cover Design.

For Shaun

Thank you for your never-ending support.

Prologue

December 1918

The cold snaked down my back as I shivered in the early morning air while pulling my threadbare cardigan tighter around my shoulders. My eyes were drawn to the fireplace where the grate lay empty and bare, and I realised I had forgotten what it felt like to be warm.

The sound of the door opening jolted me out of my sombre thoughts, and I went quickly into the small, dark hallway to see Da disappearing out of the front door. He had gone out as usual, without saying goodbye, but I was used to that; these days he barely noticed me at all.

I opened the door, feeling like a ship adrift on the open sea with no sail as I watched him hurry down the street without a backward glance. My hands were clammy, despite being able to see my breath in front of my face, and my heart thudded as I remembered how I'd waited patiently for him to come home from the war.

During that dark time, Belle had looked after me as best she could, making me feel better by hugging me close and telling me everything would be fine once

Da returned. She reminded me of Mama, the way she used to comfort me in the middle of the night after a nightmare. But I soon learnt that Belle had lied, because everything was not fine when Da arrived home from the war.

The coldness running down my spine now seemed to be telling me I must shout loudly after Da and tell him to come back, but the words wouldn't come. They were stuck in my throat and refused to leave my mouth.

Suddenly I made a decision and, grabbing my coat, I followed my father out of the door. But instead of heading towards Brighton beach where his little fishing boat was moored, I ran full pelt towards the graveyard, where my instinct told me he was more likely to be found.

Breathlessly, I stopped at the wrought iron gates, my chest aching and the crisp morning air biting viciously into my face. Squinting across at the many gravestones which stood out at different angles in the ground, I saw his stooped figure standing alone in the distance.

After pushing the creaky gate open, I walked quickly along the path towards him, pulling my coat around me to keep out the cold. As I got nearer, Da must have heard me approaching, but he didn't look up. Instead he kept his eyes cast down, as if frozen to the spot.

Taking my courage in my hands, I took a long, deep breath. 'Da, what you doing here?' I asked, trying not to incur his wrath, and knowing full well what the answer would be. 'Please, won't you come home?'

Da continued to stare at the gravestone, then after a moment he tore his dull eyes away and looked at me. His dark hair was standing up on end and his lips were closed tightly together.

'What am I doing here, Lettie?' he shot at me, his face reddening and his fists clenched by his sides. 'Visiting yer ma, that's what,' he added stonily.

The sound of his pet name for me made my stomach clench, but it was not said in an endearing way. Nothing my father said to me had been endearing since his return from the war. He had come home, after years away fighting, to find nothing was the same and everything had changed.

Now, as Da continued to glare at me, I was regretting the impulse to follow him here. It were silly of me to forget that this man was not the caring father I had known before he went away, but someone I no longer recognised.

I squared my shoulders and faced up to him, standing up as tall as my ten years would allow, and gathered my courage together once again. 'Don't go out on the boat today,' I said bravely, knowing I couldn't bear to lose Da as well. He was all I had left in the world, even though it seemed he didn't love me no more.

As I said the words, I knew it would make no difference. Da wasn't listening to my childish warning, the disbelief was written all over his face. 'It were just a dream,' he'd told me earlier this morning when I awoke crying over the nightmare. And perhaps he was right, but somewhere, right down in the very depths of my soul, I doubted this were true.

The fight seemed to leave Da's body, and he let out a long sigh and leaned against Mama's gravestone. Swiping at my own face, I fought back the tears, longing to hold him close and draw comfort from his once strong body. But the man he was now would not allow this, and knowing I would be pushed away only made me hold back.

After a moment, Da stood up and straightened his shoulders. 'Go home now, Lettie,' he ordered, pointing towards the gate before turning around and hurrying in the direction of the beach and his little fishing boat.

As I stood there in the graveyard watching him disappear from view, I knew without a shadow of a doubt that I would never see him again. Then, with a jolt, I realised that this time when I found myself alone in the world, the lovely Belle would not be there to save me.

Chapter One

Scarlett

12th May, 1930

Waiting in line with the other passengers at the Port of Tilbury, my heart was pounding with excitement and I could hardly breathe. The atmosphere was charged with anticipation and the sounds around me faded away as I peered up at the towering side of the *RMS Viceroy of India*.

Mr Charles Sawyer leaned towards me and placed his face alongside mine. 'Are you excited, Scarlett?' he whispered, squeezing my hand.

I returned the gentleman's smile, and stopped myself from admitting that I had never before sailed on a ship, let alone one like the *Viceroy*. The day before, thirsty for knowledge, I had questioned Charles on our impending trip, and he had indulged me.

'The *RMS Viceroy of India* was only launched last year so it's my first sailing on her, too,' he told me with a lift of his eyebrows. 'She is a luxurious Royal Mail steamer, and Britain's first turbo electric passenger ship.'

It was hard to believe that I was actually here on

a business trip with Charles, and about to board this beautiful ship, which would be sailing all the way to India.

If only Mama could see me now. Would she approve of what I had to do to earn this trip among the privileged? I liked to think she would. Remembering her final words to me the night of her death, I lifted my chin higher and stepped onto the gangplank.

'When things are tough, don't ever give up hope, even when you think there isn't any,' she had told me, while struggling for breath. 'Find a way, there will always be one…' her voice had trailed off as she closed her eyes for the last time.

'You were right, Mama, I took your advice and managed to find a way,' I whispered under my breath when a few moments later, Charles and I were directed towards our cabin. While we waited for the steward to unlock the door, I could feel Charles's intense gaze on me.

'What do you think so far, my sweet?' he breathed seductively into my ear, as the door closed on the steward.

I stared around me at the shining mahogany interior, the pale grey bedding, and the bedside lamp casting a soft glow over the room. 'Oh, Lord, it's beautiful,' I replied, but then turned in surprise towards Charles. 'Why is there only one bed in this cabin?'

'This ship has only single-berth cabins, but don't worry I'm not far away. My cabin is right next door to yours,' he said, indicating behind him towards a connecting doorway. 'There are extra rooms available through there for your personal use. They are usually for servants travelling with passengers, and as we have none with us, they are at your disposal.'

I clapped my hands together, unable to contain my joy; the thought of having this gorgeous room all to myself made my heart sing. 'Thank you!' I told Charles as I offered him a beaming smile.

I longed to tell Charles how unused to this kind of luxury I was, but of course he already understood that. And, I reminded myself, just like working at Madame Sloane's, I was acting a part and needed to be aware that the mask I was wearing must never slip.

'For you, my love, nothing but the best,' Charles returned, taking me in his arms and running his hands smoothly over my body.

I responded to his advances with my usual enthusiasm, eager to repay Charles for all he had given me. Then, after our lovemaking, he left me alone in the cabin and I stretched out like a contented cat on the bed.

Charles would be gone for hours, discussing sugar exportation with business associates. And it was time to take pleasure in unpacking my beautiful lingerie and my new dresses whilst revelling in this luxurious comfort.

I swung my legs off the bed as the ship's horn rang loudly through the air, followed by the sound of a bell being rung. I took this to mean that this was the start of the journey, and the chugging of the ship beneath my feet confirmed this.

Peering out of the porthole, I watched for a moment as the landscape began to disappear into the distance, and I looked forward to my unfolding adventure. Letting out a long sigh, I intended to savour every single moment of the seventeen days it would take the RMS *Viceroy of India* to reach her exotic destination.

Chapter Two

1st June, 1930

Squinting against the bright afternoon sunlight, I took in the cacophony surrounding me. The city of Calcutta was buzzing, the noise near to deafening with motorcars, rickshaws, and trams crowding the streets. There were women in brightly coloured saris, street sellers, and children with baskets of bread balanced on their heads.

Exploring this exciting city was like a dream come true for me, as echoes of another dream clung stubbornly to my thoughts.

Pushing aside feelings of disloyalty to Charles, the image of the tall, dark-haired stranger seen regularly in my sleep once again flooded into my mind. The man bore no resemblance to Charles, who was short in stature, and the mystery of his identity continued to haunt me.

As I pondered on this for the millionth time, I became aware that something around me had changed. The breath caught in my throat as the hairs lifted at the nape of my neck and, despite the intense heat of the day, a cold chill was now working its way slowly down my spine.

Panic flared inside me as I peered urgently this way and that in an effort to pinpoint the danger, but I could see nothing untoward in the melee that surrounded me. I needed to concentrate and be still, because the visions could sometimes be fleeting and disappear before I had a chance to understand their meaning.

However, the crowd would not allow me to linger, and they continued pushing past me while going about their daily business. I was buffeted along the street, now deaf to all sound except the rapid thumping of my heart. Standing to one side, I let the people pass by me while trying hard to concentrate on what was happening up ahead.

Gripped by the familiar dream-like state I knew so well, the scene in front of me faded away while another one quickly took its place. I was unable to do anything but watch as events unfolded before me. A young boy, no more than three years old, materialised from the crowd. Before I could take a breath, he ran towards the busy road, heading straight into the path of an oncoming motorcar.

Moving was impossible, as a disturbing image flashed before my eyes and I could now see the boy's small body lying motionless and broken in the road. This faded away as the feeling returned to my limbs, and my breath came in short bursts.

I'd been left with a sense of urgency, which pounded in my head, that I must find the child and prevent this tragedy from happening.

But where was the boy now, and how would I find him? My mind was racing, and my gaze was darting this way and that as sweat gathered on my forehead. Perhaps this time I wouldn't be able to help, but even so I was driven to try. And it was only as I took one last look around me before giving up that I saw him.

I stared at the boy whose wide brown eyes were full of mischief as he jumped impatiently from foot to foot. The adults around him were chatting amongst themselves, standing to my left around a market stall, which was selling all sorts of colourful bric-a-brac.

The women were in brightly coloured saris, next to the men in dhotis, while they laughed and talked animatedly. And the sound of their chatter, silent to me only a moment ago, seemed to be magnified in my ears now.

As the overhead sun beat down on my head, I could see the child searching for his escape route. Unsure what to do, but knowing I had to do something, I stepped towards the boy and tried to gain his attention before bowing slightly and bringing my palms together.

'Namaste, little one,' I greeted him with a word I'd heard many times since my arrival in India. But he simply stared uninterested back at me, and then in a flash he pushed roughly past me and quickly disappeared in the crowd.

Knowing that I could not leave him to his fate, I raced after the boy, weaving in and out of the crowd as I went, and keeping his bright yellow Kurta in my sights. As he approached the edge of the road, the sound of a motorcar approaching reached my ears.

Despite my best efforts, as I tried to catch up with the child he was still just out of my reach. I was desperate to get hold of the boy before it was too late and he disappeared under the wheels of the car.

Eventually I lunged towards him and made a grab for his sleeve, and we both tumbled clumsily onto the hard ground and landed in an untidy heap.

For a moment it was difficult to breathe, because the

fall had knocked the wind out of my sails. Attempting to get air into my lungs, I could feel the boy sobbing against my body and struggling to be free of my grip. Holding him even tighter against me, I looked up to see that we were surrounded by a small mob of people who were staring down at us in a curious fashion.

A man, who had pushed his way out of the throng, was now standing in front of us, looking down at the child with a concerned frown. He had a turban around his head and was wearing a dhoti tied up with a belt around his waist.

Bending towards us the man quickly held out his arms towards the boy and the child's face lit up. The child obviously recognised him, so I immediately loosened my grip. Then I watched the boy rush headlong into the man's arms without a backward glance at me.

A sense of relief flooded my body as tears burned at the back of my eyes. There were many times I'd been powerless to prevent bad things from happening. But luckily, this time I'd succeeded in saving the child.

After pulling myself up to a standing position, I found myself looking into the eyes of the man who was holding the child. I could see the boy was safe now, so I nodded at the man, feeling a sudden need to get away, to escape this near tragedy, and take a moment to catch my breath. But the man was talking quickly to me in an animated fashion and had focussed his dark eyes on my face.

'I'm sorry,' I told him, shrugging my shoulders. 'I don't understand the language.' Just then, a passer-by appeared by my side and, seeing the problem with communication, began to translate.

'This man says to tell you a thousand thanks for

saving his child, Memsaab,' the interpreter explained, while indicating towards the child's father.

'Thank you, but I was pleased to help the little one,' I answered him truthfully, while smiling down at the boy where he was sitting on the ground clinging to his father's legs.

The linguist repeated my words to the man, and there seemed to be a collective sigh in the air as the crowd began to disperse. But as I brushed down my dress and turned to walk away, the boy's father took hold of my arm. I looked towards the translator, who asked me to wait a moment.

Hesitating, I watched the boy's father as he unhooked a necklace from around his neck and held it out to me. I shook my head again, indicating that there was no need for him to pay me for my trouble. But the man, it seemed, would not give up, and he began pushing the necklace towards me.

With the translator still hovering by my side, I turned and asked him to explain to the man that I could not accept this valuable gift.

'I am so sorry, Memsaab,' the translator said to me, while bowing low. 'The custom here in India is that saving a life must be rewarded. If you do not accept this gift from the child's father, then this man's honour will be at stake.'

The last thing I wanted to do was jeopardise anyone's honour; it seemed I had no choice but to take the necklace. So I held out my hand to the man, who then dropped the trinket into my open palm.

I gazed at the necklace. Its large purple stone glinted in the bright sunlight overhead, sending shafts of light bouncing off the stone, which was attached to a long silver chain. The man was explaining something to the linguist, who turned to me again.

'This is an amethyst stone cut from the depths of the Himalayas,' the translator reported. 'The child's father wants to tell you that it holds the power to protect the wearer from harm,' he added.

Once again, I thanked the man for the unnecessary gift before slipping the necklace into my pocket. But I shivered as a dark feeling hovered nearby, making me long to return the necklace to the child's father. Instead, I bade them both farewell before pushing my way through the crowd and back to the safety of the ship.

Chapter Three

The waves were lifting high into the air and the ship was listing heavily from side to side. Dark clouds overhead had blocked out the light, and it felt like the middle of the night instead of mid-morning.

The cold wind whipped tendrils of hair across my face, as I clung desperately onto the railings of the ship in an attempt to steady my feet.

The nightmare had come to me in the middle of the night, robbing me of much-needed sleep. And the black feeling of dread still clung to my skin. It brought back a long-buried memory from years ago, and being outside even in this storm was much easier than facing the horror inside the ship.

'Mrs Sawyer? Please come inside. It's not a day for being out on the deck.'

The steward's words were barely audible against the loud crashing of the waves and the roaring of the wind. Nevertheless, I could hear the urgency in his voice. It was clear he could not understand why I was out here, open to the elements, in the middle of this terrible storm.

How could I tell him that the black, clawing fear was sucking me mercilessly into its depths, forcing me to attempt escape from the inevitable outcome? The thought of history repeating itself was now overriding any worries I had for my own safety.

My first instinct was to ignore the man, hoping he'd go away and leave me to face the storm alone. Manners, however, had been instilled into me from an early age, forbidding me from this far easier course of action.

I turned towards him and almost lost my footing as the ship lurched heavily to one side. As I righted myself, I realised for the first time that I was completely alone on the ship's deck.

The steward waited patiently, and was now holding out his hand to me with a concerned yet puzzled expression on his face.

'Mrs Sawyer, please come on inside,' he repeated, taking a step towards me.

I knew when I was beaten, so I nodded at him, feeling frozen with cold and rigid with fear as I took his outstretched hand.

Numbly, I let the steward lead me back inside the ship. In order to stay upright, I clung to the stair rail as the storm outside raged on. Once inside the ship, everywhere was eerily quiet, apart from the sound of the ship battling the waves and the low rumble of distant thunder.

I followed the steward mutely down some steps and along a corridor, until suddenly I realised where he was taking me as a flash of lightning lit up the dark passageway. 'No...' My chest tightened, and I felt sick with dread. 'I'm not going back in there,' I said, as we stopped outside the door to the sick bay.

The steward turned to me and spoke in soft tones. 'I'm sorry, Mrs Sawyer, but your husband is very sick and has been asking for you,' he reasoned, putting his hands out in a gesture of concern.

I couldn't move, and the sound of my own heartbeat was now thrashing in my ears. 'I'm just frightened, you see…' my words trailed off.

I hated to admit my fears to a stranger as I dipped my head and swallowed, wishing myself anywhere but here on this ship with the steward's steady gaze still on me.

It was nothing to do with this man what I did or did not do, but something in me needed to voice the torment that was ripping me apart.

'Charles has the influenza,' I managed to say, as I fought back the tears which were now threatening to spill down over my cheeks.

'I understand that, Mrs Sawyer. But right now the doctor who is with your husband needs to speak with you about his condition,' he said a little more firmly now before lifting his chin and nodding encouragingly at me.

He was looking at me with sympathy in his eyes and I couldn't bear it, because I didn't want sympathy. It was courage I needed to get me through the days ahead.

Understanding I had no choice but to face what was happening, I straightened my back, took a long inhale, and readied myself for what was to come, before pushing open the door and walking briskly into the sick bay.

The small area was airless and thick with the smell of disinfectant, and I instinctively covered my mouth with my hand. In the semi-darkness, my eyes rested on Charles lying unconscious in one of the three beds in the room, the sound of his laboured breathing echoing off the walls.

Charles looked the same as when I'd last seen him,

deathly pale, although now he had a slightly yellow tinge to his face and a glisten of sweat covered his brow. A man dressed in a white coat stood by his bed, writing on a chart.

As the steward shut the door behind me, every instinct warned me to turn around and run away from this turn of events and away from the danger within.

'Good afternoon, Mrs Sawyer,' the doctor greeted me, lowering the chart and regarding me with a thoughtful look.

'I'm not Mrs Sawyer,' I said needlessly, while watching the slight rise and fall of Charles chest and wishing with all my heart he was well again. Then, for me at least, everything in the world would be back in its rightful place.

'You are his companion, are you not? The steward told me you're together on this trip.' The doctor lifted his eyebrows at me quizzically and sighed heavily.

He was staring at me the way the steward had and I began to feel foolish, as if I were trying to deny being with Charles and that wasn't my intention at all.

'Sorry for any confusion here,' I told the doctor, lifting my chin and trying not to look over in the direction of poor Charles. 'You're right, I am his companion.'

The doctor nodded gravely at me and pressed his lips together. 'Well, Miss…?'

'It's Cunningham, Scarlett Cunningham,' I answered, dreading what he was about to tell me, while trying to internally shut out the sound of Charles's laboured breathing.

'Miss Cunningham, I'm sure you're aware just how very sick Mr Sawyer is?' He glanced across at the bed, and then at me. 'Malaria is a terrible disease.

I should know, as I've seen many cases in the past, and unfortunately his condition is worsening by the hour.'

My heart missed a beat at his words. 'Malaria, Doctor? What do you mean? Doesn't Charles have influenza?'

The doctor placed the chart back down on the bed and shook his head. 'Not influenza, Miss Cunningham. He has malaria,' he told me firmly.

Letting out a long sigh of relief, I could hardly believe what I was hearing. And as the doctor's words began to sink in, some of the dread and fear fell away.

'Are you certain about that? I mean, he was shivering and had a temperature and...' I couldn't finish the sentence.

'I'm completely sure, Miss Cunningham. The symptoms of malaria can be similar to influenza, but he definitely has Malaria. There's no doubt about that.'

A feeling of calm had descended on me at this welcome news, despite Charles still lying seriously ill in a bed just a few feet away. 'Flaming heck,' I heard myself say, before quickly apologising to the doctor for my language.

'Is there anything else you want to ask me?' he asked, lifting his eyebrows.

'Has Charles any chance of surviving this?' I asked. I knew I was clutching at straws, but I had to ask this question.

The doctor shook his head sadly at me. 'If he's lucky, he will survive. You can stay here with him if you want to. We'll do all we can for him,' he replied, staring at me with a furrowed brow.

I thanked the doctor, wondering if he really believed Charles had a chance to live when I knew otherwise.

'I'll stay with him until the end,' I said. I pulled up a

chair and took Charles's clammy hand in mine, feeling stronger in the knowledge that he wasn't suffering from influenza. The doctor nodded at me and then left the room, as I settled down beside Charles to watch him die and offer him comfort in his final hours.

Chapter Four

The rain was coming down in sheets, and I was drenched to the skin and shivering with cold from my hiding position under the clump of trees, on the edge of the graveyard at Chelsea Old Church in London.

The branches were scant protection from the elements, but at least from here I could watch the funeral service from a distance. My tears mingled with the raindrops as the coffin was lowered into the gaping black hole in the ground, and I found it hard to believe that Charles was lying dead inside that cold wooden box.

The realisation that I was alone in the world, with very little money, had hit me hard the day after Charles's death. I had overslept that morning, which was hardly surprising.

My mind had been going round in circles all night, wondering how I would survive without him. The bottom line was that he had given me pocket money while on board the ship, but that money was all I had, and it wouldn't last long.

I had woken to the sound of a knock on my cabin door and, on opening it, had been summoned to the Captain's quarters by the steward. Once there, I learnt that Charles was lying in the ship's morgue, and I asked if he would be buried at sea.

'As we are only a few days away from docking at Tilbury, this will not be necessary,' the Captain had told me formally. 'I've sent a radio message to Mr Sawyer's wife informing him of her husband's death, so everything is in order.'

The Captain then asked me a few more questions, which I answered as best as I could, while trying to ignore the judgemental look in his eyes. Refusing to let him intimidate me, I left his quarters a few minutes later with my head held high.

When the ship docked a few days later, I had no idea where to go, as I packed everything into my suitcase. Watched by the steward, I walked away from my privileged life and back to the trapped, miserable world of poverty I used to know. The suitcase and its contents were all I had left of Charles now.

Boarding a bus, I soon found myself in Bethnal Green. There, I found lodgings for a week, which would give me time to look for work and think about what to do next. The landlady was scruffy, the hallway smelt of rotten cabbage, and the bedroom was full of cockroaches, but I had no choice but to take it.

Yesterday I had been wandering the streets feeling lost, when I sat down heavily on a park bench. There I had picked up a discarded *Times* newspaper, and begun glancing through it when I found myself on the obituary pages. The words had danced in front of my eyes as I read the announcement about Charles.

Mr Charles Sawyer, a local entrepreneur, died peacefully on the 18th June, 1930, while on-board the RMS Viceroy of India. He was a much-loved husband to Angela Sawyer, and beloved father to Robert and

David. The funeral service will be held at Chelsea Old Church on…

The date of the funeral had been this morning, so I got up early and packed my case. There was no more money left, and I had no alternative but to return to the place from where Charles had saved me. But before following that path, there was one more thing I had to do.

Now, as I watched the small party of mourners standing by the graveside, I edged further beneath the canopy of trees, away from prying eyes, while trying to merge into the dark foliage.

At last the service was at an end and people were turning away. The small dark-haired woman I presumed to be Charles's wife was staring dismally down into the grave, while her two young sons stood beside her with their heads bowed.

A man nearby, who seemed concerned, pulled at her arm, urging her to leave Charles behind and follow the rest of the congregation away from the graveside.

The woman turned towards him and nodded slowly before taking his arm. Suddenly, I realised too late, they were all walking towards my hiding place. Attempting to still my racing heart, I bowed my head, knowing I should have made my escape before the service finished.

My limbs were frozen with cold and grief, and I was barely able to breathe as I watched the mourners make their way slowly towards the parked cars. As they walked on talking quietly, I waited with bated breath for Charles's wife and young sons to pass me by unnoticed.

As they came near, the woman hesitated then she

glanced up in the direction of my hiding place. Holding my breath, I kept very still, hoping my dark clothes blended in with the trees. After a moment, one of the boys tugged gently on her arm and she looked down at him and, encouraged by those supporting her, she walked on.

At last all the mourners had gone, and I was still underneath the trees. I could not leave until I had spoken to Charles one final time.

As I approached the grave, a lone gravedigger was now shovelling soil onto the coffin. And although the rain had stopped, the ground was sodden. The man heard me approaching, and he turned and gave a small nod of understanding. Leaving his spade wedged in the wet mud, he retreated from the graveside.

Silence surrounded me, and the air was damp and heavy as I stood by the side of the grave. The sides of the wooden coffin were still visible under the soil, and no doubt it was a beautiful box made of the best-polished wood the family could afford.

Overhead, the skies were darkening once more, and I had only a few minutes to speak before the heavens opened once again. My eyes were red and sore from lack of sleep as I stared sadly down at Charles's final resting place.

'Thank you for coming into my life, Charles, and for giving me so much. I know you can't hear me,' I glanced up towards the moody sky. 'Perhaps you can…' I said, lowering my eyes again. 'Either way, please know that you were a good man.'

I sniffed into my hankie and wiped away the tears. At the distant sound of thunder, I turned from the grave and began striding quickly away.

Eager to escape now, I made my way through the

gravestones in the direction of the gate. But before I reached it, I made a detour back to the canopy of trees where the suitcase, which held all my worldly goods, was hidden.

As I lifted the case, the reality of my situation hit me firmly between the eyes. I had no money to my name and nowhere to live. That left me with only one alternative; if I were to avoid the workhouse, I would have to return to the dreadful place I'd escaped from only a year earlier.

Chapter Five

I looked through the window of number twenty-one King's Street, at the numerous furs lined up on a rail inside the shop, and a cold shiver passed through my body. The shop was closed as it was Sunday, but Madam would be overseeing her second, more profitable business which was run from the rooms above the shop.

My heart was pounding as I fought the urge to run, reluctant to knock on the door. However, there was no choice but to throw myself on Madam's mercy.

When the reality of my situation had first hit me, I had been weighed down by fatigue. The amethyst necklace, gifted to me after I saved the little boy, had seemed like part of the solution to being penniless. Despite it being a treasured possession, I was willing to sell it and use the money to help me avoid a return to Madam Sloane and her seedy establishment.

However, to my horror, when I went to retrieve the necklace on the day the ship docked, it had disappeared. And despite searching through all my possessions, it was nowhere to be found. Maybe it had been stolen, but that seemed unlikely, as nothing else in our cabin had been taken.

Now, I straightened my spine and knocked on Madam's door again, louder this time. For now, or until I could find a way out of my predicament, I would have to accept my fate, the same way I had on the day I had arrived at St Agnes's Home for Girls in Hove.

Then, like now, I had nothing but my suitcase, which was packed tightly with my few belongings by my side, and my heart thudding hard with apprehension at what lay ahead. As I waited for Madam to answer the door, the anger burned deep within me at how my father had eventually come back from the war, and within a few short months had gone again.

I was jolted out of my sombre thoughts as Madam suddenly appeared at the door. I watched her over-made-up face as it creased into a surprised frown, and her eyes widened at the sight of me. Madam hadn't changed in the year I'd been away; her eyes were still small and beady, and her hair styled in tight, brassy curls about her head.

'It's you! Ha, well, I knew you'd be back,' she sneered spitefully. 'You're too late, though, I don't need another shop assistant no more.'

I flinched as Madam slammed the door hard in my face and I heard her heavy footsteps retreat through the hallway. Panic filled me as I banged loudly on the door. 'No wait!' I shouted, desperate for her to let me in. 'Please, Madam… please, I'll do whatever you want me to do!'

For a moment, there was only silence. Then I heard her walking back through the hallway, and she slowly opened the door again. Madam's jaw was tight as she looked at me with a hard expression, and her hands were firmly planted on her ample hips.

'What was that you said? Miss prim and proper,' she sneered.

I braced myself for a convincing explanation. 'I

don't have to work in the shop,' I told her, trying not to sound as desperate as I was feeling while endeavouring to forget how truly awful it was working at Madam's second business.

'I'm happy to work as one of your upstairs girls,' I said, trying to smile at her mean face. Now, more than ever, my life depended on this woman.

Madam hesitated and narrowed her eyes before glancing furtively out into the empty street behind me. Then, after looking me up and down and lifting one pencilled eyebrow, she opened the door wider and stepped aside.

'You'd better come in then,' she invited. 'At least you have your womanly curves now,' she added sarcastically as she quickly disappeared into the hallway.

Swallowing my pride, I tried not to remember the last time I had been here, and the argument I'd with this fierce woman. She had caught me, case in hand, trying to leave her establishment by the back door, and had been enraged that I was trying to escape.

A tussle had followed, but somehow I'd managed to get away from her. But as I had run quickly down the street, her screams that I would soon regret my actions had echoed behind me.

Shaking these thoughts from my head now, I lifted my case and stepped across the threshold, pushing away the thought that I'd come full circle, back to working for Madam and the dismal fate of being one of her 'upstairs girls'.

Chapter Six

'It ain't like that,' Nell said, while studying her long manicured fingernails. 'She won't give you none of the money, and that's the end of it.'

I had come into Nell's room to discuss how to improve our situation here at Madam's, but it was proving fruitless so far. She had refused to listen to reason, and was giving me one of her 'for goodness sake, wise up' looks from under those long dark lashes of hers.

'Madam keeps it all,' she continued with pursed lips. 'There ain't nothing you can do about it. Bed and board is all you'll get here however hard you work.'

'That must be why she's so bloody rich then!' I retorted as I paced the room, my blood boiling with rage over how Madam was treating us girls. 'It isn't fair; we earn that money, not her. I understand she has to take a percentage, but not *all* of the money!'

It hadn't taken me long to realise that with Madam keeping the profits of my earnings, I had no way of escaping from her house of ill repute. Finding a better life was becoming a distant dream for me, and I was more trapped than ever.

Nell gave me a resigned nod, and hauled herself off the bed before standing upright to admire herself in the mirror. After a moment she noticed me watching her and turned back towards me.

'I know what you're saying, Scarlett, but I can't see a way out, and believe me I've tried,' she said with a half-hearted shrug in my direction.

My heart sank as I remembered the old Nell, the person she used to be. I'd known her a long time, and the two of us went back many years. I first met her in St Agnes's after Da died. I wondered when she had lost that spark she used to have, and become so resigned to her fate.

At the age of ten, the future had been like a long dark tunnel to me – empty, bleak, and endless. Standing next to the straight-faced woman who was delivering me to the orphanage in Lansdowne Road that fateful day, I had shivered as the icy November wind bit into my face, frightened at what lay ahead.

As I stared up at the tall, red-bricked building in dismay, the thought of living in this home had filled me with despair. From the outside it looked cold and unwelcoming, and vastly different from the small, terraced house I had shared with my family.

After I was shown to the endless dormitory, where there were rows of beds along each wall, facing each other, and all looking exactly the same, my heart had sunk even further.

There were no pictures on the walls, no curtains at the windows, no floor coverings, and everything was black and white. Not that our family had anything of value back in Albion Hill in Brighton, but there had been a little comfort to be found sitting by the fire of an evening, or being warm and cosy in bed at night.

That first night in St Agnes's, I was unable to sleep, and was weeping in my bed at 3am in the morning when the mattress dipped and a small voice spoke to me in the darkness of the dormitory.

'What's the matter?' the voice whispered into my ear. 'And why are you crying?'

Looking up, I saw the silhouette of a girl staring intently down at me. The whites of her eyes stood out in a questioning gaze as she waited patiently for my answer.

'What do you think is the matter?' I retorted angrily. 'I miss me family, o' course, and I don't want to be here neither!'

I looked around me to where the other girls were sleeping soundly, their bodies hidden under thin blankets in the darkness. Lord knew how they managed to sleep in this cold and dismal place. And I was saddened that this was what I had been reduced to, all alone, with my family gone, and living with total strangers.

'Me name's Nell,' the girl told me, while continuing to stare at me. 'I been 'ere for years,' she said sadly, shrugging her shoulders

The resignation was clear in Nell's voice, and there was also the glint of tears in her eyes. I immediately stopped crying, feeling foolish. How had she survived this bleak existence for years? I leaned towards her and pushed away the self-pity threatening to engulf me.

'I'm Scarlett,' I told her. 'Have you seen that shop Foxy Furs on the King's Road?' I asked, suddenly desperate to find a light in this dismal world where we both found ourselves.

Nell shook her head and I warmed to my theme, feeling slightly better now. 'It's a magical place full o' lovely furs,' I gushed. 'I seen coats made out of mink, foxes, and once I even saw one with a rabbit's head on it!

'I'm going to work there one day,' I continued, as Nell widened her eyes in awe at this revelation. Then, lifting my chin, I imagined myself serving the well-to-do customers in the posh furrier's shop.

Nell gasped and shuffled closer on the bed. 'Sounds exciting to me. Can you take me there sometime, too?' she asked. 'I'd love to see it, and maybe I could work there?'

After that night, the two of us became firm friends, and I learnt that Nell was around my own age. When I looked at her properly the next morning in the cold light of day, I saw she had brown eyes, dark hair, and a ready smile.

Nell told me how she had been brought to the home at six years old, after her mother died. Listening to her made me realise that this girl had suffered a far worse deal in life than me. At least I had once known a loving family, a mother and father who had loved me – before fate took a turn for the worse. But Nell's life had been hard, it seemed, from the moment she was born.

The next day Nell took me along with her to the canteen for breakfast, where all the children joined an orderly queue and waited their turn to be fed. Then, when it was our turn, we sat down on hard benches and were told to eat in total silence.

There was an unnatural hush in the large eating area, but I soon learned that was normal for mealtimes. I was acutely aware that the nuns, with their sombre expressions, were watching us children from the edges of the room, just waiting for us to step out of line.

Despite this no talking rule, Nell leaned in close to me and whispered behind her hands. 'When we going to Foxy Furs then, Scarlett?' she'd asked, eager to see the shop I'd described so well, the excitement dancing in her eyes.

I whispered back that we could talk about it later in the dormitory. I was secretly pleased that I had a new friend in this cold, unwelcoming place, where I could add a bit of excitement to our dull lives.

Every day, on the way home from school, we made our way to King's Road to stare longingly in through the window of Foxy Furs. Nell and I were filled with envy watching the women going into the shop empty-handed, and then leaving with their expensive furs, before stepping into their chauffeur-driven cars.

Even at that young age, I knew how much I wanted the wealth that women like them had, and I vowed that one day I *would* have all those material possessions.

As the years passed, I noticed many of the customers were escorted by wealthy, older looking men, and a new determination was born in me to have a better life… whatever that took.

If only we had known then what we knew now. How we'd end up working for Madam – not selling her beautiful furs, but instead providing a service for some of those wealthy men we had glimpsed over the years.

Nell's voice interrupted memories of the past. 'Six long years it's been,' she said, letting out a long sigh and running her fingers through her dark hair. 'And let's face it, Scarlett, I ain't never going to escape now!'

I sat down on the bed and regarded Nell, who had such a mournful expression on her face that my heart lurched. Through all the years of being her friend, I had always seen Nell's fighting spirit. But that determination not to be beaten had gone, and there was only defeat left on her face now.

'There has to be a way,' I said to her, determined

to think of something to help us both get away from the evil, money-grabbing Madam. 'Don't you want to have a better life?' I asked, knowing we needed each other in the plan to escape.

Nell didn't answer my question immediately. Instead, she sat down next to me on the bed, and stared dismally into the middle distance.

'Madam promised me that when I leave 'ere I'll get all the money she owes me,' she said with a trusting expression on her face. 'Apparently she's saving it up for me,' she added, lifting her brows hopefully.

'Surely, Nell, you don't really believe that, do you?' I said, shocked that my friend could be so gullible.

Out of all the girls who worked for Madam, Nell had been the only one who showed any inclination to escape. The other girls were aloof and refused to give me the time of day, let alone plot a way to escape. But recently Nell had changed beyond recognition.

She gave me a steady look then dropped her head and rubbed at her eyes, causing black eyeliner to smudge across her cheeks. 'No, I guess I don't believe it, but the thing is, Scarlett, she took me off the streets, and I kind of owe her in a funny kind o' way.'

'Oh, Nell. Just because she's given you a roof over your head doesn't mean she can keep all of your earnings, that's just not fair. Has something else happened lately to make you so despondent?'

Nell gazed up at me with her eyes wide. 'Yeah, I got pregnant,' she said bluntly, giving a little sniff. 'Madam got me sorted, paid for the abortion – and I know I were lucky that she did this for me.'

'Was that when you disappeared for a few days?' I asked, not surprised at this revelation; sometimes it happened, even though we all took precautions. When

Nell nodded sadly, I realised that if I wanted to escape from Madam, I would probably have to do this alone.

Later that night as I lay in bed, my mind was running in circles, trying to think of ways to get the better of Madam. I had no idea how to outwit the devious old witch, especially as she watched us girls closely every day, but I was determined to find a way. Madam's words were ever-present in my head after my return to Foxy Furs.

'You 'ad better work your arse off now you're back, and make up for lost time, girl,' she told me. 'And don't think you'll escape me a second time round neither.'

There was the threat of retaliation in her words that day, meaning it would be even harder to get away from her now. If only I could find another gentleman, someone I could rely on to look after me… and someone kind like Charles.

Determined to find the answer to this problem, I resolved never to end up like Nell, who had given up on living a different kind of life. It seemed she was resigned to spending years working for Madam Sloane. But when her looks faded, where would she be then? The workhouse was the likely place, and I shuddered at the thought.

Eventually my mind stilled, and I slept that night. And this time, instead of the tall, dark-haired man I often dreamt of, my dreams were filled with a man who had prominent features and a large Roman nose.

Chapter Seven

I opened the door to the furrier's shop and hurried in out of the cold, hoping not to be seen by Madam. Her 'upstairs girls' were supposed to stay out of sight of customers, and I would face her wrath if I were caught.

Something, though, had urged me to take the risk today, and it was to do with the strange dream from the night before. The shop was quiet, and the older woman Martha was standing behind the counter. She looked up as I walked in, obviously surprised to see me defying Madam's direct orders in such a blatant way.

Hesitating in the doorway, the skin prickled at the back of my neck, and a slight shiver ran down my spine as a customer in the shop drew my attention. He had his back turned towards me and was wearing a fedora hat, which was hiding his dark hair underneath its wide brim.

The man was studying a row of furs on a clothes rail, and as the door pinged shut behind me, he swung around in my direction. Our eyes met. And I immediately saw that he had a Roman nose and a prominent chin. As he maintained eye contact with me and tipped his hat, his smile drew me in, making me feel less uncomfortable under his intense gaze.

'Don't I know you from somewhere?' he asked,

tilting his head to one side and regarding me with a furrowed brow.

For a moment I was unable to answer. How could I tell him that he might be part of my destiny, and that I didn't know whether that was good or bad?

Taking a deep breath, I glanced uneasily across at Martha who was now giving me an odd look, and the thought nagged at me that Madam could appear at any moment in the shop.

'I've never seen you before,' I quickly replied. 'Apart from in my dream,' I wanted to add.

The man was still gazing at me with an endearing expression on his face, but he made no further effort at conversation. And I could feel him watching me as I walked quickly past him, through the door towards the stairs.

However, before I could get further than the bottom step, Madam appeared and roughly grabbed hold of my arm. 'What do you think you're doing, my girl?' she said, digging her long nails painfully into my flesh and pushing her face towards mine.

Lifting my chin, I glared at her, refusing to be cowed. 'Going back to my room is what I'm flaming doing, Madam. Nothing wrong in that, is there?' I said cheekily, while staring defiantly into her hawk-like eyes.

Madam continued to glare at me, and our dislike of each other pulsed in the air between us. Then, before I had time to dodge out of the way or see it coming, she lifted a hand and slapped me hard across my cheek.

Staggering on my feet, I almost fell backwards, stunned by the stinging slap. And as a look of triumph crossed her face, anger flared inside me. Fighting back the tears, I lifted my chin higher, determined not to give in to this woman's bullying ways.

'Now don't bloody use the shop floor again. The back entrance is for trollops like you!' Madam yelled, before turning on her heel and stalking away.

My breath came in short gasps as I stood for a moment trying to regain my composure. I held my palm over my sore, burning cheek, while telling myself that very soon I would escape from Madam. Although how this would happen, I had no idea.

A sudden movement drew my attention towards the door I'd just come through. The Roman-nosed man was still standing in the shop, but now he was staring at me through the tiny window in the door, a look of utter horror on his face.

Humiliated by Madam's attack, I turned away from him and ran quickly upstairs, where I shut the door to my room and sobbed quietly into my hands. I was not beaten by Madam's behaviour, never that. But as usual I was angry at the way she treated us girls.

After a while I sat up and looked in the mirror to see the livid, red hand-mark that she had inflicted across my cheek. One day, I vowed, Madam Sloane would get her comeuppance. And if I had anything to do with it, that day was not far away.

Chapter Eight

Early the next morning, Madam barged rudely into my room unannounced to stand by my bed, where she glared angrily down at me.

'You have a new client today, Scarlett, so get up now, girl! And make sure you look your best, if you know what's good for you.'

Rubbing at my eyes, I shook myself awake. 'I'm blinking getting up,' I told her mutinously, while trying to keep my tone neutral. The last thing I wanted was more trouble from Madam.

'It's a bit early for clients, though, isn't it?' I said to her retreating back.

Usually, we girls entertained men only during the hours of darkness, not first thing in the morning in the cold light of day.

'Don't argue with me!' she retorted from the doorway. 'This man is returning to London this afternoon, and he's booked you in before he goes home. You have less than half an hour to get ready.' With that, she shot me a threatening look and hurried out, slamming the door hard behind her.

I quickly dressed, knowing that to defy Madam was only risking further abuse, but I was tired and had barely slept last night. Anger at Madam had consumed me as I plotted my revenge far into the night.

Barely fifteen minutes later, I was ready, and I waited for my visitor while trying to ignore my rumbling stomach. There had been no time for breakfast before my new client's arrival this morning, so I must go hungry for now.

When there was a knock at the door, I opened it to see the Roman-nosed man standing in the doorway. Having no idea why I had dreamt about this man, I shivered in the doorway. From past experience, I've learnt that things could go either way – this man might be a good person or a bad one, and right now I had no way of knowing.

'Good morning, Miss Cunningham,' he said, looking a bit awkward. 'May I come in, please?'

The man was not handsome, but as I ushered him into the room, I noticed that his smile lit up his face. As he walked in and glanced around the room, I braced myself for what came next. For what always came next.

'Madam Sloane told me your name was Scarlett? Is that right?' he asked, straightening his shoulders. And before I could answer, he added, 'Mine's Eric Johnson.'

Eric Johnson was short in stature and had a large, rounded stomach which strained against his smart pinstriped shirt. I had always been tall, and I towered over him in the middle of the bedroom as he ran a hand through his dark hair.

'That's my name,' I told him, finding this puzzling and a strange way to go on.

My customers didn't normally take the time to tell me their names, or to act so formally around me. We usually got on with what the customer had paid for, without any such pleasantries getting in the way of business. 'Pleased to meet you, Eric,' I returned, before taking his outstretched hand.

There was a strange silence in the room, as if Eric didn't know what to do next, so I took matters into my hands and began to undress. But Eric put a hand up to stop me.

'Scarlett, please don't do that...' he said hesitantly, before looking around the room towards the bed. 'Why don't we sit down first?' he asked unexpectedly.

Whatever way worked for him, I supposed, and I stopped taking my clothes off and sat down on the bed as he'd asked. When Eric sat next to me, I forced myself not to flinch as he lifted one hand and ran it gently down my sore, reddened cheek.

'I saw that woman do this to you yesterday, Scarlett, and I'd like to know why you stay here?' His hazel eyes narrowed as he stared intently at me.

Eric was waiting for an answer, and anger – red and hot – rose in my chest at his words. 'Surely you know, *Eric Johnson*, that no-one would choose this life if they had a choice?' I replied, wondering what this man's game was, because it must be a game he was playing.

'What do you want, and why are you asking me questions about myself?' I snapped, aware that my bad night's sleep was making my temper short and my patience thin.

Eric continued to look at me steadily. 'I'm sorry, Scarlett, but I think you've misinterpreted my intentions, which are strictly honourable.'

What was going on here? This man, who had paid for a whore's services, was telling *me* that his intentions were honourable! Eric was either joking with me or completely insane.

After a moment I became aware that he looked a bit hurt. 'I'm sorry, but what are those intentions?' I asked, trying to understand.

As I waited for Eric to explain, a niggling feeling had started in my stomach that this man *was* kind, and that he meant everything he said.

He frowned uneasily at me. 'I've come to talk to you, Scarlett,' he explained. 'I know that's not the normal way of things in this kind of establishment, but I honestly don't want anything else from you right now.'

He held his hands up to indicate how genuine he was. 'I saw you yesterday in the shop, as you know, and I haven't been able to stop thinking about you since. And as I'm leaving Brighton today… I had to see you again.'

Despite this explanation, I still didn't quite believe that Eric only wanted to talk. As I thought about this, he lifted his hand to run his fingers through his hair again, and I noticed the wedding ring.

'What does your wife think of you coming here today?' I said, surprising myself with my bluntness, but knowing there was no other way to get to the bottom of what Eric was up to.

He shrugged before following my eyes and looking sadly down at the third finger on his left hand. 'She wouldn't be happy, that's true, especially as I've never strayed before, despite it being an arranged marriage.'

He looked up at me with a soft gaze. 'You have to understand, Scarlett, that as soon as I saw you, I knew you were different to other women. In the past, I've never given into temptation, but somehow… with you… I simply couldn't resist.'

For a moment I was totally speechless, but I was beginning to see that there might be a reason for Eric to have been in my dream after all.

'Go on then, Scarlett,' Eric encouraged as I pondered

on his fancy words. 'Take a chance on me and tell me all about yourself,' he pleaded. 'I want to know everything, but mostly about how you ended up here at the *wicked* Madam Sloane's house of ill repute.'

'All right, Eric,' I began. If this wealthy man wanted to pay to hear my life story, then that's exactly what I'd give him, I told myself.

'I was born in Albion Hill in Brighton, the eldest of five children, and my father was a fisherman, my mother a laundress,' I told him truthfully.

A puzzled expression flitted across Eric's face. 'You don't sound as if you come from that area of Brighton, if you don't mind me saying, Scarlett,' he observed, lifting his dark eyebrows.

Eric was right there. My mind went back to when Nell and I used to stand in the shadows of Madam's shop, staring in through the window of Foxy Furs at the rows of furs set out on rails, all those years ago. Nell had been mesmerised by the sight of all those rich women with diamonds dripping from their necks, but I had done more than merely watch them.

Through listening to the way the women spoke, I soon realised that to have a chance of working in this upper-class shop, I would have to change my accent. So I had practised daily after that, trying out my accent on Nell whenever I could.

Eventually, I had fooled Madam into thinking I came from a well-to-do area of Brighton, instead of the rougher part of town which was Albion Hill. I explained all this to Eric now.

'Of course, I didn't know then that Madam was running two businesses from these premises,' I told him ruefully.

'I see, so through lying about the area which you

came from, and by putting on a posh accent, you gained employment in Madam's shop?'

'That's about the measure of it,' I replied. 'I told Madam I was from the Clifton Hill area. The years I spent watching the women gave me an insight into how they spoke and how they acted. Then, at fourteen, when I left school, there was a sign in Madam's shop window for a shop assistant.'

Eric leaned back against the wall and looked impressed. 'That's very enterprising of such a young girl,' he told me with a gleam in his eye.

I tilted my head thoughtfully. 'I suppose it was, but you have to understand I had no choice if I wanted a better life,' I told him, swallowing hard as I remembered how naïve I had been in imagining that Madam's business was solely to sell furs to her rich clients.

'And did you get to work in Madam's shop in the end?'

'Oh yes, I did for a while,' I said, remembering how it was then. 'I was very young, and for the first few weeks, unbelievably, I didn't realise what was going on here.'

I could clearly recall the day when I realised what I'd got myself into. By then, though, I was in too deep. I had left the orphanage, and was living in an attic room at Madam's, with nowhere else to go but the workhouse.

'That must have been pretty awful for you,' Eric said, placing a hand on my arm. 'How did you find out about the brothel side of things?'

I hesitated, because I was opening up about my life for the first time, which was hard, but he seemed to genuinely care so I ploughed on.

I told how once I was living at Madam's, I had begun to notice things weren't all they seemed. My room was at the very top of the house, and there were three other girls living on the second floor – and *none* of them worked downstairs in the shop.

'Another girl here, called Nell, came soon after I did, but she was put to work upstairs straight away. Madam told me I was too skinny and needed to fill out to be one of her upstairs girls. And it was then I realised what was going on.'

'And Nell hasn't managed to escape from Madam either?'

'I don't know if Nell has ever tried to get away, it's almost as if… she's lost all her fight. She used to be quite brave when we were at the orphanage together. And when I came back here after Charles died, I told her I'd help her get away, too.'

'Madam wouldn't let you keep working in the shop?'

'I pleaded with her to let me, but she wouldn't give in, saying that as soon as I was fifteen, I would be expected to give up the shop work and be part of her team of girls. The older women in the shop – the ones who had once worked upstairs, but were past the age of attracting men – were put to work in the shop.'

My chest was heavy as I remembered how fearful I had been at the thought of being with a man for the first time and, worse still, a man who had paid for my services in that dirty way.

Eric shook his head and pursed his lips together at this revelation. 'That evil old bat!' he said angrily. 'You and Nell… you were so young.'

I couldn't help smiling at his description of Madam. 'You're right, she is an old bat, there's no mistake about that,' I told him, warming to him as each moment passed.

'By the time my fifteenth birthday came along, Madam was desperately trying to feed me up,' I told him, staring into the middle distance.

'Ah yes, so that you filled out?' Eric said with a disgusted snort.

I met his gaze with a heavy sigh. 'Exactly. As I said, she wanted me to have my womanly curves so that I could better attract her clients. Nell had a buxom figure long before I got my rounder shape,' I explained.

'Looking back, I was lucky I met Charles before Madam could force me into prostitution.' Eric's brows rose in curiosity at this, so I explained, 'Charles was an entrepreneur, and in the business of exporting sugar from India. He offered to make me his mistress.'

Eric nodded slowly. 'Well, I'm glad you had Charles,' he said. 'But what happened to him? Why aren't you still with him?'

I swallowed and gazed down at my hands, feeling a lump in my throat as I recalled Charles's last hours on board the ship.

'I was happy for a while with Charles, but I had nowhere to go after he died. I ended up back here, begging to be allowed to work for Madam in whatever way she needed.' I looked up into Eric's sympathetic gaze. 'That was a sad day for me,' I told him dismally.

'That's bad luck, Scarlett, and I'm sorry to hear about Charles dying that way,' he said, leaning towards me. 'But you still haven't told me why you couldn't go back to your family home, after you found out that Madam's shop wasn't all it had seemed.'

I hesitated at this question. It was much harder to talk about than Charles and why I had come back here after he died. There was still so much pain inside me over what happened at that time in my life, and Eric must have sensed my unease.

'You don't have to talk about it… I mean, if it's too painful,' he offered soothingly.

I took a deep breath and pushed away the feeling that I needed to keep all this inside of me forever. 'I don't mind…' I began tentatively. 'We were just an ordinary family, like so many others. After my father went off to war, things got harder, but together we managed… that is until the autumn of 1918…'

Eric hesitated before asking, 'Was it the Spanish flu? Take your time, Scarlett,' he said. 'There's no rush to tell me anything.'

Recalling that awful time made my body tremble and my heart beat faster, but I gathered my courage together and tried to tell him how it had been.

'I were nine years old when the epidemic hit Brighton,' I told Eric as I gazed into the middle distance. 'Watching my younger brother die first broke all of our hearts.' Tears pooled in my eyes. 'He was only three years old, you see,' I said, aware that I'd never spoken these words aloud to anyone else before.

The tears began to roll down my face then, and I could do nothing to stop them. The telling of my story sounded strange, as if I were looking down on myself from somewhere high above me.

Eric narrowed his eyes and pulled his brows in. 'Go on, Scarlett, what happened next?' he probed gently.

'We… that is my mama and me, tried our best to save the others, but one by one they died. It was devastating, Eric, I really can't tell you how much it hurt, or how much I regretted that I was the one who survived when the others died.'

My voice sounded shaky as I spoke, but I was determined to tell him everything, despite the breaking of my heart all over again.

'It was when me mama died, that was the worst, because then I was completely alone in the world.' I could hear my accent slipping back to Albion Hill as I spoke.

'What about your father, Scarlett? Did he return from the war when all this happened?' His face looked hopeful.

I hated to disappoint Eric, and wished with all my heart that had been the case, because at the time I was desperate to see my da, but I shook my head dismally.

'It was impossible for my father to get home, and especially worse because it was the end of the war when this all happened. It meant there was chaos everywhere. On his return, my father was a different man to the one I remembered, and he was completely devastated about my mother's death. He looked at me as if it should have been me to have died, and not her.' I bit down hard on my lower lip, remembering.

'Within months of returning home, he too was dead. He drowned at sea while trying to make a living for us both, after turning to the drink.'

For the first time in a long time, I was properly crying now. Great heaving sobs racked my body, causing me to lift my knees and hug them tightly into myself.

Whilst I sat rocking myself in this sorry state of overwhelming grief, I became aware of Eric wrapping his arms around me. And against my better judgement, I sank gratefully into the comforting depths of his embrace.

Chapter Nine

Eric slowly undressed me, and when I was laying naked beneath him, his gaze roamed the length of my body. He had appeared at my bedroom door this morning, and this time he was happy to do more than just talk.

For once, I didn't inwardly flinch at a man staring at me in this way. I was not used to this kind of tenderness from my clients, but had become very good at hiding my disgust. Usually, the men would come and go very quickly, and the dirty deed done within minutes.

There was no talking or lingering over the pleasures of the sexual act, and I'd come to accept that this way was best. After all, they'd paid for the service I was providing, and even though inside I'd be crying with the shame of it all, we would go about the business of coupling in a mechanical way.

However, everything was different today with Eric, because already he felt more like my lover than a paying customer. By no stretch of the imagination could he be called good-looking. His nose was too large, his belly too round. But in those hazel eyes I could see compassion and understanding, and I was soon relaxing in his company.

Our lovemaking was slow and tender, and when at last Eric let go of me, there was something niggling at the back of my mind. Would Madam come crashing into my bedroom demanding that Eric leave in a minute? I was already in her bad books, and couldn't risk anything else happening.

'Eric...' I began, needing to voice this worry. 'Madam will be here in a minute, I'm sure of it,' I told him tentatively. 'We have limited time with clients, and she doesn't allow us to go over that; if we do, we are in big trouble.'

Eric smiled lazily up at me and pulled me quickly back into his arms. 'Don't you worry about that, my love,' he whispered into my ear. 'Madam made me fully aware of that silly rule, and I've paid her double the going rate for you,' he said, a smile twitching at the corners of his mouth.

Pulling out of his arms, I quickly sat up. 'Now, why on earth would you do that?' I asked, my heart beating fast at this revelation.

Eric's eyes softened and that smile was back on his face again. 'Because I like you, Scarlett,' he said, and then he added, 'You know, you're a special lady.'

'I don't know anything of the sort, and you barely know me at all,' I told him, but despite myself I felt a warm glow inside at his words.

'Honey, I've seen enough for me to know how I feel about you,' he answered. 'Scarlett, I'm serious. I might even be in love with you,' he admitted.

This admission was making my head spin. 'That won't do, though, will it, Eric?' I said, sensing his eyes on me as I stood up to get dressed. 'The thing is... us two, we are worlds apart.'

Eric retrieved his cigarettes from his jacket pocket and, after lighting up, he blew out a puff of smoke and looked at me thoughtfully.

'Does that mean you can't be loved by me or by anyone else then, Scarlett? Even though you are truly the most beautiful woman I've ever seen,' he said evenly.

There was a strange feeling in my stomach as I pulled on my dress, and I realised it had been a while since I had felt as if I was loved. 'Of course not,' I replied, flattered by his smooth words. 'But it does mean you have to share that love with lots of other men.'

I heard the bitterness in my own voice, knowing I was pushing him to clarify what he meant or where this liaison could lead… if it were to lead anywhere.

Eric seemed to be thinking hard about this. 'What do you want most in the world, Scarlett?' he asked. 'Is it love you are searching for, or is it something else?' he said, crossing his arms over his chest.

This was a strange question to ask someone in my position. I certainly didn't love Eric; how could I? I'd only just met him. And anyway, I wasn't in the business of falling in love. I had loved my family once, and I'd loved Charles, but they had all gone and left me, so love was pretty pointless really.

But Eric, it seemed, was a kind man, and I had to be truthful here. 'Freedom is what I really crave, Eric. To be able to escape from this kind of life and have all the things that money can buy,' I told him truthfully, wishing I could have both of these things. 'Not much to ask, is it?' I said, throwing back my head and laughing, before doing up the suspenders on my stockings.

Eric shook his head. 'Quite right,' he answered seriously. 'Well, I can offer you all of that, if you'll let me.' He looked steadily across the room at me as he spoke.

My heart leapt at his words. Had dreaming about

Eric been a good omen, after all? 'Are you serious?' I asked, desperately needing to make sure he wasn't toying with me here.

'You're what I've been looking for, Scarlett. I understand you don't love me, but maybe you could learn to love me in the future? In the meantime, I could save you from all this,' he promised, gesturing wide with his hands.

Was I being given a second chance of escape? Aware I had to tread carefully, I waited for Eric to tell me what exactly he was offering me.

When we were both dressed, and he still hadn't told me anything more on the subject, I knew I needed to be blunt. 'What do you mean exactly, Eric? You'll need to explain to me what you *could* give me, before we can move forwards here.'

My heart was beating at a furious rate, and the breath was caught in my throat, but I dampened down the excitement. If Eric's promises came to nothing, I would be left with only bitter disappointment.

He stubbed out his cigarette in the ashtray, and then, taking a comb from his pocket, stood up and walked over to the mirror. After a moment of running the comb through his dark hair, he turned back to me.

'Isn't it obvious, Scarlett? I'd love to marry you, but I can't, because I'm already married. Instead, I'd like you to be my mistress, and that's my offer.'

Eric had no idea that he held all my hopes and dreams in his hand that day. Escaping from Madam was like a dream come true for me, and my heart soared at his words. Still wary of his intentions, though, I tried not to show how much the thought of escaping meant to me.

I took a deep, slow breath. 'I'd like that, too, Eric,'

I told him calmly. 'But there would be conditions attached to any arrangement that we make between us; things I would need to put in place.' Holding my breath, I waited for Eric to change his mind.

He offered me a questioning gaze. 'Conditions? What conditions are those then?' he said, giving me a straight look.

Lifting my chin, I stood my ground. 'One of those conditions would be security in the form of a house,' I told him evenly, and waited for his reaction to this request.

However tempting Eric's offer was, it would be worthless if he wouldn't play by my rules. My mistake with Charles was that I had not set 'conditions' and I'd learnt to my cost that this was not the way to do business.

Eric looked conflicted as he rubbed at the bridge of his nose. *Was this the end of his offer?* I wondered. *Maybe I'd asked for too much?* I forced myself to breathe deeply, and fought the urge to retract what I'd said.

'Let me think about how best to do this,' he said eventually. 'I'd like you to live in Brighton ideally, that way I'd be able to visit you whenever I am here on business, which is quite regularly. And it's a fair distance from where I live in Kensington, so it wouldn't arouse suspicion with my wife or my family.'

I nodded, not trusting myself to speak in case I said the wrong thing and Eric's offer would come crashing down around my ears. I could see his mind ticking over the problem, and I hoped he could work this out in a way that would be of benefit to us both.

'What line of work are you in, Eric?' I ventured, feeling odd again; we never asked client's personal questions. But if I was considering this man's offer, I needed to know more about him.

'I own a shipbuilding company in the Docklands, it's called Johnson and Johnson. And the last few days I've been staying in Brighton on urgent business,' he told me, glancing down at his pocket watch.

'That's interesting,' I said, thinking I needed to be alone to think about what he had said and to mull over whether he was genuine or not. Hopefully, my gut instinct would lead me in the right direction. 'I think you'd better go soon,' I told him, aware that my attitude would either make him keener or put him off me forever.

Eric walked over and took me by the shoulders. 'All this might take a while to sort out, Scarlett,' he said with a frown. 'But you'll agree, once your conditions have been met?' he asked, looking hopeful.

Relief flooded through me. 'Once the house is in my name and everything is in order, Eric, I'll leave Madam's to be with you,' I told him truthfully. 'But *not* until that happens.'

His face lit up at this news. 'That's good to hear, honey,' he told me excitedly. 'Now, I do need to go, or I'll be late. But rest assured, I'll be back.'

When Eric left a short while later, promising to see me the following week, it was all I could do not to shout with joy at my apparent good fortune.

Chapter Ten

'So, you're leaving then?' Nell was sitting at her dressing table where she paused in her application of make-up to look across at me and narrow her eyes.

Eric hadn't visited this week as he'd promised, but a letter had arrived telling me he was sorting out the purchase of a house in Lewes for me. I was very excited. However, I'd made a grave mistake. In my joy at the thought of escape, I'd confided in Nell, and as I watched her reaction to my news, I now realised that could have been the wrong decision.

'Listen, Nell. Once I've escaped, I'll find a way to help you get out of Madam's, too,' I told her, wondering how I was going to achieve this, but knowing somehow I would.

Nell wasn't pleased for me in the least. Instead, her eyes brimmed with tears as she stared at me dismally. 'I doubt that very much. You'll disappear and leave me to my fate, just like you did last time! Nothing changes around here, Scarlett,' she said resignedly.

My heart lurched. Nell was my friend, and I didn't like seeing her upset; I also knew how she felt being trapped here at Madam's. Years ago, she had watched me leave with Charles, with a solemn look on her face. She had said nothing, but her expression had filled me with guilt back then.

I placed my hand on her arm, but Nell stiffened beneath my touch. 'I promise I'll do all I can to help you once I'm living as Eric's mistress. You're my best friend, Nell, and I won't leave you to the mercy of Madam,' I promised.

My mind was working overtime in its pursuit of how exactly I was going to do this, but somehow, I would find a way. I owed Nell for the friendship she'd shown me in the orphanage all those years before.

Nell's eyes hardened as she swiped away the tears. 'If you say so,' she said, pursing her lips before turning back to the mirror to continue applying her make-up.

Her back was ramrod straight as she continued to paint her face, and I tried to reassure her. 'Once I've left, I'll ask Eric if he can find you employment in his shipyard, maybe even in the office,' I cajoled, hoping that this might be something he could do.

Eric was a businessman and entrepreneur, so surely he could help me find a place for Nell in the outside world? But Nell continued to ignore me, and there didn't seem to be anything I could say to convince her right now. Leaving her to her make-up, I went back to my own room.

That night, I dreamt Nell betrayed me to Madam and I woke up sweating, with my heart racing. Sitting up, I looked across at the wall that divided Nell's bedroom and mine. *Surely she wouldn't do that*, I wondered, *would she?* I hoped the bad dream was my over-anxious mind playing tricks on me, but there was no way of knowing.

In the next few days, Nell took to totally ignoring me whenever we came across each other. She also seemed on more friendly terms with Madam than ever before, and one evening I hid on the landing and watched her go furtively into Madam's room.

Putting my ear to the door, I tried to listen to what the two of them were saying, but only a muffled exchange reached my ears. However, everything pointed to Madam knowing of my plans to leave, and this thought made me nervous.

Eric became my sole focus now. I couldn't wait for him to give me more news on the house, so that the day I left would come round quicker.

At last, a week later, Eric returned. As Madam showed him up to my room, I quickly closed the door, ignoring Nell who was watching with interest from her doorway.

'I'm pleased to see you, Eric. How's the house purchase coming along?' I asked him eagerly, and I waited with bated breath to hear his news.

Eric's eyes sparkled as he told me he'd found a property in the nearby market town of Lewes. 'I'm in the middle of securing the deal, Scarlett darling, and it shouldn't take long now,' he said, taking me in his arms. 'You only need to be patient for a few more weeks, honey.'

Nell was listening through the doorway, but I couldn't tell Eric this. I knew he would advise me to leave now, and not wait for the house to be signed over to me. But I'd made a pledge to myself not to go until the security I craved was firmly in place.

When Nell cornered me a few days later and asked when I was leaving, I could see the jealousy shining in her eyes, and understood I had to be cautious.

'Our plans have been put on hold because his wife found out about me,' I lied. 'So I won't be leaving after all.'

I got the distinct impression that Nell didn't believe

me. But at least she was talking to me again, and when I did leave, I knew I had to do it secretly and without her knowledge.

A whole month went by, and I was beginning to get very jittery waiting to hear from Eric, but also trying to act normally around Nell and Madam. Eric returned at last, and this time as soon as he walked into my room, I told him how urgent it was that I leave Madam's.

'She can't stop you going,' he reassured me, not understanding my concern.

To Eric, it was simple, and I was forced to admit my suspicions that Nell had told Madam about my escape plan. 'Madam will find a way to stop me leaving, I feel sure,' I said, wringing my hands nervously, knowing that he hadn't really grasped how nasty Madam could be.

'Calm down, Scarlett. I've bought the house for you in Lewes, and the contract will complete in a few days.' He was looking at me now with an intensely worried gaze. 'Do you need to leave right now? Is that what you're saying?'

Taking a deep breath, I reminded myself that although I trusted Eric implicitly, I had to leave Madam's only *after* the house in Lewes was signed over to me. I couldn't risk it any other way. 'I'm sorry, Eric, I'm overreacting and I'm sure you're right. Madam can't stop me from going with you,' I said, not believing this for one minute.

That night, I thought about how Madam had taken to restricting the movements of us 'upstairs girls' more closely recently. Any time we left the building, we were followed by one of her men. I hadn't told Eric about this, but they watched our every move. This meant that when the time came to go, I would have to leave under the cover of darkness.

It was unclear why Madam had begun this rule, and no-one had dared to ask her, but I had a sneaking suspicion it was something to do with Nell. It had all started after I saw Nell sneak into Madam's room that night.

Chapter Eleven

In his letter, Eric had promised to send any further correspondence to me via a PO box number at the local post office in Brighton, as I didn't trust Nell or Madam not to intercept my post. If Nell had told Madam of my plans, I was convinced that they would both be waiting for me to get word from Eric.

That morning, I went for a short walk to the post office to check for any mail from Eric. I was always followed by one of Madam's men, who waited outside the building for me each time I went in, and then watched my every move.

This particular day, to my excitement, I found that Eric had sent me a parcel. I opened it inside the post office, away from the prying eyes of Madam's spies. There was a letter inside, some paperwork, and what looked like a key. I quickly stood to one side of the counter and read the letter.

> *My Darling Scarlett,*
> *You'll be pleased to hear that today I signed the house in Lewes over to you. I have included the deeds, which you will see have your name on them, and as the owner you just need to put your signature at the bottom of the page. I have also enclosed a front door key to the house, and am pleased to say you can move*

in as soon as you like.

I hope you'll be very happy in the property. I am tied up with work at the moment, but I will look forward to us spending many happy hours together in the future.

All my love,
Eric

After looking furtively around me, I tucked the small parcel inside my coat. Madam's spy was still loitering outside, and I ignored him as I came out of the building, and strode back to Madam's with my head held high.

Now that I had the address and the key to the house, it was time for me to leave, but I was again feeling jittery. I would have to secretly pack my suitcase without the others knowing what I was doing, and I knew that wouldn't be easy.

That evening, after my last client had left, I pulled my empty suitcase out from under the bed so that I would be ready to leave as soon as I could escape the hawk-like eyes of Nell and Madam.

Opening the empty suitcase, I was just about to place one of my dresses inside it, when I noticed a small, round shape standing proud of the lining of the case. Placing the dress on the bed, I quickly ran my fingers over it, feeling a solid form beneath my touch.

My heart began to race. Quickly, I searched for an opening in the lining and found a small corner was slightly ripped, and then noticed that here the material was quite frayed.

Turning the case upside down, I shook it vigorously until whatever it was had travelled nearer to the hole in the fabric. Then, as I made a grab for it with my fingers, I gasped in surprise as the object fell out onto my open palm.

Everything else faded into the background as, to my surprise, I stared at the amethyst necklace which glinted at me in the dim light of my bedroom. It must have been there all the time, and somehow got wedged in the lining of the suitcase while I was still on board the ship with Charles.

No wonder I couldn't find the necklace before; it had been well hidden under the lining of the case. But to find it now, just as I had at last found an escape from Madam's, was ironic, as I would have sold it instead of coming back here. In truth, it wouldn't have given me enough to live on after Charles died, but it would certainly have softened the blow of being penniless for a while.

Just then, the sound of Nell moving around her room jolted me out of my thoughts, and I was acutely aware of the empty suitcase lying on the bed. Quick as a flash, I hid the necklace under my clothing and finished packing my belongings.

I would stay in my room for the evening and go to bed fully clothed tonight. That way I could leave quietly in the middle of the night. How I would get past Madam's guards I still had no idea.

Sweat beaded my brow as I lay in bed wide awake long into the night. By three o'clock in the morning, I could wait no longer. The house was in total darkness, and time was running out. I had to attempt my escape now.

As I swung my legs out of bed, Nell's loud snores echoed through the thin walls, and I grabbed hold of my case and placed my wool coat loosely over my shoulders. In the darkness, the creak of the door opening echoed through the house, and I froze for a moment and waited for Madam to appear.

When nothing happened, I opened the door as quietly as I could and tiptoed out onto the dark landing. Suddenly, light flooded the area, blinding me with its brightness, and my case fell to the floor with a loud thud. I groped for its handle with my heart thumping wildly in my ears.

'Where do you think you're going?'

I turned to see Nell standing close by me. Holding tightly to the handle of the case, I tried to run past her, but she was faster. She lunged towards me, and I found myself pinned painfully beneath her on the hard floorboards of the landing.

'Madam!' she yelled at the top of her voice. 'Scarlett's bloody trying to escape!'

I wasn't giving up without a fight, and I began grappling with Nell. I pulled at her hair, biting into her arm, and kicking her hard, just as Madam appeared on the landing.

'Stop that!' Madam yelled. 'Or I'll get one of my men to restrain you!'

Realising that I was beaten, I let go of Nell and staggered to my feet. She was staring at me with her eyes narrowed, while rubbing at her arm where I'd sunk my teeth into her flesh. With my mind whirling, I tried in vain to see where my escape route was, but I could see there was none; it seemed I was trapped.

Nell had squashed my lungs against the floor and winded me, and I found it hard to catch my breath as I turned towards Madam.

'You can't stop me if I want to leave,' I said shakily, and I heard Nell let out a loud spiteful laugh from beside me.

I swung around to face her. 'Why have you done this, Nell?' I asked, hating the sound of regret in my voice, but unable to help it. All the years of friendship we had both shared had come down to this. But Nell simply stared back at me with her lips pursed and her fists clenched by her sides.

Madam crossed her arms across her chest. 'Maybe you should take a leaf out of Nell's book,' she said smugly. 'She knows where her bread's best buttered,' she added, lifting those pencilled brows at Nell.

Nell shook her head and glared at me. 'It's cos she thinks she's better than everyone else here,' she said, finding her voice at last.

'That's not true, Nell,' I told her, tears pricking my eyes. 'You're a fool. I would've helped you, don't you know that?' I was telling the truth, because somehow I would have found a way to help Nell if she hadn't told Madam of my plans.

Nell dropped her gaze and shrugged her shoulders before looking across at Madam for further instructions.

'Get her back into the bedroom!' Madam ordered, and Nell sprang into action immediately. The two of them manhandled me roughly back into my room and threw me, and my case, onto the floor.

'You're going to work extra hard now until you've paid the debt you owe me,' Madam said, pulling a key for the room out of her pocket.

Pushing myself upright on the floor, I glared back at her. 'And what debt is that?' I demanded. But Madam merely shot me a look of hatred before passing the key to Nell and striding out onto the landing.

'Just so you know, Scarlett, I'm now getting every penny I earn and every penny *you* earn, too. So you've done me a favour by trying to escape.' Nell grinned spitefully and stared towards Madam's retreating back, before stepping outside and locking the bedroom door behind her.

Chapter Twelve

I was losing track of time. Each day was exactly the same as the one before, and I was trapped in Madam's house with no way of escape. It must be at least a week since Eric sent me the key to the house in Lewes, and since then Madam had kept me locked in my room.

Whenever I needed a bath or to use the toilet along the corridor, Nell or one of the other girls escorted me there, and then waited outside the door until I came out again. One of the girls also brought me my food each day, and if it was Nell, I tried to reason with her, but she refused to engage in any kind of conversation with me.

Every day Madam brought me a client, with a warning beforehand. 'If you spill the beans to the coppers, then I'll deny your accusations. I'll tell them you've been stealing from me,' she told me with hatred in her voice. 'Nell will back me up with this, too,' she added, and I knew she would.

As I lay wide awake at five o'clock one morning, I tried to stem the panic, telling myself that somehow Eric would find a way to rescue me. If only he knew of my predicament.

In the silence of the morning, the low murmur of voices coming from outside reached my ears. I swung my legs out of bed and walked across to the window.

Through the early morning half-light, I could see Madam on the pavement below, talking to one of her guards.

My window was locked, and Madam had the key so I couldn't open it, but by placing my ear to the glass, and with little or no traffic at this time of the day, snippets of their conversation reached my ears.

An icy shiver ran up my spine as the words 'do away with her' and 'needs to be done soon' and 'coppers will come knocking on me door' came floating up to my window. I didn't need to hear any more; it was obvious what Madam had planned for me.

My mind whirled. *Who could help me out of this deadly situation I found myself in?* There was no doubt that if I didn't act soon, I would be murdered in cold blood.

I slumped down on the bed, and thought about Nell and how kind she had once been to me. I was saddened at how things had changed between us. She was now my archenemy, someone who despised me, and my eyes filled with tears, because finally my luck had run out.

Sobbing into my hands, the dark days of the Spanish Influenza filled my mind, and I saw again the first of my family to die. My brother Benjamin who was so young, and then the rest of my family had succumbed to the influenza one after another. It was hard to understand why I had been spared the same fate, as I lay back on the pillows feeling helpless.

Digging deep inside myself, I tried to find a glimmer of hope, something to show me the way forward. There had to be a way out of this situation, and if there wasn't, I would go down fighting.

Would my gift – which had always been a curse – be able to help me now? Closing my eyes, I tried to clear my head of fear and waited for a sign.

There was nothing, and I bit down on my lip, fighting disappointment. Just as I was about to give up, an image swam into my head, and I could see a hazy picture of Eric. I concentrated hard and focussed solely on the image.

Eric was in an office and he had his head bent low, studying some paperwork. Keeping my eyes shut tightly, I watched him moving around the room, as he got up from his desk and pulled a file out of a nearby cabinet.

'Eric…' I began urgently under my breath, aware there might be ears listening at my bedroom door. 'Come to Madam's and don't delay, please. She's holding me against my will!'

However, Eric simply carried on with his work and, as expected, couldn't hear me. But I didn't want to give up just yet.

'Eric, it's me, *Scarlett.* Come to Madam's and bring the police before she…' I couldn't finish the sentence, I couldn't say 'has me killed' or 'commits murder'.

Keeping my eyes closed, I tried to keep the hope alive that somehow I would find a way to escape. But there was no sign that Eric had heard my pleas, as the scene in my head faded away.

Chapter Thirteen

I must have dozed off, because the next thing I knew the clock at the side of my bed said eight o'clock. And I quickly realised the tread of footsteps outside my door had woken me up.

Sitting up in bed and listening intently for any further noise, I heard the distinct sound of a key being turned in the lock and, unexpectedly, Nell's voice.

She pulled the door open and appeared in the doorway looking agitated. 'Scarlett, you need to get out now!' she urged.

A jolt of fear went through me and I considered ignoring Nell, but her next words made me think again.

'Please! You're in grave danger and I've come to help you!' she added urgently.

Jumping off the bed, I rushed across the room and eyed her warily, and she stared back at me, her expression unwavering. *Was this a trick?* I wondered. *Another ploy by Nell, instigated by Madam, to trap me in some way?*

'What is it, Nell?' I asked. 'I won't be falling for your lies again!' I blinked at her and took in a deep breath. 'I don't know what your game is,' I said evenly, staring at her steadily. 'But don't you think you've done enough to make things difficult for me? After all, we were once good friends.'

'We need to get you outta 'ere now,' she hissed, her frightened gaze darting from me to the landing area behind. '*Madam*… she's going to have you done away with, you know, taken care of…' Her words trailed off as she gave me an intense stare and bit down nervously on her lower lip.

The conversation between Madam and one of her men came back to me. *But why would Nell try and help me now?* My thoughts were jumbled, and I couldn't think straight for the sound of my heartbeat thrashing in my ears.

'Scarlett, I'm sorry, I really am,' Nell said with tears in her eyes. 'If you want the truth, I were jealous of you leaving without me, but I don't want you to be harmed in any way, course I don't. Cos, as you say, we were friends once.'

Despite the way Nell had betrayed me, my heart went out to her now. 'I would've blinking come back for you,' I told her truthfully. 'You didn't believe I would, though, did you, Nell?'

She shook her head sadly, and then quickly indicated towards the stairway. 'Nope, you're right. Didn't think you would. I thought you'd disappear out of me life, never to be seen again. That aside, you need to get dressed now, there ain't no time for this, Scarlett. No time for anything but you getting away from Madam!'

Something in Nell's tone made the hairs lift at the back of my neck, and I knew then with a deep certainty that I *could* trust her. Galvanised into action by this, I turned back into the room and quickly dressed. The amethyst necklace was on my bedside table and I put it around my neck, hiding it under my clothing, before retrieving my packed case.

'I'll check the coast is clear first,' Nell said urgently, before poking her head out of the door and looking left and right on the landing.

I followed her out onto the landing as quietly as I could, but we had only taken a few steps when Madam's door flew open.

'You can stop right there, you two!' she shrieked.

Madam's eyes glowed like hot coals and I froze under her penetrating glare. Beside me, Nell took matters into her own hands and gave me a hard shove towards the staircase.

'Run, Scarlett!' she yelled. 'Go on, get going now afore it's too late!'

The suitcase was knocked out of my hand, and I wasn't going anywhere without my precious few belongings. I grabbed the case and made a run for the stairs, but Madam was quickly upon me. Taking hold of my arm, she screamed for one of her men to come to her aid.

As I wrestled with her, Nell moved in to help me. However, she was soon overpowered by one of Madam's heavies, who had arrived on the scene within seconds. Between the two of them, I was shoved unceremoniously back into my bedroom.

Madam's verbal abuse of Nell reached my ears, followed by the unmistakable sound of her administering one of her slaps. I was sorry for my former friend who had, in the end, tried to save me, and was now being punished for her trouble.

With the door locked again, I wondered where to go from here, when another sound reached my ears. And this time it was coming from downstairs.

For the second time that morning, I rushed to the

door to listen. Quick, heavy footsteps echoed on the stairs, and I could hear Nell calling out that I was being held prisoner.

Then a miracle happened! I could hear a man's voice, which sounded remarkably like Eric's, telling Madam in no uncertain terms to let me out this instant. He must have been outside my door, because the words were very clear.

'Eric! Eric! I'm in here!' I shouted, and I banged on the door with both of my fists, desperate to be heard now.

A stunned silence was followed by the sound of the key being turned in the lock, and then Eric was standing in the doorway with a policeman by his side. His face was alight with pleasure at the sight of me.

'Scarlett!' he said breathlessly. 'Has that wicked old bat hurt you? If she has, I'll have her guts for garters!' he said, reaching out to me.

Relief coursed through me at the sight of him. 'I'm still in one piece, thanks, Eric. But I'm bloody glad to see you!' I said before stepping into his outstretched arms.

As Eric hugged me tightly against his pinstriped suit jacket, I could see Madam over his shoulder. She was being handcuffed to a policeman while Nell hovered uncertainly in her bedroom doorway.

Nell looked up and caught my eye. Her face was still red from Madam's earlier assault, and I thought about how she had initially betrayed me to Madam. However, if I told the police that she was in on the kidnapping, she'd be arrested along with Madam. It was nothing less than she deserved, but for old times' sake I couldn't do that to her.

'Come on, Scarlett,' Eric said, releasing me and

holding me at arm's length. 'It's time to leave this house of ill repute and start a new life in Lewes where you'll be safe.' He lifted my case from the bed and took hold of my arm before steering me out of the room.

As we passed Nell, who was still standing in the same place on the landing, I silently mouthed the words 'thank you' to her, and in return she gave me a small shaky smile.

We stepped out into the cold morning air to see Madam sitting in the back of a police van parked up outside the house, and I walked past her with my head held high. Once we were safely on our way to Lewes, I leaned against the back of the seat, feeling quite shaken by events.

I turned my head in Eric's direction as he steered the car. 'What happened?' I asked. 'I haven't seen you for ages and then you turn up today, thankfully, just when I flipping needed you most.'

Eric glanced at me and then at the road before replying. 'I'm sorry I haven't been in touch for some time, Scarlett. There's been a crisis at work. My manager had an accident and died from his injuries. It's been absolute chaos dealing with all that and making sure his widow and children were alright, as well as keeping up with the workload.'

'Oh Lord, Eric, that sounds pretty bad. Sorry to hear about that,' I sympathised, feeling for the manager's widow. 'It must be hard managing without him at work.'

'It's incredibly hard, Scarlett. And I can't stay away long now. The man I've left in charge is not really capable of coping on his own without me, and my son's too young to leave holding the fort.'

The mention of Eric's son set me on edge. He hadn't

once told me that he had children in the short time I'd known him, and this thought made me uneasy. 'How old is your son, Eric?' I asked, trying not to picture him in a happy family scene.

Eric didn't answer this question straight away, but instead changed the subject and spoke of trivial things such as the weather. Some time later, he pulled up outside a small Victorian terraced house, and parked the car before turning around and taking me in his arms.

His kiss was deep and comforting, like a warm blanket being wrapped around me, and afterwards he cocked his head thoughtfully to one side.

'Scarlett... about my son,' he said, entwining his fingers in mine. 'His name is Frankie and he's only ten years old right now, but he's mad keen on working at the shipyard with me.' Eric had a proud smile on his face as he spoke of his boy.

'That's good he's keen on the business. So one day he'll take over from you?'

'Frankie often accompanies me to work when he isn't at school. And the truth is, he probably knows more about the company than the man I've left in charge today.'

I could see how much Eric loved his son, but I was feeling uneasy at this knowledge.

'Eric, there are things I need to know,' I told him, trying to choose my words carefully. For the first time since meeting Eric, I realised how very little I knew about him. 'It may seem a bit late to be asking... but...' I began tentatively.

Eric tilted my chin up towards him and looked into my eyes. 'There's nothing you need to know, rest assured of that, Scarlett Cunningham. Except that I want to be with *you*,' he said firmly.

'I love my son dearly, but he isn't the reason we're together. You're the woman I want to be with, Scarlett, and only you. It's true we have a business arrangement, but it's more than that for me.'

Tears pricked the back of my eyes. How could I ever repay this kind man? Especially as I was sure I would never feel the same way about him as he did about me.

'Thank you, Eric. I'm overwhelmed with gratitude for what you've done for me,' I reassured him. 'And I'm grateful for the house,' I told him. 'And most of all for sending me the key, and for turning up today just when I needed you.'

Eric nodded slowly, and a small frown appeared between his brows. 'That was the odd thing, Scarlett,' he said, giving me a searching look. 'You won't believe this, but I had the strangest feeling this morning while I was at work.'

The breath caught in my throat at Eric's words. *Had my attempt at reaching out to him this morning worked, after all?* I wondered.

'I have no idea why, but I had the odd sensation that I needed to get to you quickly, before it was too late.' He paused, as if deep in thought. 'Which sounds absolutely ridiculous, I know. But honestly, Scarlett, it was almost as if you were in the room with me pleading for my help in some way.' He leaned back on the seat and laughed at this.

I laughed too at the ridiculousness of this, while trying to hide how I really felt. 'You're right, it does sound silly. I mean, how could you possibly have known I was in danger? But I'm glad you took notice of *that feeling* and came to my aid anyway.'

That was an understatement if ever there was one,

because without Eric's intervention this morning, things could have turned out very differently for me. And I shuddered at this thought.

Eric shrugged in a non-committal way. 'To be honest, I took a chance on it. It was the nudge that I needed. I hadn't heard back from you after sending you the key to the house, and I wanted to make sure you were all right.'

I thought about this. 'But what about the policeman you brought to Madam's, and how did you know she was holding me against my will?'

'I didn't know, but as I got nearer to the house, I heard the old dragon shouting and I guessed it would be at you. After all, you've never followed orders when it came to Madam before, have you?'

'You've got the measure of me then.' I laughed at this observation, because it was true.

'It was pure chance there was an officer of the law walking his beat along that road. And, as you can imagine, he knows what kind of establishment Madam runs. So he's often in that area. Nell did the rest. She must have been watching out of the window, because just as we were about to knock on the door, she quickly opened it and lost no time in explaining what was going on inside the house.'

My heart was full of gratitude towards Nell, but I reminded myself that if she hadn't snitched on me to Madam in the first place, I wouldn't have been in that awful predicament.

Eric stepped out of the car and opened the door for me. 'The thing is, you're safe now, Scarlett,' he said, while lifting my case out of the boot of the car. We walked towards the house together, and he unlocked the front door. 'Welcome to your new home,' he said.

'Thank you so much, Eric,' I replied, sounding like an old record, and feeling a rush of affection for this man who had rescued me from certain death.

With the future bright, I understood my life would now be quite different, and I told myself not to waste a second of it looking back at my past. The disturbing image of the tall, dark-haired stranger that I still dreamt of nightly, was pushed to the back of my mind as I stepped over the threshold into my new home.

Chapter Fourteen

September 1933

It was Sunday morning, and I was decorating. As I moved the paint brush slowly up the walls of my narrow hallway, applying a light buttermilk colour in long, even strokes, I reflected on how much I loved this house.

It was hard to believe I had lived here in Lewes as Eric's mistress for two years. The time had flown by. With the dark days of poverty behind me, and the knowledge that I wouldn't end up back on Madam's doorstep again if anything happened to Eric, I was happy and content.

I was just admiring my handiwork on the newly painted wall when there was a knock at the door. Visitors were rare on a Sunday. Eric always spent the Sabbath with his family, and I rarely saw anyone else.

Recognising the young girl from next door standing on my doorstep, I beckoned her into the house.

'Hello there,' I said, aware that I must look a sight with my apron spattered with paint and my face bare of make-up.

The girl regarded me from under long, dark eyelashes. 'Good morning, I'm sorry to disturb you on the holy day,' she said uneasily. 'I'm Ruby Summers and I live next door...' she widened her large brown eyes at me as she spoke. 'Could I borrow some sugar, do you think?'

I knew Ruby by sight. She was a pretty young girl with a halo of dark hair, who was often seen out with her parents. Mr and Mrs Summers were very sombre-looking, always dressed in dark clothing, and they rarely, if ever, smiled. They had both gone out of their way to turn away if I came upon them in the street since my move into Lewes.

'Hello, Ruby, pleased to meet you. I'm Scarlett, and I have plenty of sugar,' I told her, opening the door wider. 'Come in, and mind the wet paint.' I indicated the walls of the hallway as she stepped over the threshold. 'Why don't you have a seat in the front parlour for a moment?

'Are you on your own today then?' I asked Ruby a moment later, as I handed her the bowl of sugar.

'My mum and dad are at a church service,' she replied. 'And I made up an excuse not to go.' She turned the corners of her mouth down mutinously as she spoke.

This didn't surprise me, as I'd often seen Ruby trailing reluctantly behind her parents on their way to church on a Sunday morning. 'Well, in that case, would you like to stay for a cup of tea?' I offered, quite liking the idea of some company today.

Ruby said she would love a cuppa, and I disappeared into the kitchen to make it. When I returned a moment later, she swung around guiltily from where she'd been staring at a photograph of my parents taken on their wedding day.

'Is that your mum and dad?' Ruby asked, sitting

down on the settee and indicating the picture. When I told her it was, she said, 'They look lovely. Do they visit you often? I bet you've got a nice family.'

I placed the tray of tea on the side table and straightened up. Lovely wasn't the word I would have used for my parents; my mother had a hard streak, and my father had been aloof.

'That photograph was taken a long time ago,' I told her. 'But you could say that I had a good family, as families go,' I said with a heavy heart.

I swallowed the lump in my throat and watched Ruby as she gazed around the room in adoration. And even though I barely knew this girl, something in me wanted her to know the truth. That sometimes life was hard, but whatever cards you were dealt by fate, there was a way to survive.

'All my family died in 1918...' I began, sitting down next to Ruby, and her head quickly turned in my direction. The words were hard to find, because I rarely spoke about my past. 'It was the Spanish Influenza, you see,' I continued meeting her gaze. What I didn't tell her was that my father had been spared this fate, but had perished soon after his return from the war.

Ruby looked shocked at this. 'Oh, my Lord,' she exclaimed. 'That's tragic, to lose everyone! I'm sorry to hear that. How perfectly awful for you!'

This was the hard bit, seeing the sympathy in other people's eyes. 'It was a long time ago, Ruby,' I said with a resigned shrug, while ignoring the feeling of emptiness I often had when thinking about my family.

She watched me get up and pour out the tea, and I sensed she wanted to know more.

'I hope you don't mind me asking, Scarlett, but what happened to you after your family had gone? You must have been quite young.' She glanced across at the photograph again then back at me with a questioning gaze.

After I had handed Ruby a cup of tea and placed mine down next to me, I took a deep breath and began to explain the past as best I could.

'I was nine years old when my mother became sick, and I hoped she wouldn't be taken from me as the others had been,' I told Ruby, remembering how much I'd prayed for Ma, but it had all been in vain. 'My Aunt Belle, who was my father's sister, took me in and looked after me when Ma died.'

Ruby's face looked hopeful that this was my happy ending. 'Was Belle a nice person, and did she look after you well?' she asked, placing her cup down on the table and lifting her eyebrows.

I thought about this for a moment. 'Belle *was* a nice person, Ruby,' I explained, thinking about my aunt's kindly manner. 'Although, there were things I didn't know about her, being so young.'

It had been a mystery to me, before the Spanish Influenza epidemic, why my family had shunned Belle for years. Of course, I was too young to understand the real reason why I was forbidden to associate with her, and it only became apparent to me years later.

However, as young as I was, I had eyes in my head. And it was obvious to me that Belle was different to the other women in our street. At the time, it was puzzling being told she was a sad, lonely figure, when it was obvious she had a stream of visitors every day.

'It's good you weren't all alone at that awful time then,' Ruby said now, giving me a steady look.

I could see from her face that she wanted to ask me what it was I hadn't known about Belle. But I chose not to enlighten her that day on Belle's occupation, or her eventual fate, and how I had ended up in the orphanage a year later.

'The thing is, Ruby, I survived that time in my life and moved on,' I said, eager to change the subject now. 'Do your parents often leave you behind when they go to church then?'

Ruby shook her head slowly. 'I do my best to get out of going to church,' she said solemnly, but then her eyes lit with excitement as she looked up.

'I'm starting work at Hanningtons' Department store in Brighton next week, now that I'm fifteen,' she lifted her chin proudly. 'But I have to admit to being a bit nervous about it,' she added, biting down on her bottom lip.

I sipped at my tea and gave her an encouraging smile. 'Don't worry, I'm sure you'll be fine,' I told her. And even though I had only just met Ruby, I was warming to her endearing personality.

'I hope so, I really do…' Ruby replied, looking quite doubtful about this.

Placing my teacup down, I leaned towards her. 'What is it about working in the store that worries you?' I asked, thinking she'd have no trouble fitting into the big, posh department store, which was known as *the* place to shop, and nicknamed 'the Harrods of Brighton'.

Ruby shifted on her seat and frowned. 'I don't know. Really. Even though it's what I dearly want to do, it's frightening.' She gazed into the middle distance as she spoke. 'There'll be lots to learn, and I'm worried I won't get it right.'

'But you seem like a bright girl to me, Ruby,' I said, trying to think of the right words to reassure her. 'I'm sure you'll be fine working for Hanningtons. What do your parents think about you working in the department store? Are they supportive?'

Ruby shook her head vigorously at this. 'They wanted me to work in Lewes in a boring hardware shop, and they tried to stop me from finding a position in Brighton. But I dug my heels in and insisted.'

'Good for you, that's the spirit,' I told her encouragingly.

Ruby took a long, deep breath. 'The thing is, my parents are very religious, and I don't share their beliefs,' she said, lifting her chin. 'Which makes it hard for me, because they don't want me to have any freedom.' She looked at me as if to say this was a sorry state of affairs.

I regarded her worried frown, and it seemed to me that she needed a friend – something I understood only too well.

'You're welcome to come here and see me anytime,' I told her, and was rewarded with a beaming smile, which spread right across her pretty face.

'Really? Oh, that's very kind of you. I'll look forward to that,' she replied, looking much happier than when she had first walked into my house.

'That's settled then,' I told Ruby, and we began discussing the weather, and how cold the evenings were becoming now we were into the month of September.

Looking back on that day, later in my life, the first thing I realised after Ruby had gone was that she'd forgotten to take the bowl of sugar home with her. And the second thing was how that first meeting with Ruby had been the start of a deep and close friendship between us, which would last a whole lifetime.

Chapter Fifteen

September 1939

I had been looking for a stray earring in my jewellery box when I came across the amethyst necklace. There it was, glinting in the daylight, and hidden amongst the other bits of jewellery.

I took a long, deep breath as I lifted it out, and then stared at the beautiful purple stone hanging on the long silver chain. Memories flooded back of the day I had been gifted the necklace while in Calcutta with Charles.

My mind whirled as I thought about Ruby's imminent departure into Brighton, and the recent announcement on the radio. The week before, the whole country had listened to Neville Chamberlain's radio announcement as he confirmed that the deadline for withdrawal of troops from Poland had expired. Therefore a state of war existed between Great Britain and Germany.

This momentous event had coincided with Ruby's decision to leave home. With her twenty-first birthday only days away, she would no longer be governed by her strictly religious parents. The time had come for her to move out of the family home in Lewes and live in Brighton.

Now, on the eve of her departure, Ruby had come over to say goodbye, arriving on my doorstep a few minutes ago.

'This necklace is a good luck charm, and originally from India,' I explained to her as I waited for her reaction, remembering how the child's father I'd saved had told me that the necklace had the power to protect the wearer from harm.

Ruby stared at the necklace, looking a bit mesmerised by the stone. The late afternoon sun streamed through the window, catching the colours, and making it shine in different shades of violet.

'The Hindi name for it is "Taabeej",' I continued, trying to spark Ruby's interest in the necklace and feeling desperate, despite myself, for her to accept this precious gift.

I placed the necklace down on the small table between us and waited. In the deepest recesses of my heart, I understood that if there was the slightest chance Ruby might escape injury, or death, during this most frightening of times, then I was ready to take it.

Right now, I would bargain with the gods for her survival. Over the past six years, since the day she had first appeared on my doorstep under the pretence of needing a bowl of sugar, we had become very close. Ruby was now a very dear friend, and I didn't want to lose her.

Letting out a long sigh, she regarded me with those big brown eyes of hers. 'It's too precious, Scarlett,' she said simply. 'Honestly, how can I take this valuable necklace with me to Brighton? What if I lose it?' She gave me a half smile and lifted her eyebrows questioningly.

Since hearing of Ruby's decision to move away, which closely followed the announcement that the country was now at war, I had found myself in turmoil. And the thought of losing this young woman from my life was almost unbearable.

'You won't lose it, Ruby,' I told her, lifting my chin. 'I want you to have it,' I added, wondering how to persuade her to take the necklace with her.

Ruby knitted her brow and leaned towards me. 'Listen, Scarlett, I'm sure I'll be fine in Brighton. You know what everyone's saying, that this war will be over within a few short months,' she reasoned.

I didn't have an answer for that, nor did I know how to explain to Ruby, this girl I had taken under my wing six years ago, that my fears for her were escalating. She may well have come of age and now be twenty-one, but the life she had led so far had been more than a little sheltered.

Taking a deep breath, I tried again. 'I was gifted this necklace on a business trip to Calcutta, with a man I knew before Eric,' I told her truthfully. 'It was a thank you present from a man who was grateful to me for saving his child from injury.

'I was told that the necklace has the power of protection, and that's why I want you to have it,' I continued, hoping this would convince her. 'You might think this is merely superstition, and maybe it is, but take it as a keepsake if you like?'

Ruby nodded and smiled at this, then she picked up the necklace from the table, before placing it carefully around her neck. 'I'll take it with me if it means that much to you,' she said, running her fingers slowly across the smooth stone.

I didn't trust myself to speak. Seeing the necklace

around Ruby's neck was making me feel like crying again, but I had to let her go. I had to allow her to spread her wings and live her life to the full, because this was her chance.

'How are you feeling about moving into Brighton, Ruby?' I asked.

'I can't believe my case is actually packed and already hidden under my bed,' she said excitedly, and then she pressed her lips together and gazed into the middle distance.

'It's a shame I'm sneaking away and having to hide that I'm moving out,' she added regretfully, looking back at me and shrugging her shoulders.

'They'd try to flaming stop you leaving, if they knew of your plans, you know that, Ruby. And you'll be fine, I'm convinced of it,' I told her, knowing this was the only way she could escape her overbearing parents and make a different life for herself.

'Brighton will change with the declaration of war,' I said, stating the obvious, and attempting to make light of my fears for her in these troubled times.

'I don't doubt that, Scarlett,' she replied, giving me a searching look. 'But living in Regency Square will be good for me, even with what's happening right now. My friend Harriet said the landlady was nice, and she should know; she's been living in that lodging house for a whole year now,' Ruby said encouragingly.

'You've been good to me these past six years, Scarlett. And I hope you know how much I appreciate that. But we both know if I don't go now, it'll become harder to escape from my parents.'

She rolled her eyes dramatically heavenwards before adding, 'I'd end up married to the local curate, and living exactly the same life as them. And what an awful fate that would be!'

Ruby was completely justified in escaping while she still could, and while everybody's mind was on the war. However, there were times when I found the thought of letting her go very hard.

'God forbid it should ever happen again,' I murmured, feeling a hard lump in my throat. I hadn't meant to dampen Ruby's enthusiasm for the adventure that lay ahead, but the words were out of my mouth, and hanging awkwardly in the air between us, before I could stop them.

Ruby gazed at me steadily and then shook her head. 'Oh, Scarlett. When you moved here six years ago, you helped me see past my old fears, perhaps now I need to help you see past yours?'

'Thanks, Ruby, but I'm absolutely fine,' I reassured her, lifting my chin and swallowing hard. 'It's just sometimes, it's the thought… of it happening again.'

Ruby frowned and leaned back in her armchair. 'That's understandable. I mean, you did lose all of your family in that flu epidemic.' She spoke softly, her eyes wide with understanding. 'I can't think of many things worse in life than that.'

Unshed tears pricked at the back of my eyes, and I had to say what was in my heart. 'You're my family now, Ruby. And you should be proud of who you are. A beautiful, confident woman, quite different from that awkward fifteen-year-old girl who knocked on my door years ago,' I told her, smiling through my sadness.

Ruby laughed at this, but her dark eyes were serious. 'Thank you, Scarlett. I don't know about a beauty, though.'

I knew Ruby *was* beautiful, even though she didn't

know this herself. 'Well, anyway, I hope I've been able to help you over the years.'

'One of the most important things you've taught me, Scarlett, was that my parents' way wasn't mine. That I'm different to them, and even though it was painful at times, with your help I got there in the end.'

Her face was shining with happiness as she spoke, and my heart lifted. 'Thank you, but I may not have been the best influence on you, despite what you say,' I said, looking at her with affection. 'I love my life in Lewes, and Eric is a good man,' I said ironically, 'but at the end of the day, I'm still a kept woman.'

Ruby shrugged as if this was of no consequence. 'That's never mattered to me, Scarlett. I've always admired you for being you; even wished I could be more like you,' she said, lifting her eyebrows.

In the future, when I was lonely, I would hold those kind words close to my heart in Ruby's absence. 'Right, well, enough sentimentality, my girl. Have you got the letter ready?' I asked her firmly.

Ruby nodded at me with a wide grin. 'All done. It's written and lying under my pillow to leave for my mum and dad to find after they've gone off to church tomorrow morning.'

Together, we had hatched the plan. Ruby was to feign illness the next day, so that she wouldn't be able to join her parents for the usual church service. Then she would use the time to escape to Brighton while they were gone.

As Ruby walked towards the door, I remembered something else I was going to give her. 'I'll have the gramophone delivered to Regency Square for you, if you still want it?'

Ruby said she definitely wanted the gramophone.

Like me, she was remembering the times we had listened to Glenn Miller, Judy Garland, and the wonderful Ella Fitzgerald together.

The next moment we were hugging each other as if our lives depended on it, before I pushed her gently towards the open front door. And for the first time since Eric set me up in this house, I found myself looking forward to his arrival that evening.

Chapter Sixteen

November 1940

I hovered outside the ward where Ruby was a patient at the Royal Sussex County Hospital, in Brighton. Reluctant to go in, sweat beaded my brow as I peered through the small window in the double doors and saw the patients' beds lined up next to each other in a world of white.

After receiving a letter the day before, telling me that Ruby had been injured, I had come to the hospital as soon as I could. But now I was afraid of what I might find beyond these doors, and I pulled the letter out of my pocket and re-read it.

Dear Miss Cunningham,

I have been led to believe that Ruby Summers is a friend of yours, and I regret to inform you that she is a patient here at The Royal Sussex County Hospital. Ruby's recovery from injuries sustained in a bomb blast, outside Hanningtons' store, is extremely slow, and I suggested she needed visitors to lift her spirits. Ruby is reluctant to see anyone, but then she mentioned your name…

The journey to the hospital had passed in a blur, with my mind racing in circles. I was unable to stop the worst-case scenarios being played out in my head over and over again. *What kind of injuries had Ruby suffered? Would she make a full recovery? Would she still be able to walk, talk, and do all the normal things in life?*

And most of all, I wondered how I had not known about the bomb that had dropped outside Hanningtons' store. There must have been a report in the *Evening Argus* or another local newspaper at the time of the bombing, but somehow, I'd missed it.

Gathering my courage, I took a long, deep breath and pushed open the double doors. I gazed around the ward for a sighting of Ruby's pretty face and dark head of hair, as my heart raced.

Walking slowly through the ward, with the smell of bland food and carbolic soap filling my nostrils, I searched for Ruby while sick with dread. Then suddenly, one of the patients waved at me from a bed at the end of the ward. *Was that Ruby underneath the swathe of bandages covering her forehead?* Quickly, I hurried towards the bed with my stomach churning.

When at last our eyes met, I could see it was my friend, and relief flooded through me. 'Hello, Ruby, how are you feeling?' I asked shakily, as my jumbled thoughts settled a little and I took a deep breath.

'Oh God, Scarlett, I'm so pleased to see you,' Ruby replied, her chin trembling.

She was sitting half propped up against the pillows, and her face below the bandages was almost as white as the sheets on the bed. With my heart thumping hard, I stepped towards her and said the first thing that came into my head.

'Oh blimey, Ruby, you poor thing,' I sympathised,

and watched her eyes fill with tears as she gazed dismally back at me.

'Harriet died in the blast,' Ruby gulped, and the sadness in her voice tore at my heart.

Taking hold of her hand, I noticed that not only was her forehead covered in a bandage, but also one arm was encased in plaster. 'That's terrible, but whatever happened? I mean… I know it was a bomb blast outside Hanningtons, but I don't have any more details about it.'

Ruby was gripping my hand tightly, and my mind was back on its circling again. Poor Harriet had died in the explosion, which was bad news indeed. Thank God Ruby had not suffered the same fate.

'Why weren't you both in the air raid shelter then?' I asked Ruby the question that was spinning round in my head.

She took a deep, shuddering breath and looked steadily back at me. 'I tried to save Harriet, I really did,' she said falteringly. 'But she suffered from claustrophobia and wouldn't go down into the shelter, and she was so stubborn that I couldn't convince her…' She lowered her eyes and wiped at her wet face with her free hand.

Digging deep into my pocket, I pulled out a handkerchief and handed it to Ruby. 'Take your time,' I told her soothingly. 'There's no rush to explain anything. I'm not going anywhere for a while.'

Ruby nodded before blowing her nose hard. 'Harriet had been in the Odeon cinema in Kemptown when it was bombed recently. Do you remember the report about it?' she asked urgently, her words falling over themselves. 'Oh, Scarlett. Harriet panicked and ran before I could stop her, and there was nothing I could do… nothing!'

Ruby began sobbing noisily into her hands, and all I could do was lay a comforting hand on her shoulder. For the first time since meeting Ruby when she was just a girl of fifteen, I had no words of comfort or any advice on how to make this better. 'I'm so sorry, Ruby, I really am. That's really tough. *Poor* Harriet.'

While Ruby cried out her grief, my thoughts returned to how I'd felt when I'd received the letter, reluctant to read the words dancing on the page, in case it was the worst news imaginable.

When I'd finally plucked up the courage to read it and found that Ruby was in fact alive, the relief had been immense. Now I had to make Ruby see that this was not the end of the world.

'Ruby…' I began tentatively. 'I understand it doesn't seem this way at the moment, but in time you'll accept what's happened.' I was searching for the right words to bring her comfort, but in the end all I had was the truth.

'You know me,' I told her, lifting my chin. 'I often think fate has a part to play in this kind of thing.' I nodded encouragingly, because this was something I truly believed, and I wanted Ruby to believe it, too.

She stopped crying and her hand went to her chest. 'Fate?' she echoed disbelievingly, her eyes wide. 'What do you mean by that?'

I sat up straighter on the edge of the bed. 'Well, I know more than most that fate can deal some pretty cruel blows,' I told her, trying to find a way of explaining this so that she would understand.

'Scarlett?' Ruby's concerned voice cut through my gloom. 'Are you alright?'

'Fate can be cruel. You know that yourself,' I said.

99

'Look at what's happening here in Brighton right now. This town has been reasonably lucky so far, but those poor sods in London are getting it something right rotten.'

Ruby pursed her lips and gave a little nod of understanding. 'God, it must be bad living in London right now,' she said and picked agitatedly at a loose thread on the bedspread.

'There's no two ways about it, it's pretty dismal there,' I agreed, remembering the daily reports on the radio of relentless night bombing raids. There were thousands dead and countless fires raging in the capital. The tube stations, it seemed, were crammed tight with people every night, desperate to stay safe. It sounded a lot like hell on earth to me.

Ruby ran her fingers over the amethyst stone hanging on a chain around her neck, and my body tensed.

'It was supposed to be a blinking good luck charm, but it didn't help you much did it, Ruby?' I inwardly flinched, hearing my old Albion Hill accent returning, which often happened when I was upset about something.

Regret mixed with sadness was making my stomach knot, because I had given Ruby false hope. I had led her to believe the necklace might help protect her in times of trouble. But it had failed miserably on that score.

'If only I'd known when this awful thing would happen, I could have given you a more precise warning. You did get my letter, didn't you, Ruby?' I asked, suddenly aware that the letter might have gone astray.

Sudden tears sprang to Ruby's eyes, and I watched

as she swallowed hard. 'I did get the letter but… Scarlett, the thing is, I didn't tell Harriet what you said or about your premonition,' she admitted dismally.

'Perhaps, Ruby, you didn't believe me?' I said, trying not to sound judgemental. 'It probably wouldn't have made any difference,' I shrugged, trying to make light of it now.

I struggled to recall then what exactly I'd seen of the explosion before writing the letter to Ruby. I'd been browsing in a local antique shop when the familiar prickling sensation had begun to creep slowly up my spine.

Leaning against the shop doorway, I'd fought against the images pushing their way into my head in this most public of places. Shuffling my body back into a corner of the doorway and trying to hide from prying eyes, I had tried to understand what I was seeing.

Two young women were running away from a shop doorway. Their faces were obscured, and the picture in my head was unclear and very hazy. The sound of a bomb exploding had then filled my head, along with the very real feeling that dust and debris were flying everywhere.

For a moment, I had been lost in that terrifying chaotic scene surrounding me, and that night I had agonised over telling Ruby about what I'd seen. I couldn't be sure of her reaction and I didn't want to frighten her. After all, she hadn't been in Brighton long, and as usual, I had no clear idea if this premonition involved Ruby or not.

However, the next morning I had put pen to paper and written Ruby a long letter. Come to think of it, she had never actually answered that letter. I'd received correspondence from her the following week, but she hadn't mentioned my letter with the warning about the explosion.

Now, Ruby shook her head and then winced at the pain she'd unintentionally inflicted on her head. 'To be fair to me, Scarlett, you've never mentioned this strange gift to me before, have you?' she said, looking at me intently.

'I kind of thought that the letter was probably more to do with your old fears coming to the surface again,' she went on. 'And the way you were before I moved into Brighton, you know, a bit overprotective of me... made me think that was what was happening here.'

I had to concede that Ruby had a point. 'The truth is, I've never told anyone before, because somehow I couldn't,' I admitted.

The warning I'd had that Da would die on that fateful fishing trip, when I was ten years old, had been the first time it had happened.

I glanced up from where I'd been gazing sadly into my lap, lost in long ago memories, and smiled weakly at Ruby.

'You don't have to tell me now, or explain anything,' she told me sympathetically.

Despite this reassurance, the time had come to tell Ruby about the secret I had been harbouring, because this young woman was the closest thing to family I had.

Slowly, I began to explain how Da had returned from the war a changed man, how I'd dreamt about his fishing boat tragedy not long after his homecoming, and how eventually, after Da died, Belle had succumbed to the influenza, too.

'It was *tough*,' I told Ruby. 'But I didn't give up, and somehow, God knows how, it made me stronger.' I lifted my chin determinedly. 'You have to see, Ruby, that although it's a terrible tragedy that Harriet's dead, life must and will go on for you.'

Ruby nodded and gave me a meaningful look. 'You're right, Scarlett, but the nightmares are just relentless,' she said, biting down on her lower lip.

Thinking hard, I could think of only one way that Ruby could be helped with this problem. 'You need to go away for a while and have a change of scenery,' I told her. 'Give yourself a break from familiar surroundings.'

Where in the world Ruby would go and convalesce for a few weeks, while the country was at war, was another problem altogether.

'What? I can't do that!' Ruby clutched at the sheet with her good hand and looked full of panic. 'Although the very thought of working in Hanningtons again...' her voice trailed off miserably.

'I think you're trying to look too far ahead here, Ruby. Couldn't you do a few more hours at the pub when you get home instead?'

Ruby had been working at the Fortune of War pub in Brighton with Harriet in the evenings, and had thoroughly enjoyed it by the sound of things. Returning to the pub and keeping busy could be a good thing for her, but the problem of how to escape Brighton for a while still hung heavily in the air.

'Hello, ladies, and how are we today?'

We both looked up as a nurse suddenly appeared by Ruby's bed, and began adjusting the pillows and generally tidying the bed. Her name badge said the word Ella on it, and I realised this was the woman who had written to me about Ruby.

'Hello, Ella, pleased to meet you. I'm Scarlett.'

I stood up and faced the fair-haired nurse. 'Thank you for telling me about Ruby,' I said, grateful to this woman for her intervention because I would not known about Ruby's fate without her help.

Ella said she was pleased to help, and then she paused in her work to regard Ruby, looking thoughtful. 'I couldn't help overhearing your friend's suggestion about you getting away from Brighton for a while,' she said.

Then she explained that her daughter Jude was studying with The Royal College of Art, which had been relocated to the Lake District for the duration of the war.

Understandably, Ruby looked puzzled as to what this had to do with us, and I too wondered where the conversation was leading. That was until Ella explained further while taking Ruby's blood pressure.

'Poor Jude wasn't happy about this at first; after all, Ambleside's quiet after the liveliness of London life,' she said, while writing on Ruby's chart.

'Thankfully, she's settling in now, though. But I was thinking, it might help you to go and stay with Jude for a while?' She lifted her brows questioningly at Ruby, and then looked across at me with hope in her eyes.

'That sounds a flaming good idea,' I agreed, seeing the logic in this. 'What do you think, Ruby? This could be just what you need. To get away from Brighton for a while.'

I found myself hoping Ruby would agree to this kind offer, because Ella seemed a nice person, which meant that the chances were high of Jude being a good sort, too. However, Ruby didn't look too sure about the idea, and I could see the doubt in her brown eyes.

'Perhaps... I don't know...' she said, knitting her

brow and staring dismally down at her arm in plaster, as if it would stay that way forever.

'Have a think about it. There's no rush for an answer,' Ella replied with a smile, and then she quickly disappeared down the ward to help the other patients.

For a moment, Ruby didn't speak. She watched Ella's disappearing back before turning to me with a deep weighted sigh. 'I'm not sure I want to do that, Scarlett,' she whispered. 'Go to Ambleside all on my own? I'm not convinced that's a good idea.'

I tried to choose my words carefully, aware of how fragile Ruby was right now. 'Think about it, Ruby,' I told her. 'You don't know Jude, that's true, but you'll soon get to know her once you're in Ambleside. And a short stay in the countryside might help you recover your spirits.'

Ruby nodded, then laid her head back on the pillow and closed her eyes. I could see how exhausted she was, so a short time later I said my goodbyes.

'I'll be back to see you soon,' I told her, giving her a gentle hug, then I walked out of the hospital to make my way towards the bus stop.

On the journey home, I stared out of the window at the rain running in rivulets down the glass. As Brighton turned into Lewes, it was hard not to think about the terrible events which had led to Harriet's death.

Regret stabbed at me for not telling Ruby before about my special gift. Maybe if she'd known about it, she would have taken my letter more seriously, and even been able to warn Harriet. But as these thoughts crowded my head, I understood that it was too late now, and sadly I would never know whether Harriet could have been saved or not.

Chapter Seventeen

Frankie

The envelope hadn't looked anything out of the ordinary, and there had been nothing at first glance to warn Frankie that it was addressed to his father's mistress.

Eric had gone into work at the shipyard early that morning, and Frankie was following him to the office an hour later, as usual. Frankie had been on the way out of the house when he spotted the envelope lying on the doormat, and picked it up, intending to give it to his mother to post.

However, something made him hesitate. The envelope was written in his father's hand and was addressed to a Scarlett Cunningham, whoever she was. As he neared the postbox, he stared at the writing for a moment, noticing the seal was coming slightly adrift.

Before he realised what he was doing, he had finished unsealing the envelope and was reading the contents of his father's letter. He didn't know why he did so, because he knew it was wrong, and he had never read any of Eric's private correspondence before.

However, Frankie had been curious for a long time

about where his father spent so much time when he was frequently away from home, and he suspected Eric was keeping a mistress. Or perhaps the name Scarlett written on the letter made him want to know more about who exactly she was. Frankie was intrigued by the thought of this woman whose name conjured up images of a beautiful woman in a bright red dress.

The journey to Lewes seemed interminably long to Frankie, and he was aware that Eric would be wondering why he hadn't turned up for work. Instead, he was heading from their family home in Kensington to a small market town called Lewes, ready to confront his father's mistress.

Chapter Eighteen

Scarlett

The loneliness has crept up on me in recent days, making me restless at night and unsettled in the daytime, especially since I haven't seen or heard from Eric in weeks.

The recent bombs dropped over Brighton have had the effect of making me fearful about venturing into the seaside town. And travelling into Brighton on the bus has only highlighted how the seaside town has changed since the outbreak of war.

Walking on the beach was now out of bounds, after it had been mined and closed off to the public. And both of the piers were now no-go areas, after having had sections of their decking removed. This would stop them being used as landing stages in an enemy invasion, which was a terrifying thought, but one that could become a reality.

With Brighton being declared unsafe, thousands had been evacuated and it was more like a ghost town than the thriving shopping area it used to be. The only place that people gathered now was outside the food shops. There, they formed long queues and waited patiently, while clutching their ration books close to their chests, as if they would be snatched away at any moment. As well they might by some unscrupulous people.

After my visit to see Ruby in hospital last week, she wrote me a long letter. Eager for some good news, I quickly tore open the envelope to read her familiar sloped handwriting.

Dear Scarlett,

After our conversation last week, I've decided to join Ella's daughter Jude in Ambleside. Seeing you was a tonic, and I know you and Ella are right, that I need a complete break from Brighton and a change of scenery as soon as possible.

You never know, maybe I'll become an artist like Jude. But joking aside, I've felt much better since your visit, and Ella thinks I'll be ready to leave in about a week's time, so I may not see you before I leave for the Lake District.

The letter went on to tell me how Ruby was looking forward to Ambleside with some trepidation, but was nevertheless convinced it would help in her recovery.

Pleased that she had made the decision to leave Brighton for a while, I pushed away the thought that the loneliness would be even harder to bear once she left for the Lake District.

Now, as the day stretched ahead of me, I picked up a small pile of clothes, which needed mending, and began the task of sewing up the hem of a dress. With the generous allowance Eric gave me, I usually bought new dresses whenever I needed them. But with clothes as well as food now being rationed, there was no choice but to make do and mend.

By eleven o'clock, with the mending finished, I made a cup of tea, then gazed out of the window to see the rain coming down heavily, and my heart sank even further.

As I watched the passing traffic and people hurrying through the rain, the figure of a man appeared out of the landscape. He walked quickly towards my gate and hovered there for a moment, looking a bit uncertain as he peered towards my front door. I stepped away from the window and watched him from the shadow of the curtains.

My first thought was that he could be a salesman, but they were far and few between with so many men serving in the armed services right now, so I came to the conclusion that this was unlikely.

The man pulled up the collar of his overcoat against the torrential rain, and pushed open the back gate before knocking on my front door. I opened the door and regarded my visitor, who towered over me on the threshold. He stared at me intently from under his hat, which was pulled down low against the onslaught of the rain.

'Can I help you?' I asked, my gaze focussed on a single drop of water trickling slowly down his cheek towards his chin.

'I do hope so,' he said, pushing his hat further back on his head. 'Are you Scarlett Cunningham?' he asked rather abruptly.

That voice and those eyes – now that I could see them – were so recognisable and so like someone else I knew. My heart missed a beat. There was something else niggling at me, too. Something I was struggling to make sense of as I gazed back at the man.

'That is my name, how can I help you?' I answered,

dreading the answer to my question. Prickles of unease began creeping up my spine. Here was a man who looked like a stranger, but was at the same time somehow familiar to me. His next words sent shock waves racing through my body.

'The name's Frankie Johnson,' he said, before glancing behind him furtively, as if checking for passers-by in case he was seen speaking to the likes of me.

'Frankie Johnson?' I echoed. Seeing this man up close, he was much younger than I thought he would be – not yet eighteen years old, by the looks of him. His large hazel eyes were regarding me with a frown etched between his brows, and what I could see of his dark hair under the hat was stuck damply to his forehead.

'Well… can I come in then, Miss Cunningham?' he ventured. 'Especially as I'd rather not conduct our business in full view of the neighbours,' he added impatiently. And without waiting for an answer, he pushed past me and strode right into my house.

'Now wait a moment!' I snapped, following him quickly and thinking what a damned cheek he had barging into my home that way. By the time I caught up with him, he had reached the front parlour, and was now shifting from foot to foot impatiently.

'Look here, who do you think you are?' I demanded with my hands on my hips. I felt wrong-footed with him standing in front of me this way. 'You've no right to come in here uninvited, even if you are—' I stopped abruptly. *Frankie Johnson?*

Planting his feet, Frankie glared icily back at me. 'Yes, that's right. I'm Eric's son,' he said, narrowing his eyes at me. 'So you're the woman *he* risks everything for then?'

Frankie was looking me up and down with such a look of contempt that I shivered under his scrutiny. This was too much, and anger rose in my chest at his audacity. Even if he were Eric's son, he had no right to treat me in this way.

'You're going to have to explain yourself, Frankie,' I told him, matching his tone and determined not to show weakness in the face of his bullying ways. All the while the question of what he was doing here was hanging in the air between us. 'Otherwise you can just leave! And where is Eric, anyway?' I took a step towards him, aware that this young man must be hurting deeply. 'Has something happened to him?' I said, a little more gently now.

'My father is very well, thank you, Miss Cunningham,' he said, emphasising the word 'father'. 'That's not why I'm here.'

'In that case, what do you want?' I demanded, fed up with going around in circles.

Frankie sighed heavily and looked a little less sure of himself than when he'd first walked in. The bravado was diminishing as he gazed awkwardly past me. Then he glanced down at his hands, and for the first time I noticed that he was holding an envelope.

'This letter is for you, Miss Cunningham,' he said, lifting his chin defiantly. 'It's from my father, but he didn't send me here with it, if *that's* what you think.'

'In that case, how did you come by it then?'

'It should have been posted, but in his haste to leave the house this morning, my father must have dropped it, because I found it lying on the doormat.'

Suddenly the look on Frankie's face changed. He looked even more youthful and a bit vulnerable all of a sudden, and a younger more handsome version of his father gazed back at me.

'Frankie…' I said, trying to put together a few words of comfort for him, and attempting to imagine what it felt like to come face-to-face with your father's mistress.

However, I had no words of reassurance here, and I realised there was nothing I could say which would help this man right now. He shouldn't be here, standing in Eric's place, in the home that Eric bought for me – and he really needed to leave.

Frankie shrugged and held out the letter to me. 'Here you are. You may as well have it, as I've come all this way.'

I nodded at him and took the envelope from his outstretched hand before noticing that it had already been opened. 'Why don't you sit down for a moment?' I said, trying to keep my patience.

My voice sounded far off in my own ears, and I wondered whether Frankie's mother knew about me, and had perhaps sent her son to confront her husband's mistress. If so, I would be sorry for her suffering, but it wouldn't alter anything.

'Have you tampered with your father's letter?' I asked, as Frankie lowered himself onto the settee. But he ignored my question as I pulled the letter out of the envelope and began to read Eric's words.

  Dearest Scarlett,
  I'm sorry I haven't seen you for a while, but work has been demanding of my time recently, or lack of it, but I miss you terribly and hope to visit you soon.

Heaving a sigh of relief that the letter was not bad

news, as far as I could tell, I glanced across at Frankie. Before I read any more of the letter, I needed to know what was going on with this young man and why he was here.

'What do you want from me, Frankie? This letter could easily have been posted; it even has a stamp on it,' I said, needing to put a stop to whatever game he was playing.

Frankie's anger burst from him like a dam as he stood up. 'It could have been posted, you're right there, Miss Cunningham!' he blustered. 'But I wanted to take this chance to find out exactly who you are and what you are doing with my father!'

Pacing the floor agitatedly, he turned back to me and scowled. 'I've suspected my father had a mistress for some time, although my mother seems oblivious to it. Either that, or she's turning a blind eye,' his voice was thick with sarcasm, but then he stopped his tirade and rubbed wearily at his forehead.

I sighed and then walked over to the window where I stared out sightlessly for a moment. 'Look here, I'm really sorry,' I said, turning back towards him. 'But you have to remember things happen for a reason. Your parents live their lives the way they see fit, and things can often be more complicated than they look to others.'

I stopped myself saying more, because it wasn't my place to tell this young man why his father had no passion for his mother, or how Eric loved his wife more like a sister than a lover.

Frankie's voice cut through my thoughts. 'I wanted to understand for myself what he sees in *someone like you*,' he said unkindly, pulling his mouth into a tight line. 'You're nothing but a tart, so it's still a mystery,' he added spitefully.

My best response to this was to say nothing at all, because Frankie's dislike for me showed in his clenched jaw and his face taut with anger.

'You're a beauty, I'll give you that,' he growled, as if he could hardly believe this to be true.

Anger, red and hot, flared inside me. 'Enough! I think you'd better leave right now,' I said, pointing to the door. 'Insults are not what I need to hear in my own home, *Frankie Johnson*,' I snapped, matching his tone. 'My relationship with your father is flaming well nothing to do with you.'

Frankie openly flinched as if he wasn't expecting this, and he took a step towards me.

Refusing to move, I stood up straighter and faced him with my heart racing. He might be young, but he was tall and broad. But, I reminded myself, he was Eric's son and therefore he had been properly brought up, so I should have nothing to fear from him here.

Then it happened. As we locked our gaze defiantly, each of us it seemed was unable to look away. And as the seconds ticked by, I began drowning in those hazel eyes. With a jolt I realised that this was the man I'd been dreaming of for years, the man who in my dreams had loved me more than life itself.

Breaking the spell, Frankie tore his eyes from me and shook his head vigorously. Then, turning on his heel, he hurried back through the hallway, leaving me gasping for breath and wondering what exactly had just happened.

As Frankie reached the door, he spun around and glared back at me. 'Women like you don't know what harm they're doing!' he bellowed, before striding angrily down the footpath and banging the back gate shut behind him.

Watching Frankie disappear from sight, I stepped back inside the hallway and slumped against the wall for support. Something painful was pulling at my chest as Eric's voice echoed in my head. 'I needed passion in my life,' he had told me with his gaze soft. 'And then you came along.'

I understood that I filled a gap that Eric's wife couldn't. However, I could see Frankie found this hard to accept, and I understood that, too. Determined to push the guilt aside and read Eric's letter to the end, I returned to the front parlour and continued where I had left off.

Things are so unsettled at the moment, as orders have been slowing up because of the war. Also President Roosevelt will be putting in place the building of the liberty ships, which is much needed for our country to replace the ships lost in battle. The first of these liberty ships will be built by the Americans next year, so our ships won't be needed so much as they are in peacetime. As you know, my passion is in building ships, so I've been increasingly unhappy in my work since the war began, and I'll explain more when I see you.

I hope you are well and not missing me too much, and I promise I'll see you very soon.

Please take care of yourself, and until we meet again, I send all my love to you, my darling.

Eric xx

As I folded up the letter, I felt breathless and shaky. Since the age of sixteen, the man I now knew to be Frankie Johnson had been a part of my dreams. But who he was had always been the unanswered question in my head.

Now that I knew him to be Eric's son, at least a part of the puzzle had been solved. Feeling thoroughly unsettled by Frankie's visit, which had left me reeling, the mystery still remained of how his future was tied up with mine.

Chapter Nineteen

Frankie

Eric's chair fell to the floor with a clatter as he stood up abruptly, and glared across the office at Frankie. 'Where the hell have you been?' he demanded, his hands planted firmly on his hips.

Frankie avoided eye contact with Eric and walked casually through the door. He was aware that the other employees had their heads bowed over their work, and were pretending not to notice the tension in the air between the two men. He wished his father had confronted him away from everyone.

He didn't immediately answer his father. Strangely, he hadn't even thought about what he would say to Eric on arrival at work. Instead, his mind had been full to bursting with thoughts of a woman called Scarlett, and as his father continued to glare at him, he searched his mind for a valid excuse.

Sitting down at his desk, Frankie looked across at Eric. 'Sorry, I overslept this morning,' he said weakly, meeting his father's angry gaze and giving him a beseeching look.

Eric huffed at this, but decided to leave the matter there for now. He shot one more disbelieving look towards Frankie before sitting down at his own desk and shuffling through some paperwork.

Frankie heaved a sigh of relief and thanked his lucky stars that Eric had been up before him this morning, making it perfectly feasible that he had overslept. However, he was sure his father would have something further to say on the matter when they were alone at home later. Frankie was always on time to work, and was well known as his father's most conscientious worker.

As the hours wore on that day, Frankie found it hard to concentrate on his work. There was a voice in his head saying he should not have interfered in his father's life by going to see Scarlett Cunningham.

The scene when he had knocked on her door kept coming back to him. Frankie had hardly been able to conceal his surprise when Scarlett answered his knock. And as he took in her appearance, anger on behalf of his mother had vied with complete admiration for his father.

Scarlett was strikingly beautiful. She had a slim waist and blonde hair that flowed to her shoulders in waves, and she'd looked at him with surprise from startlingly coloured turquoise eyes. And even though he tried not to, he couldn't help comparing her to his mother, who had iron-grey hair, a thick waist, and plain features.

Frankie had seen that Scarlett was reluctant to ask him in once she realised who he was, but he had been determined he wasn't having that. What he found most unbelievable was that during their uncomfortable conversation, she'd offered him no excuse about why she was conducting this affair with his father. The woman had no shame, it seemed.

Over supper that evening, Frankie was surprised

that his father seemed to have forgiven him for oversleeping that morning.

'Don't let it happen again, son,' was all he said on the matter while his mother dished up dinner for the family. 'It's not like you, Frankie, to lie in bed and be lazy when you should be at work,' he had added, lifting his eyebrows.

Frankie watched his mother waiting on them all, and the unfairness of the situation hit him hard. As the hours ticked by, he became more incensed about his father's behaviour, and decided he had to spill the beans to her. But when at last he found the right time to speak to her, her response was not what he had expected.

He had expected tears, or at the very least anger, but his mother looked back at him with an understanding nod.

'I know about the mistress, Frankie,' she'd said simply, her round face flushed from the kitchen where she had been baking all afternoon. 'Of course, I don't know her name, but I do know your father has another woman, and I'm glad he has someone to love in that way,' Amy told him.

Frankie was speechless, and stared at his mother in surprise. 'What? But why do you put up with it?' he asked, looking at her steadily.

'Sit down, Frankie, and please listen,' she told him in a tone he had never heard her use before.

Frankie felt as if he were a little boy again, being told off for misbehaving, and he did as he was ordered. Amy sat down opposite him and regarded him uneasily.

'Things are not always as they seem…' she began, looking thoughtful and echoing Scarlett's words.

Frankie was instantly appalled. 'Mama! Really, what possible explanation could there be for father being unfaithful to you in this way?' His blood was boiling on behalf of his kindly mother, and he was determined to put a stop to his father's misdeeds.

However, Amy set her jaw, and stared at him with a furrowed brow, ignoring his anger. 'Johnson's Shipbuilding may be doing well now,' she began. 'But when your father first inherited it, the debts had mounted up,' she paused at Frankie's surprised expression.

'Your grandfather was not a good businessman; in fact, when he died the company was on the verge of bankruptcy,' she said, shaking her head sadly.

Frankie could hardly believe this to be true. 'But how did Father turn it around to what it is today then?' he asked in utter disbelief.

Amy pulled her brows in. 'Eric needed capital for the business, but instead he had nothing but debts. It was devastating. But my father stepped forward and offered Eric the money to save the business. You see, my father and your grandfather had been close friends for many years before they died.

'This money would save the business, but there was one condition. Part of the deal was that your father had to marry me.' Amy's shoulders visibly drooped as she said this. 'That was the agreement,' she added, lifting her eyes to Frankie.

Frankie's heart went out to his mother. 'You mean your father sold you as part of the business deal?' It was unbelievable that this kind of thing still went on – after all, they were not in the Dark Ages. 'Why did your father do this to you?'

Amy shrugged as if she had been resigned to her

fate. 'I was twenty-nine years old and unmarried, with no chance of matrimony. My father meant well; he wanted me to have a family to care for, and to be secure before he died.'

Frankie could see his mother wanted him to understand, but he still struggled with how she had been used in such an awful way. 'It was an arranged marriage then?' was all he could find to say to her.

And as he spoke, Frankie realised that this explained the lack of affection between his parents, and the odd relationship they seemed to have, which was more like siblings than man and wife. It was all becoming clear now.

'Couldn't you have found your own husband?' Frankie asked, but even as he spoke, he already knew the answer to this question.

Amy laughed, breaking the tension between them, and laid a tender hand on his arm.

'My darling son, my family were wealthy, and I could have married any number of men. But I'm no oil painting, and they all wanted me for my money. With Eric, my father had found someone who would look after me. And as for love, well, that didn't come into it,' she smiled good-naturedly.

After the conversation with his mother, Frankie saw his father in a different light. He understood how well he had done in providing a good life for them all over the years. And he recognised how hard he had worked to get Johnson and Johnson back in the black all those years ago.

However, the one thing that did surprise Frankie was that he couldn't stop thinking about Scarlett Cunningham. And despite trying his best to forget her, he longed to see her again.

Chapter Twenty

Scarlett

Frankie was proving hard to forget, as I dreamt about him nightly now. And with the dreams becoming more intense, I knew he needed to stay away from me.

Life had settled into an uneventful pattern after his visit, and when I saw Eric the following week, I chose not to mention his son's appearance.

Eric walked into my house that day looking downcast, and confirmed what he had said in the letter. 'Business is drying up, Scarlett,' he told me, 'and the government are expecting us to begin building field guns instead. My heart's just not in it,' he added, shaking his head.

Having no words of comfort for Eric, I was saddened to hear he wasn't enjoying his work anymore. And when I asked him how the family was, and in particular Frankie, he looked at me in surprise and assured me they were all fine.

Maybe I had been disloyal to Eric not telling him about Frankie's visit, but I understood how it would upset him to know that his son had confronted his mistress. And I vowed that if Frankie turned up again, I would quickly turn him away.

When the weeks went by and there was no sign of Frankie, I was conflicted. Part of me longed to see him again, while another part of me was glad he'd chosen to stay away.

Eventually, three months later, Frankie appeared on my doorstep again, and this time he seemed older and more mature somehow. There was no letter in his hand this time, and he stared down at his feet before lifting his gaze to mine, and apologising for his previous behaviour.

'I'm sorry for how I went on the last time I was here, Miss Cunningham. I've had time to think about things now,' he told me awkwardly.

My heart turned over at the sight of those beautiful hazel eyes and that thick dark hair, and I was pleased that he seemed to have accepted the situation.

'Please come in, Frankie,' I invited, telling myself I wouldn't let him stay long.

It was only afterwards that I realised I should have turned him away that day. But there was something inside me, which said I owed this young man an explanation, and I realised that I wanted him to have a better opinion of me.

Frankie followed me through to the front parlour where he made himself comfortable on the settee. 'I've spoken to my mother,' he said uneasily, leaning his elbows on his knees. 'She told me how things are with my father.'

Perching on the edge of the armchair, I nodded encouragingly and waited for Frankie to finish explaining what was clearly hard to talk about.

'This made me understand their lack of affection for each other,' he reflected sadly, 'and made me realise why father needed someone like you.' He leaned back on the settee and looked slightly uncomfortable.

'Frankie…' I said, wondering where to start. 'I admire your father's sense of humour, and I'm grateful for the kindness he showed me, which came at a time when I badly needed it.'

There was a glimmer of understanding in Frankie's eyes as he nodded at me with a soft expression. 'So, what is happening with you?' I asked, changing the subject and realising I knew nothing about him apart from the knowledge that he worked with Eric.

Frankie's face brightened, and he sat up straighter on the settee. 'I like working at the shipyard with my father,' he said, with a tilt of his head.

'We don't discuss your father's home life,' I told him truthfully. 'But Eric has told me what a good employee you are,' I added encouragingly, and watched him glow with pride.

'Did he really say that? I work hard, and to be honest, he's not one to offer up any praise.'

'Why don't you tell me more about the company, Frankie?' I said, wanting to engage him in conversation and curious about Eric's shipbuilding business.

Frankie nodded enthusiastically. 'It's called Johnson and Johnson, and it's based at London Docklands. My parents grew up together because their grandfathers were close friends, and my father inherited it from my grandfather on his deathbed.'

Frankie paused for a moment and then explained how his mother, Amy, had told him the business had been full of debts when Eric took it over. However, his mother's father had stepped in and saved the day, but part of the deal was that Eric had to marry Amy.

'Eric said as much when we first met, although he didn't explain it the way you have,' I told Frankie, thinking how Eric had obviously been coerced into a marriage in order to save the family business.

'It's a strange way to go on...' Frankie reflected, gazing into the middle distance.

'It sounds as if your mother wanted to get married, and your father needed her money to save his business. Not all that strange when you think about it,' I reasoned.

Frankie glanced across at me and shrugged. 'That's exactly how it was,' he said thoughtfully. 'Maybe not then,' he conceded.

'Do you have siblings, Frankie?' I asked, wondering why I hadn't asked Eric this question before.

The answer to this was obvious. I was Eric's secret; a woman hidden away from prying eyes, which meant I didn't have the right to know anything about the other life he lived with his family. But Frankie, it seemed, had no such reservations.

'Just one sister, her name's Beverley,' he explained, then he told me how he had grown up in Kensington and had enjoyed the best education money could buy. He'd only ever wanted to do two things when he grew up: to follow his father into the shipbuilding industry, or go into aviation.

'On another note, I've joined up, and am currently waiting for my papers to come through from the Royal Air Force,' he told me proudly. 'It means I won't be working at Dad's company for much longer. I'm very excited about it, as I've always longed to fly a plane, particularly a Spitfire.' He offered me a knowing grin as he spoke.

My heart lurched at the thought of Frankie being in the middle of the conflict. 'Does your father know about this?' I asked, worried now for his safety.

Frankie casually crossed his arms over his chest. 'Not yet, but I'll tell him when the papers come through. There's plenty of time, and now that I'm eighteen it's time for me to make my own decisions.'

I thought about Eric and how he would feel once he knew his son was going to war; it wouldn't be easy for him. Just as it wasn't for all the parents up and down the country whose sons were away fighting.

As the hours passed, we drank tea and chatted, and I found Frankie easy company. When he eventually stood up to leave, I found myself reluctant to see him go.

Trying to ignore the growing attraction between us, I pushed away the longing to be in Frankie's arms, although hiding this wasn't easy as I ushered him out of the door.

'Can I come and see you again, Scarlett? You know… to say goodbye before I go off to fight?'

Frankie stood on the doorstep, drawing me in with that intense gaze, and my cheeks flushed, and my heart raced. *How could I deny him one last visit when he was going off to risk his life fighting?* I knew I could not, so I found myself agreeing to his request, while ignoring the niggling worry that it would be a grave mistake.

As I closed the door on Eric's son, I told myself that we had nothing to hide and that we were merely friends. But the look of love on Frankie's face as he walked out of the door matched how I was feeling about him.

With that first shiver of excitement came the realisation that I would fall in love with Frankie. Somehow, I knew my destiny was linked to his. As I drifted off to sleep that night, I vowed to make sure nothing romantic ever happened between us, in order to stay loyal to Eric.

Chapter Twenty-One

My feelings for Frankie were growing, despite my best efforts at denial, and it was proving hard to stop thinking about him since his last visit.

When Eric came to see me, he told me how Frankie was leaving for the RAF manning depot in Toronto soon, to begin his training. I took a deep breath and asked him how he felt about his son going off to fight.

Eric shook his head softly. 'I'm worried about him, Scarlett,' he told me. 'Of course I am. But I can't stop him going, and after all, Hitler must be defeated.'

The expression on Eric's face was a mixture of pride and regret, and my heart went out to him. I understood his pain. But at least for me the temptation to see Frankie would be gone once he left for Canada.

It was early evening a few weeks later when I opened the door to find Frankie standing on the threshold. 'Hello, Frankie...' I said, unsure whether I should let him in or not. 'I'm expecting to see your father here tonight, so I think it's best if you don't come in this time.'

He shifted awkwardly on his feet. 'Dad's still busy at work, as we received more shield gun orders from the government today. I left him knee-deep in paperwork,' he explained, lifting his eyebrows at me. 'I won't stay long,' he promised, his hazel eyes alight with hope.

The feeling that this would end badly persisted, but Frankie would be gone after today so what harm could it do to see him one last time? 'All right, you can come in for a moment or two,' I conceded, opening the door wider, before glancing out into the street for any sighting of Eric in the distance.

'What's this about, Frankie?' I asked as we walked through to the front parlour. And when he didn't immediately answer, I turned towards him.

'You know you've got to stop coming here, don't you?' I told him, but my heart was racing at the sight of him looking so handsome, and I was struggling to ignore the desire coursing through my veins.

'Scarlett,' Frankie said hesitantly, standing in the middle of the room. 'I'm leaving tomorrow,' he told me urgently.

'And what has that got to do with me?' Frankie's leaving was everything to do with me, but I didn't want him to know that, and it was hard to keep up the pretence.

'For goodness sake, Scarlett!' He ran his fingers through his hair agitatedly. 'Stop doing this, please!'

'Stop doing what, Frankie?' I said calmly, torn between wanting to push him away, while at the same time longing to hold him in my arms.

Frankie shook his head at me and stepped closer. I could smell his masculine scent, a mixture of lavender and citrus, and I was acutely aware of the short distance between us.

'You know what I mean,' he accused. 'Stop pretending that you don't feel the same way about me that I do about you,' he said, with his gaze fixed on my lips. 'I love you, Scarlett. I knew it the first moment I saw you,' he continued softly. 'I know it's complicated, but…'

I couldn't speak, and as Frankie's voice trailed off, I knew he had to leave now before we went any further. 'It's not complicated, Frankie,' I told him hoarsely. 'It's impossible. Now you must go before…' Despite the words, I was unable to move away from him.

Frankie continued to gaze at me, and before I knew what was happening, his lips came down on mine, and he was kissing me as if his life depended on it. I became lost in Frankie's kiss, unable to tear myself away or to stop what was happening between us.

As all resistance left me, I understood that I'd finally found what I'd been looking for all my life. Here, in the front parlour of my house, with this beautiful man whose red-hot passion matched my own.

Hardly aware of anything but Frankie – his smell, his lips, and the feel of his body on mine – we tore desperately at each other's clothes. And my heart soared as Frankie loved me just as I'd seen him do in my dreams many times before. As we lay together afterwards, limbs entwined, I finally admitted to myself how much I loved Frankie Johnson.

Later, as we drew apart, Frankie gazed at me longingly while I began adjusting my clothes. Keeping my head bowed, I had no idea what to say to him. There were no words about what we had just done together, but I could not deny even to myself that I didn't regret a single moment of our lovemaking.

'Frankie, you must go now,' I told him urgently, taking his hand and leading him through the hallway. He nodded at me mutely and followed me to the door.

He stared at me tenderly as we stood together on the threshold. 'I don't know when we'll see each other again, but will you write to me, my darling?' Frankie asked hoarsely, as he pulled me into his arms and held me close.

I clung to him and tried to find the words to send him away for good, while at the same time knowing that was impossible. This all-consuming love for him was something different. It was passionate, raw, and made me completely wretched in the knowledge that I could never love Eric in the same way.

Through these conflicting thoughts, the sound of Eric's voice echoed somewhere in the distance, and my worst nightmare was realised. As I wrenched myself out of Frankie's embrace, I turned to see Eric standing a few feet away from us on the garden path.

He was staring at us both, his face a mask of shock, and his mouth set in a grim line. The flowers he was holding fell to the ground, landing in a heap of dishevelled colour scattered around his feet.

'Oh no, Eric…' I whispered, pulling further away from Frankie. I watched in horror as Eric staggered backwards, turned around, and then fled.

I wanted to shout after Eric, but what could I say? There was nothing, no words of comfort for him, as he ran down the path as if the devil himself were after him, leaving Frankie and myself to stare guiltily after him.

Chapter Twenty-Two

Frankie

After he left Scarlett's house that evening, Frankie was reluctant to go home. Worried about the thought of facing his father, he had driven to Brighton seafront, parked up, and sat on a wooden bench.

Frankie had never considered that his father could be deeply in love with someone like Scarlett, and had simply drawn the conclusion that their relationship must be purely physical.

Too late he realised he had made a terrible mistake. And yet, it was a mistake he could never regret. As soon as he had set eyes on Scarlett the day he'd confronted her over his father's letter, he had known himself to be in love.

When he eventually arrived home, he was dismayed to find his father was still up. Even though it was nearly midnight, Eric was waiting for him in the front parlour.

As Frankie hesitated in the doorway, Eric turned from where he had been staring out of the window into the blackness of the night, and their eyes met.

'Hello, Father,' Frankie greeted Eric hesitantly, trying to gauge the expression on his father's face.

Eric pulled his brows in and rubbed a hand through his hair. 'Come in, Frankie,' he said. 'I think we need to talk, don't you?'

The two men sat down on opposite sides of the room, and for a moment neither of them spoke, until Frankie could bear it no longer.

'I'm sorry,' he blurted out, unable to bear the tension in the room.

Eric had his head dipped and was rubbing the back of his hand repeatedly across his forehead.

What else could he say to his father? Frankie had no idea how to make amends, and was aware that he must have hurt Eric badly, but he had no excuse for his actions.

Eric eventually lifted his face to Frankie. 'How did you know?' he asked, as he looked steadily across at his son.

'Know what?' Frankie said stupidly. His heart lurched and his mind whirled. *Should he deny everything? Deny finding the letter and taking it to Scarlett? Or maybe make out she meant nothing to him? Would that save Eric's feelings?* As he wrestled with these conflicting thoughts, he watched Eric shake his head in despair and stand up.

'About bloody Scarlett, of course!' his father bellowed. 'What do you think I meant, son?'

Frankie's mouth had gone dry, and a hard lump had formed in his throat, as he watched Eric pacing the floor. He was a little boy again, being reprimanded for some misdemeanour and waiting to hear what punishment he would receive.

Eric stopped pacing. 'How did you even know where she lived?' he said at last, sitting down on the armchair and staring across at him through narrowed eyes.

Frankie leaned forwards and put his elbows on his knees. 'It was the letter,' he began, knowing he had to tell the truth here, because there was nothing else, and because his father wasn't stupid.

'The letter? What flaming letter?' Eric repeated, blinking at him.

Frankie took a deep breath and lifted his chin high. 'The one you didn't post to Scarlett, the one where you told her you wouldn't be able to see her much in the future,' he babbled, unable to stop talking now that he'd started. 'The letter I found lying on the doorstep.'

Eric simply stared back and looked confused, so Frankie was forced to keep going, keep saying the words, which were causing so much pain on his father's face.

'I took that letter to Scarlett, and that's when I met her,' he explained. Then, feeling braver, he added, 'I don't know what made me do it. I think I was curious because I'd suspected you had another woman, and well…'

Frankie dropped his gaze and couldn't finish the sentence. He couldn't say that he was angry on behalf of his mother; after speaking to Amy about this, it all seemed rather futile.

'I wondered what had happened to that damned letter,' Eric said, shaking his head. 'I convinced myself that I had posted it… but I obviously hadn't.' His face darkened as he lifted his eyes to Frankie. 'Not only did you take the letter, but you bloody read it, too, by the sounds of it!' he accused.

Frankie had run out of words, so he simply nodded at his father. To his complete surprise, Eric began to laugh.

'What's so funny?' Frankie asked, niggled. As far as

he could see, there was nothing to laugh about when two men loved the same woman.

Eric leaned back in his chair and regarded Frankie with a smirk. 'Don't you see, Frankie, how Scarlett Cunningham has taken you in? She's using you the way she used me. Scarlett was a common prostitute when I set her up – a woman of the night.'

Frankie's body tensed at Eric's words. 'Don't talk like that about Scarlett,' he said, even though what his father said about her being a prostitute was probably true.

Eric shrugged his shoulders and confirmed this. 'It's the truth, son,' he said, and then he raised his voice and repeated emphatically, 'Scarlett is nothing but a tart!'

Frankie had heard enough. He was angry at his father's cruel words, and confused. 'She's still a beautiful woman,' he said in defence of Scarlett. 'And I love her,' he added proudly, and rose from his chair.

Frankie walked quickly upstairs to his room, unable to believe what his father had just said. Eric's words were at odds with the devastated look on his face when he had found him with Scarlett. But if Eric really did not love Scarlett, then it worked in Frankie's favour; he wouldn't have to feel guilty anymore.

As he reached the top of the stairs, Frankie realised he needed a glass of water. The confrontation with his father had made his throat parched and sore. Retracing his footsteps, he walked past the front parlour, on the way to the kitchen. And when he glanced into the room he had just vacated, he felt sick to his stomach.

Eric was sitting with his head bowed low and his hands covering his face. His shoulders heaved up and down, and the soft sound of his muted sobbing reached Frankie's ears, while his tears dripped silently onto the floor below.

Chapter Twenty-Three

'You've done what?' Amy's knife and fork dropped to the dinner table with a clatter.

It was the evening after Frankie and Eric's confrontation over Scarlett, and Frankie had just announced to his mother that he had joined up. He eyed Amy with sympathy over the dinner table, feeling her pain.

'I received my call-up papers a few weeks ago, Ma, and I'll be on a plane to Canada to begin my RAF training in a few days' time.'

Amy stared back at him and then turned towards her husband. 'Did you know about this?' she asked, pursing her lips.

Eric nodded as he regarded his wife, then glanced across at Frankie with an unreadable expression.

Frankie had known his mother would be upset about him joining up, and when he got his papers through the post to register, he had said nothing to her. Telling his father had been much easier, as Eric had accepted this was the way of things. He wondered if perhaps his father was glad that Frankie was going; at least then he would be miles away from Scarlett.

Amy sat back down at the table and picked up her knife and fork. 'I suppose I knew it was coming,' she admitted with a resigned sigh.

'None of us can stop Frankie joining up when he's been ordered to by the government,' Eric reasoned, laying a comforting hand on Amy's arm. 'We all knew the day would come soon,' he added.

Amy glanced across the table at Frankie. 'I understand now that you're eighteen it was imminent,' she said. 'But it would have been nice to know what was going on,' she added, raising her eyebrows.

The guilt was making Frankie's chest heavy. First of all over Scarlett, which was the elephant in the room between him and Eric, and now because he'd kept his call-up papers a secret from his mother. 'I'm sorry, Ma,' he said. 'I should have told you when my papers came through.'

Beverley shot Frankie an encouraging look from across the table. 'Well done, dear brother,' she said. 'I'm very proud of you,' she said, giving her mother a concerned look.

After dinner that evening, Eric took Frankie to one side. 'Please don't worry about "the thing" we discussed last night,' he told him, widening his eyes at Frankie. 'I hope you understand that it really doesn't matter and it's not what's important here.'

Frankie shrugged this off and gave Eric a hug. His father was not telling the truth because he knew 'the thing' they'd discussed, which was Scarlett, did matter very much to Eric considering how upset he had been the evening before.

The next day at breakfast, after Eric had gone off to work, Amy took Frankie to one side and asked him what the problem was between the two men in her life.

'What do you mean?' Frankie replied, picking up his jacket from the back of the chair. 'There's nothing wrong between us,' he lied, feeling rather hot under the collar and hoping his mother would believe him.

She regarded her son with interest. 'I saw the two of you talking furtively last night, as if you're sharing a secret,' she said, as she loaded the sink with breakfast dishes.

She turned from the sink and gave Frankie a quizzical look. 'And I've seen the way he is around you, it's as if he's putting an act on – pretending or something…' she furrowed her brow, obviously baffled by her husband's behaviour.

Frankie feigned confusion, telling her it must be to do with him joining up. 'I think Father would rather I joined the army than the air force,' he said, making it up as he went along. 'Perhaps he wanted me to follow in his footsteps.'

This was an out and out lie. Eric had offered no opinion on which military service Frankie should sign up to when he was conscripted, but it was all he could think of to say to his mother.

Amy might know –and accept – that her husband had a mistress, but telling her that her son had the same lover would be, in Frankie's opinion, a step too far. And if the truth were told, Frankie was heartily ashamed of what he'd done, even though he loved Scarlett with all his heart and was sure he would never stop loving her.

Chapter Twenty-Four

'Attention! Quick march!'

The sergeant's voice cut through Frankie's thoughts at the manning depot in Toronto, and he forced his limbs to move quickly in line with everyone else as they all marched stiffly along the tarmac. He was tired and had to fight to stay alert while marching. To counteract the weariness, he took deep breaths of the cold Canadian air, hoping it would help him to feel more awake.

Frankie had arrived in Toronto two weeks ago to commence his training, and the first night he had hardly slept. He had lain awake far into the night, thinking about Scarlett and his father. The turmoil had robbed him of much needed sleep and when he had eventually nodded off, he had been woken abruptly at the usual time of 5am, feeling groggy and heavy with regret.

That first day, Frankie had made up his mind to write to his father. The physical distance between them now had made him realise he needed to reassure Eric that he would do the right thing when it came to Scarlett.

In the letter, Frankie told Eric how much he regretted what had happened, and even though he loved and admired his father's mistress, Frankie would not be pursuing a relationship with her on his return to England.

He wrote:

> *You try to deny it, Father, by telling me that Scarlett is nothing more than a whore who uses men, but I know how you feel about her. So I hope we can put this unfortunate incident behind us and forget that it ever happened.*

Frankie could never forget what happened with Scarlett, but he finished the letter by saying he looked forward to seeing Eric when he was allowed leave home, and that he hoped Johnson and Johnson was managing without him.

After writing to his father, Frankie had tried to put thoughts of Scarlett aside to concentrate on being here in Toronto and the training ahead of him. He was aiming to become a bomber pilot eventually, and to fly the Spitfire Mark VB planes, so he knew he would have to work extra hard to achieve that goal.

Later that day, in an interlude before dinner, Frankie lay down on his bed and stretched out his aching muscles, hoping that sleep would come to him more easily tonight. *What was Scarlett doing right now?* he wondered. And closing his eyes, he re-lived their lovemaking.

'What yer thinking of, mate, your sweetheart back home?'

Jimmy's voice jolted Frankie out of his thoughts, and he opened his eyes and regarded his friend who was sitting on the bunk next to his.

Since the first day of joining up, the two young men had become firm friends, despite their different backgrounds. Jimmy wanted to be a gunner and came from the east end of London, while Frankie was aiming for the pilot's seat and had been brought up in Kensington. They were like chalk and cheese, but they were already great mates.

'I don't have a sweetheart, Jimmy,' Frankie replied, sitting up, and he saw his friend lift his eyebrows at him in disbelief.

Frankie thought about all the reasons Scarlett could never be his sweetheart. *She was too old for him for a start,* he thought ruefully. That's if age mattered. Scarlett was obviously somewhere in her early thirties, while Frankie was only just eighteen. But the real reason he couldn't be with her, and the only one that mattered, was that she was his father's mistress.

'Well, you could 'ave fooled me,' Jimmy said, his eyes dancing with amusement as he grinned widely at Frankie. 'You looked like you was thinking of her right then, so you did!'

Jimmy pulled a small photograph out of his pocket and held it out to Frankie. 'Her name's Jean,' he explained with his eyes softening. 'She's a lovely gal, so she is, and we got engaged afore I left home.'

Frankie stared at the photo of Jean, who was pretty with dark hair and a nice smile. 'Jean looks very nice indeed, Jimmy, and I'm pleased for you,' he told him, handing the photo back, and wishing with all his heart that Scarlett were his fiancée.

Jimmy was still staring at him with a quizzical expression on his face, and suddenly Frankie found himself telling Jimmy all about Scarlett and Eric, even though he'd never told anyone else before. The words tumbled out of his mouth as he explained what had happened that fateful day.

'Crikey, mate! That's heavy stuff all right,' Jimmy observed, pulling his fingers through his cropped dark hair and lifting those bushy eyebrows of his.

'Yeah, I know that, Jimmy,' he said, his eyes drawn to the envelope lying on his bedside table, which had been handed to him earlier in the mess room.

Frankie gazed at his mother's familiar handwriting, and swallowed the bitter taste of disappointment that the letter obviously wasn't from his father.

Jimmy looked at the envelope. 'Is that a letter from the lovely lady named Scarlett, then?' he asked, leaning his elbows on his knees and giving him a knowing look.

Frankie shook his head sadly, dreading what news the letter contained. 'It's from my mother,' he said quickly. 'And it's probably just news from home.' He opened the letter, and scanned the contents and his heart dropped to his boots.

'Not bad news, I hope, mate?' Jimmy asked, his voice laced with concern as he straightened up.

Frankie tore his eyes away from the letter and looked across at Jimmy. 'It's my dad; he's only gone and joined up!' he said with a prickle of unease.

'Surely not. Ain't he too old for that?' Jimmy looked confused as he lit up a cigarette and then blew out a puff of smoke. 'My old man is definitely too ancient, and with his flat feet an' all, there was no chance of him getting into the army.'

'Well, it is surprising to me, too, Jimmy, I mean… my father was forty on his last birthday.' Frankie didn't want to believe Eric had joined the army, but knew why he had done it, and he swallowed nervously as he felt the heaviness returning to his chest.

Eric wasn't physically fit and, having fought in

the last war, had been lucky to come through it alive. *Would his father's luck run out this time?* It didn't bear thinking about. Frankie looked down at the letter again and finished reading the contents. One sentence stood out from the rest.

Your father is currently in the middle of his training at Crowborough army camp, in East Sussex. He left quite soon after you flew out to Canada...

Frankie noticed how his mother expressed no shock at this turn of events. Perhaps she had expected it, or perhaps she knew more than she was saying. But either way, Frankie was more than a little concerned for his father.

Eric had been dispirited about the way things had gone recently at the shipping company, and he had been deeply unhappy at work. After what had happened with Scarlett, perhaps he just wanted to escape, get away from everything. But joining up was not escaping; it was running straight from the frying pan into the fire.

Frankie let out a long sigh, folded the letter up, and put it in his pocket just as the dinner gong went, and they all began filtering out to the canteen for much needed sustenance.

As he joined Jimmy in the dinner queue, Frankie thought again about his own letter. Eric had not replied, and instead had gone off to the army camp without corresponding at all with his son. This made Frankie feel even worse about the way things had gone before he'd left for Toronto.

Frankie decided there and then he would write again to Eric, this time care of the army camp in

Crowborough. He could only hope that his father received the letter before he finished his training and was sent into battle.

Chapter Twenty-Five

Scarlett

It was early evening. I kept my small torch to the ground while walking along the darkened streets of Brighton, past the clock tower, towards the Central Free Church, and thought about Eric's letter. It had arrived only a week after he found me in Frankie's arms:

> *Dearest Scarlett,*
>
> *You know that I love you, but I think we both understand it is time for us to go our separate ways. The war has brought so much change to all of us, and I cannot bear to stay and watch my shipbuilding company become nothing more than an arms factory. But I accept that's what must happen to help the war effort.*
>
> *I have now joined up, and will be leaving for Crowborough army camp next week. You may be thinking I'm too old to fight and that they only want young men, but now the government are accepting older men for active service, too, so long as they are healthy – so they say. This letter therefore is to say goodbye and good luck to you, the most beautiful woman I have ever known, and someone I've been*

privileged to meet.
    Yours forever,
    Eric.

Tears had filled my eyes while I tried to accept this might have happened anyway; after all, Eric wasn't happy at work any more. But I didn't really believe that. Guilt made my chest heavy as I remembered how Eric had saved me from Madam years ago.

Even though I might have found a way to escape myself, Eric had arrived just when I needed him the most, and I had repaid this act of kindness by being unfaithful to him. Accepting that both men were now lost to me forever, and that I had only myself to blame for this situation, was something I reminded myself of every single day.

I regretted not telling Eric about Frankie's first visit from the outset. If I had, it would all have been out in the open and not a secret between us. When Frankie and I came together in a haze of passion, I started off a chain of events, which could never be undone.

As I pushed open the heavy wooden doors of the church, these thoughts echoed endlessly in my head. Frankie being so much younger than me meant there could be no future for us. Even if there was a possibility of being with him, how could I hurt Eric further by making a life with his son?

After the incident with Frankie, I had needed to get away from Lewes for a while, and helping in the war effort made me feel more useful. To this end, I found lodgings at Norfolk Square and made imminent plans to move into Brighton.

I wrote to Ruby and told her what I intended to do, and was comforted that I would be living near to her lodging house in Regency Square.

Finding a tenant for my house had proved easy, and I rented it out to the wife of a serving officer and her two young children, who were escaping the London bombings. Since my move to Brighton, signing up to train as an ARP warden had helped to distract me from unsettling thoughts of Eric and Frankie.

Now, as the smell of incense and the odour of burning candles filled the air, the familiar figure of the priest came into view at the front of the church. He glanced up when I entered, and I walked quickly between the polished wooden pews, the low murmur of voices reaching my ears from the back of the church.

'Good evening, Mrs Cunningham,' the priest said with a welcoming smile.

He was rearranging large candles on the altar as I returned his greeting, then I made my way towards the small group of people who were gathered in the hall where the ARP training regularly took place. As I entered the hall, the musty smell of the adjoining space replaced the smell of incense from inside the church.

Mrs Jackson, the ARP trainer, was a rotund lady with an easy smile and liked by everyone. 'Hello, Scarlett,' she gushed, her words echoing around the high-ceilinged room.

'We're just about to start, please come in and sit down, dear,' she said, indicating an empty seat next to a young lady called Betsy, who had been training alongside me for the past few weeks.

'Tonight we'll teach you what to do in case of a gas attack,' Mrs Jackson began, after gathering everyone together. 'We have protective masks and suits to show you, and the training will focus on how to cut someone's clothing off if they've suffered an attack.'

Betsy caught my eye, looking a bit horrified at what Mrs Jackson had just said, and I understood exactly how she felt. The idea of having to deal with a gas attack was not a welcome thought.

However, since I had started the training, I had taken the sensible approach of not thinking too much about what might lie ahead for us wardens on the streets of Brighton. That was something we would all have to face once the training was finished and we were let loose on the general public.

The bombs dropped here were mostly those left over from the raids on London, and usually when the pilots wanted to offload their cargo before returning to base. So, in that respect we were lucky to be an afterthought, but it was still devastating for the residents when bombs were dropped on Brighton.

Mrs Jackson's talk proved to be very interesting, and two hours later we all filed out of the church hall and I began the short walk along Western Road back to Norfolk Square.

The training always took place in the evening because some people had day jobs. We had begun by learning first aid, which included how to do tourniquets and dressings, then the admin side of things, which involved writing up reports and labels as incidents unfolded on the streets.

We also learned about snuffing out incendiary bombs with sand, about stirrup pumps and how to tackle fires. It was all really interesting, and I was enjoying being involved with the ARP.

***

That night, I slept fitfully. In my troubled dreams,

there was a ship being bombed from above by enemy planes. The horrifying sight of men jumping to their watery graves, in a bid to escape from the burning wreck, had been heart-wrenching, and I awoke with sweat beading my brow.

My heart was racing and I felt nauseous, knowing that this was another warning of something about to happen. This time, I understood that the dream seemed to concern a man Ruby had met during her stay in Ambleside.

She had come back from the Lake District two months ago, and when we met up soon after her return to Brighton, she'd told me excitedly about meeting Reilly Brownlow.

'I met him through Jude and the other artists who have been relocated to the Lake District with The Royal College of Art,' she explained.

'Is he an artist, too, then?' I asked, assuming this was the case.

Ruby had shaken her head. 'Reilly is employed by Lord Fairfield at Ambleside Manor, working the land and looking after the livestock there.'

She stared into the middle distance, her gaze far away, before looking back at me with her eyes sparkling. 'Oh my Lord, Scarlett,' she enthused. 'Reilly is so handsome.'

I could see that Ruby was deeply in love with Reilly, and I was pleased for her. On our last meet up, she had looked even happier, as she told me of her plan to get married to Reilly on his next leave home. Keeping my smile in place while Ruby's face glowed with happiness was hard, as I longed to see Frankie again.

Before we parted that day, Ruby told me how she prayed every day that Reilly would survive the dangers he faced.

'I've given him the amethyst necklace to help keep him safe while he's away fighting,' she explained, her face clouding over slightly.

On her return, Ruby had gone back to work in The Fortune of War pub on the seafront in the evenings, and I was busy with the Women's Voluntary Service. So we hadn't seen very much of each other recently.

This morning, I got up later than normal, as I had been out doing ARP duties until 3am. Last night, the sirens had sounded at 11pm over Brighton, and then a terrifying procession of aircraft had begun at midnight.

The planes had been on their way to London. And later we learnt that their targets were the Houses of Parliament, Westminster Abbey, and the British Museum, with 33 bombers brought down that night.

Feeling the bad dream still clinging to me, I knew I needed to tell Ruby what I had seen. So I quickly dressed and rushed over to Regency Square, where I banged impatiently on the front door and waited breathlessly for her landlady to answer.

Time seemed to stand still as I stood on the doorstep, anxiously shifting from foot to foot. At last Ruby appeared at the window above me, and then leaned out to greet me.

I tried to smile, but I could see that Ruby held a letter in her hand, and my heart turned over with dread as the breath caught in my throat and the hairs lifted at the nape of my neck.

'Ruby, don't open that letter!' I frantically called up to her. But she had already turned away from the window and disappeared back into her room.

As soon as Mrs Monday let me into the house, I ran up the stairs two at a time, hoping to get to Ruby in time. However, when I got there, Ruby had the letter clutched to her chest, and the amethyst necklace was lying in a crumpled heap at her feet.

I led Ruby over to the bed, where she sat down and began to sob. Taking a deep breath, I sat down next to her, noticing that she had dropped the letter. Bending forwards, I picked it up where it had landed on the floor, and read the opening paragraph with my heart in my mouth.

> *Dearest Ruby,*
> *I'm sorry to be the bearer of bad news, but Reilly is missing, presumed dead…*

Heartbroken for Ruby, I tried my best to comfort my friend as I searched my inner voice and intuition for something to tell me that Reilly had somehow survived the ship's sinking.

Clinging to the hope that one day Reilly would return to Ruby, despite this terrible news, I found only a black void where hope should have been. And I had no words of comfort to offer Ruby at this terrible time in her life.

Chapter Twenty-Six

Frankie

Frankie had completed his initial training in Toronto and progressed onto the Elementary flying school in Ontario. He was learning the basics of flying the de Havilland Tiger Moth, and would soon be making his solo flight. After that, he would go onto the Service Flying School in Ontario for sixteen weeks, where he would get his wings, and then finally the Operational Training unit in Quebec.

It was an exciting time, and he was looking forward to the challenges ahead. But all that went to pot when he got the bad news about his father. The emergency leave to go home was soon granted, and he had immediately flown home. This morning, he had been to see his mother.

It had been a difficult conversation, and although Amy had appeared calm, he could see through her façade and knew she was devastated. Words of comfort escaped him as he watched her re-read the telegram. Then she handed it back to him with tears in her eyes. The words had danced in front of his eyes as he gazed sadly down at them.

Regret to inform you that your husband 1368869, Sgt. E. Johnson, has been killed in action…

Frankie had swallowed hard, unable to read any more, knowing that his father was dead because of him. If Eric hadn't seen him kissing Scarlett, he might not have joined up – and he would still be alive today.

Before returning to Ontario, there was one other person Frankie had to see. Others might have disagreed, but he understood that Scarlett had a right to know what had happened to Eric. And he was acutely aware that, as his father's mistress, she would not have been informed through the normal channels.

First, he had gone to Scarlett's old Lewes address, and been shocked to find out she'd moved into Brighton. A harassed young mother answered the door while jiggling a baby on her hip.

'Scarlett has moved into Brighton and joined the Women's Voluntary Service,' she told him. 'She's lodging at Norfolk Square, and I'm renting the house from her,' she added, as a small child emerged from inside the house and clung to her skirts in the open doorway. 'We needed to move because we were in London, you see?'

Frankie did see. London was not safe right now for families with young children; not safe for anyone, really.

Now, as Frankie approached Norfolk Square, his heart was in his mouth. He knocked on the door and waited for Scarlett's landlady to answer, his heart pounding at the thought of seeing her again. This feeling was mixed with intense sadness at the bad news that he was about to give her about Eric.

His longing to see Scarlett had not abated with the

miles between them. But along with this intense need to see her was the dark claw of guilt over breaking his father's heart.

At last, Scarlett appeared. She was standing in front of him, looking as glorious as ever, with that intense turquoise gaze focused on him. If it were humanly possible, she looked even more striking; her eyes sparkled with health and her face was more rounded than before.

Scarlett had put on a little weight, but Frankie could see that it suited her and only served to accentuate her features even more, giving her a voluptuous look.

'Hello, Frankie,' she said. 'I've been waiting for a visit from you,' she added unexpectedly, lifting those lovely brows at him.

Frankie immediately wanted to turn around and run – away from this woman he loved too much, away from the feelings he had no right to feel. That first time he had confronted Scarlett, Frankie had had no knowledge of how much she meant to his father, or how she played an important role in keeping his parents together.

Shaking himself out of his thoughts, Frankie remembered why he had come and what he had to tell her. He attempted to steady his nerves. 'Could I come in, Scarlett?' he said, hardly able to tear his eyes away from her face.

Scarlett nodded slowly, opened the door wider, and led him through a dark hallway into the small front parlour. She indicated that he take a seat, while she perched on the edge of the settee, placed her hands in her lap, and regarded him thoughtfully.

It was then that he noticed what she was wearing. So different from the beautiful, fitted dresses he had seen her in before, she was wearing black trousers, sensible shoes, and a dark-coloured jacket, as if she were ready to go out. Despite this plain attire, she looked stunningly beautiful.

Beside her on the settee sat an ARP warden hard hat, with its trademark W in large white letters emblazoned on the front. He swallowed the lump in his throat at what he needed to say.

'I'm sorry, are you about to go out on duty?' he asked, aware that she was studying his own uniform as he removed his cap and shifted uneasily on his seat.

'I'll be leaving shortly, but I have a few minutes to spare,' she said. 'How are you, Frankie?' she asked, with a frown etched between her brows.

Frankie struggled to compose himself as he looked down at his feet and tried to delay the inevitable. Unable to begin, he abruptly stood up and began pacing the floor, before turning towards Scarlett and blurting out the truth before he lost his nerve.

'Eric... my father... is dead,' he said. His voice sounded shaky, and tears filled his eyes as he scrubbed a hand across his face. 'I'm sorry to have to tell you this, Scarlett,' he managed.

Scarlett gazed back at him for a moment, unmoving, almost as if her limbs were frozen. Then he watched her digest what he'd said, and the feeling came over him that this news wasn't a complete surprise.

Unexpectedly, she stood up and pulled him towards her, and then he was in her arms. As their lips met, every moment of missing Scarlett went into that kiss, and he held her tightly against his regulation RAF jacket and never wanted to let her go.

As they drew apart, Scarlett took in a long, deep breath and gave him a searching look. Then she dipped her head and swayed on her feet as tears began to roll unheeded down her cheeks.

Frankie reached out to Scarlett, but she pushed him abruptly away and sank slowly down onto the settee, and placed her head in her hands. Great racking sobs shook her body, and for a moment he stood awkwardly to one side, having no idea how to comfort her.

Kneeling down on his haunches, he again tried to console Scarlett. He couldn't bear to see her suffering this way, couldn't bear that he was to blame for her grief, or for his father's death. The guilt was heavy in his chest, and too much of a burden.

Eventually, Scarlett lifted those lovely eyes of hers and gazed at him with accusation in their turquoise depths, and Frankie could see then how much she regretted Eric's death.

Feeling even more awkward, and having no idea what to do, he went to stand at the window where he stared sightlessly out at the street beyond. After a while, when the silence in the room became unbearable, he turned back towards Scarlett.

Frankie wished with all his heart that things could have been different. That somehow he had met Scarlett before his father. But that would have been impossible, of course, because he was so much younger than Scarlett. As his thoughts tumbled over each other, he became aware that she was looking at him with a quizzical expression on her face.

'How did you find me?' she asked quietly, her face stained with tears.

Frankie explained how he'd gone to her house in Lewes, only to find there was a tenant there now who had directed him here to Norfolk Square. Scarlett nodded slowly and looked as if she wanted to be somewhere else, maybe somewhere far away from him.

The sheer misery etched on her face made Frankie realise just how much she must have loved his father. And that he must have been mistaken when he thought she loved him more than Eric.

Then he remembered something Scarlett had said to him earlier when she'd opened the door to him. 'What was that you said about waiting for me to arrive? Had you already heard that Eric was dead?'

As he spoke, Frankie realised that couldn't have been possible. His mother had been informed through the normal channels, and received a telegram, but Scarlett would not have received such notification.

Scarlett shook her head now without answering his question. 'How did Eric die?' she asked, a hitch in her voice. 'I mean… I know it would have been in combat, but do you know any details?' she asked, her eyes swollen and red.

Frankie had no idea if Eric had suffered at the end, or if his death had been quick, but he wanted to save Scarlett further suffering.

'He was killed at the siege in Tobruk,' he told her, lowering himself into an armchair and leaning his elbows on his knees. 'The information coming through is sketchy about exactly what happened,' he said truthfully.

'How awful. How's your mother taking the bad news?' she asked sympathetically.

'Ma's bearing up under the strain. She had a visit from another soldier who fought alongside my father at Tobruk,' Frankie lied, with his chest aching. 'The soldier explained that Eric hadn't suffered in his last moments.'

Taking a deep breath, he tried to think of something

else to help take that heartbroken expression off Scarlett's face. 'I was at home with my mother when the soldier visited her, and before leaving he took me to one side,' he carried on, lost in the lie now.

She gazed across at him steadily with hope in her eyes.

'The soldier said Eric had asked him to tell *you* how much he loved you, Scarlett.' Frankie hesitated before saying, 'I told him I would pass on the message to you.'

And then he said the words that were hanging heavily in the air between them.

'It's my fault he's dead,' he told her, his voice breaking on the words and feeling the pain in his chest intensify. 'He would never have joined up if he hadn't seen us two together.'

'You don't know that for sure, Frankie,' Scarlett said. 'Eric wasn't happy with the way things were going at the shipping company,' she pointed out.

Frankie tried to stem the grief threatening to overwhelm him. 'If we are being truthful here,' he said, running his fingers through his hair and looking up at her, 'we both know it was *you* he truly loved, and not my mother,' he told Scarlett softly.

Scarlett's body stiffened in response to his words, and she stood up abruptly. 'Frankie, I want to thank you for coming here today and… for telling me about Eric,' she said, turning quite formal in her speech and taking a step towards the door.

Frankie stared at her, trying to work out what to say, but he could see by the straightness of her back that they were done with questions. And as she began walking through the hallway, he had no choice but to follow her.

'It was very considerate of you to call on me,' she

159

said, as they reached the front door.

Frankie gripped his RAF cap and tried to stem his panic. Scarlett was talking as if they were complete strangers, and not two people who had once been lovers. His heart lurched as he watched her opening the front door with her head held high.

And even though she was now pretending they were mere acquaintances, he could not leave this way. Taking her firmly by the shoulders, he forced Scarlett to look at him.

'Don't do this,' he warned her. 'You know very well that *I love you*, Scarlett, and I think you love me,' he said desperately. 'We met at the wrong time, that's all. Please don't say goodbye like this.'

He was pleading with her now, uncaring that she might think him weak, but he had no way of knowing when he would see Scarlett again.

Scarlett's eyes hardened and she set her jaw. 'That's not true. I don't love you, Frankie, it was Eric that I loved,' she told him firmly. 'And I really want you to leave now!'

Frankie didn't want to give up, but maybe Scarlett *had* truly loved his father and not him, despite their lovemaking. And if that were true, then he'd made a right old mess of everything.

After all, he reminded himself, she was a woman of the night and could turn her affections to any man who paid her enough money. Even so, it was hard to believe that she didn't love him at all.

'Scarlett, listen, when I've finished my training, I'll be posted to active service,' he told her intently.

Knowing he was lowering himself to plead with her this way, he couldn't seem to help himself. 'I'm sorry I can't alter what's happened to my father… but…' the words died on his lips at Scarlett's cold expression.

'Please go now, Frankie,' she said, giving him a curt nod. 'There's nothing between us. You have to remember that what we did was a huge mistake. Something which happened in the heat of the moment, and nothing more.'

Frankie couldn't believe how she was acting. This was a different woman to the one he'd made mad passionate love to that day his father had arrived unexpectedly.

'Scarlett… can't we be open with each other here? What about us?' If she really didn't love him, Frankie wasn't sure how he would go on with living, and risking life and limb for his country.

But her mask of coldness intensified as she leaned towards him. 'Frankie, understand this! There is no *us*, and there never has been,' she stressed.

Frankie simply gaped at her. It was worse than he had expected, and she obviously had no feelings for him whatsoever. But she wasn't finished with him yet.

'You're far too young for me, for one thing,' Scarlett continued. 'Now, please… I need to be alone now,' she said, indicating towards the open doorway.

Frankie was determined to say what was in his heart before he left, knowing that he might never get another opportunity.

'Age has nothing to do with our love, and you know it!' he retorted, feeling as if everything was falling apart around him. His father was dead, and Scarlett hated him. He didn't know what he had expected from her, but it wasn't this.

Despite the age difference and his father's death, he could never regret loving Scarlett. Even though, apparently, she didn't love him back. He gazed at her for one long moment, waiting for her face to soften, but when Scarlett stood steadfast, he knew he was beaten.

Giving up on the fight, he shot her one last look and strode out of the door without a backward glance. Later, on his return to Ontario, he genuinely thought he was going to die – not from injuries sustained in this terrible war, but from a broken heart.

Chapter Twenty-Seven

Scarlett

For days after hearing the news that Eric had died, I walked around in a haze of grief, only half living, with my body feeling numb. Everything was done automatically, and I moved around mechanically like a robot.

After taking the bus into Brighton, I stood along with the other women in the food queues, with my ration book, trying not to let my emotions overwhelm me. When the numbness receded, I was left with a deep, clawing guilt, which was exhausting.

Even though we'd had a business arrangement from the start, and I didn't love Eric, I felt adrift – as if something solid had gone from my life.

What was hard to accept was the knowledge that after all he had done for me, I had rewarded Eric by sleeping with his son. Finding me with Frankie that day had been the undoing of him, so how could I forgive myself for that?

At night, I struggled to sleep, and when I did drift off, my dreams were full of being trapped at Madam's again, and I'd wake up with my heart racing and my stomach churning. In the middle of all this mental turmoil, Ruby paid me a visit.

'Scarlett, what on earth's the matter?' she said, looking askance at me.

Her dark eyes were full of concern as she gazed at me lying on the bed in a dishevelled state. The blame had become a lead weight, and I was unable to think of anything except Eric dying alone on that battlefield.

I tried to explain to Ruby how it was. 'Frankie came to see me,' I croaked, with my throat dry and aching. 'It's Eric… he's dead, Ruby. He died in combat.' I bit down on my lower lip to stem the tears.

Ruby shook her head sadly and made me a sweet cup of tea. 'You need to rest and let this dreadful news sink in, Scarlett,' she said with moist eyes. 'Believe me, I've been where you are now, and I understand how you are feeling. You're still in shock, and it'll take a while to sink in.'

Through the haze of my grief – *or was it guilt that was making me feel so bad?* – I noticed the hitch in Ruby's voice. She was referring to the day she'd heard about Reilly, and her wise words rang true with me. In time, I would get over Eric's death, but right now it was all too raw and a lot to take in.

Ruby had continued to bustle about the room chatting to me while I tried my best to listen, but all I really wanted to do was bury myself under the covers and shut out the world.

The next day, I lay in bed all day. By the evening, I shook myself out of my stupor and gazed at myself in the mirror. I saw someone looking back at me that I didn't recognise. She had red eyes and a downturned mouth, and I knew I had to do something to change this dismal state of affairs.

I told myself there were many other people who

were suffering in this war, and that I had no right to wallow in self-pity in this way. Lifting my chin with a determined air, I began dressing in my ARP warden clothes, determined to return to the church hall and finish my training. My acceptance of Eric's death, and my part in it, began that day.

Today, with a start, I realised that Ruby's visit had been weeks ago, and since then I hadn't been able to rid myself of the feeling, that there was something important she had wanted to tell me that day. With an afternoon free today, I decided to pay her a visit.

'Come in, Scarlett,' Ruby greeted me at the door of her lodging house in Norfolk Square in her dressing gown, and then led me upstairs to her room.

'Excuse me for not being dressed, but I've been sleeping off my evening shift at the pub. You know how it is, don't you?' she added, pulling her dressing gown tighter around her.

'Of course,' I said, following her into the room. 'How are you, Ruby?' I asked. 'I'm sorry I haven't seen you for a while. It's taken time to get back to normal after the news about Eric.'

'Oh, don't worry, I'm fine thanks, Scarlett...' Ruby began, as she opened the curtains to let the afternoon sun in. 'Actually, I have some good news to tell you,' she said, turning towards me with an uneasy smile. 'The thing is, there's no easy way to tell you this... but I got married.'

As I stood in the middle of the room, my mouth fell open at this surprising news. 'Flaming heck, Ruby, you've done what? Who have you married?' I said, staring hard at her. What was going on here? The only man she loved was Reilly, or so she had always told me.

Ruby regarded me with a frown. 'Dick McCarthy,' she said, picking up her cup from the bedside table and sipping her tea.

'I'm sorry, Ruby. This is a bit of a blinking shock. In fact, I can hardly believe it.' Then I remembered something she'd told me a while back.

'Didn't Gerald warn you about him, I mean this Dick fellow? So why did you go ahead and marry *him*? Unless…' my words trailed away as my eyes were drawn towards her stomach and I realised what Ruby hadn't told me.

She responded by pulling her dressing gown across herself even tighter, in an attempt to hide the roundness of her stomach. And I couldn't believe I hadn't noticed the last time I had seen her. How had I missed that Ruby was expecting a baby?

Thoughts spun in my head. 'Bloody hell, Ruby, why didn't you tell me? Who else knew about this, and why wasn't I invited to the wedding?' I knew I wasn't giving her any time to answer my questions, but my mind was whirling.

Ruby lowered her eyes and let out a long, drawn-out sigh. 'Dick knew about the baby, but he was the only one,' she told me, and then she lifted her head and gave me a searching look from under those long, dark eyelashes of hers.

'I did tell you about Dick and the baby, Scarlett,' she explained dismally. 'But you were so upset about Eric at the time that you didn't hear me.'

Ruby shook her head slightly and then bit down on her lower lip. 'There's something else I need to tell you,' she said uneasily, while running a hand protectively over her stomach. 'This is Reilly's baby.'

'Oh, Ruby. Does Dick know it's Reilly's baby?' I

asked tentatively.

Ruby stared at me sadly, while I did a quick calculation of when she had last seen Reilly in Ambleside. We were now almost at the end of June, and she had returned from Ambleside in March.

'Dick comforted me when I was upset about Reilly, and I told him then that I was pregnant with my fiancé's baby.' Ruby stared down at her hands as she spoke. 'A few weeks later, Dick offered to marry me.'

I nodded, understanding now why she had married him. 'Well, Dick McCarthy sounds like a good sort to me, Ruby,' I told her with relief.

Ruby smiled back but it didn't quite reach her eyes. 'I'm sorry you didn't come to the wedding, but Dick said we had to marry quickly, before he went back to the navy. So there was no time to organise a proper wedding.'

The guilt was back and creeping all over me once again. This time over Ruby who had needed me, and I hadn't even noticed. For the second time recently, I'd failed someone that I loved dearly.

I swallowed hard and took a step towards her. 'I'm sorry, you know, that I didn't hear you tell me this, Ruby,' I told her, wishing I could turn the clock back and change things.

When she had come to see me, I'd been distraught over losing Eric. But surely if she had made me understand somehow, made me see how things were, then I would have realised? Instead, she'd gone and married Dick without my knowledge.

There was something else nagging at me, something Ruby didn't know which I had to tell *her*, because I'd also been hiding it from myself. 'I'm pregnant, too,' I blurted out, feeling a lump in my throat at the thought

167

of us both being in the same predicament.

Except we weren't in the same predicament. Ruby now had Dick to look after her and the baby, and I had nobody. Nobody but myself, and I had never felt more alone than I did at that moment in my life.

Ruby stared at me in surprise, and then she reached over and hugged me tightly. 'That's unbelievable, Scarlett! This means our babies will be born close to each other. Let's hope they'll be friends, like we are, when they grow up.'

Relief surged through me that I had at last told someone what was going on. Now I just had to face up to it myself, I began to wish that I'd been able to find a way to tell Frankie the truth, that I was expecting his baby.

Ruby was regarding me with a furrowed brow, and it was as if she were reading my mind. 'Have you told Frankie yet?' she asked, holding me at arm's length. 'He has a right to know, Scarlett, you do understand that, don't you?'

I thought about Frankie and how he'd pleaded with me to keep in touch the last time I had seen him, and my heart turned over. 'The thing is, I couldn't do it, Ruby. Not after hearing about poor Eric,' I explained with a heavy chest.

She looked shocked. 'But why not, Scarlett? I understand it wouldn't have been an easy thing to say, but you're going to need Frankie to marry you,' she said, making it sound simple. 'I take it that Frankie is the father of the baby?'

I nodded and gave her a weak smile, then wondered how to explain to her what I didn't really understand myself.

'The thing is, Ruby, it didn't seem right to tell

Frankie about the baby when he came to tell me that his own father had died.' My voice trailed off as the words dried in my throat and I tried to get my head round what had happened.

'I think it was the guilt, which I just couldn't get past. I couldn't tell Frankie that I loved him or about the baby; it was impossible...' I swallowed hard, reliving that awful day when Frankie told me about Eric.

I rubbed at my forehead where a headache had begun, and tried to find the truth. 'So I denied my feelings for him and sent him back to the RAF training centre in Canada.'

Ruby gave me a sympathetic nod. 'I can understand how difficult that might have been, after all Eric had done for you.'

I couldn't answer Ruby, but she was right. That was the problem, and something I could never get away from, because Eric had loved me even though I hadn't loved him.

She laid a comforting hand on my arm. 'I'm sorry about Eric, Scarlett, but it wasn't your fault him dying that way. That was the fault of this whole bleeding, awful war.'

Hearing Ruby swear was surprising, because she had been brought up to speak nicely. 'Thanks, but you're wrong. It was my fault.'

Ruby pulled her brows in. 'I don't think that's true,' she said. 'Anyway, you'll be pleased to know that I've made the right decision in marrying Dick.'

It was good news, because at least one of us would be happy, but I couldn't help feeling that something wasn't quite right here. Had she really forgotten Reilly so quickly, the man she claimed to have loved so deeply?

'Are you sure about that, Ruby? I mean, I know how much Reilly meant to you. But if you are happy, then I'm pleased for you.'

Ruby stood tall and lifted her hand to show me the ring Dick had bought her. In doing so, her dressing gown rode up, revealing her bare arm. Quick as a flash, she pulled the sleeve down again while averting her eyes, but unfortunately, she wasn't quick enough.

'What the bloody hell is that on your arm?' I yelled, unable to help myself. And when she didn't answer me, I repeated the question. 'Ruby! What's going on?'

Instead of answering me, she turned away and walked slowly towards the window, where she began fiddling with the curtains. But I refused to be ignored. Swiftly, I caught up with her and yanked up the offending sleeve to reveal her injuries.

'What are those awful bruises on your arm?' I demanded, taking her by the shoulders and forcing her to look at me now.

'Honestly, Scarlett, it's nothing,' she shot back while pulling abruptly away from me again.

I waited for her to explain, and eventually she dropped her gaze, slumped onto the bed, and put her head in her hands. I stood over her with my hands on my hips.

'Those bruises are not nothing,' I said, pointing to her arm. Smarting with anger at whoever had inflicted this on my friend, I tried to calm myself by taking a deep breath. 'Did Dick do that to you?' I asked her bluntly, and Ruby looked up at me and nodded slowly. 'He's not such a good sort after all then!'

Being angry wasn't helping Ruby, I reminded myself, as I sat down on the bed next to her. 'Why would he do that to you? Please tell me, because I need to understand what's happening. And why didn't you listen to Gerald's warning?' I asked again, confused as to why she had married someone who was obviously a bully.

Haltingly, she explained how she had thought Gerald had been listening to gossip, and generally being overprotective of her. 'He's a good man, Scarlett,' she said, meeting my gaze. 'He looked out for us barmaids and... well... I had the baby to think of, you see, and with Reilly being dead and all... I had no idea what else to do,' she wailed.

A knot formed in my stomach at what Ruby had just told me. 'I'm so sorry that I wasn't there for you. But you do know you have to leave Dick, don't you?' I warned, coming straight to the point. 'Not just for your sake, but for the baby's as well. I mean, if Dick did that to you, Ruby, God knows what he would do to an innocent baby.'

She stared down at the black-and-blue bruises on her arm and sighed. 'Dick seemed genuine before we were married,' she muttered, lifting her face and staring past me into the middle distance. 'But after we were married, the minute we were alone... he said I would have to do as I was told.' Ruby looked at me with dull eyes, her face flushed as she stifled a sob.

That was the truth of it. Ruby had made a mistake in marrying Dick, but there was no easy way out now – even I could see that. And for once I had no idea how to help Ruby get out of the situation she now found herself in.

She looked so distressed that I tried to think of something good to say to her. 'Think of it this way,' I reassured, as I leaned forwards and touched her arm.

'At least Dick has gone back to the Royal Navy to fight, and he won't get any more leave home for a while. So for now at least, you are safe.'

Chapter Twenty-Eight

Annika seemed the right name for the baby from the minute she was born. The name had been going around in my head for weeks before she appeared. I had read somewhere that it meant 'beautiful one', and with her blue-green eyes and soft porcelain skin, she suited the name.

I had been lucky that the birth had been straightforward. Mrs Penny had come up trumps and fussed over me when I was pregnant, and she was the first person to call the midwife when I went into labour in my room at Norfolk Square.

Annika was now just over a month old, and was a bundle of joy. As I held her in my arms and she smiled up at me, once again I wished I had told Frankie I was expecting his baby when he'd come to see me about Eric back in June.

Instead, he had returned to his training in Canada, under the misguided impression that I didn't love him, and without knowing he was about to become a father. The more I thought about the way I sent him away that day, the more I regretted my decision.

'Your father doesn't know you exist, sweetie,' I told Annika, as she held my gaze. 'But don't worry, darling,' I soothed, as a frown appeared between her tiny brows, 'I'll always be here to look after you.'

As Annika's eyes fluttered shut, I carefully laid her in the cot, just as I heard a light tap on the door. I opened it to find Mrs Penny standing in the doorway. 'I've just put Annika down,' I told her quietly, putting a finger to my lips to indicate the baby was sleeping.

Mrs Penny glanced behind me and then gave me a knowing nod. 'What time are you on duty tonight, my dear?' she whispered.

I stepped out onto the landing so that I wouldn't wake Annika. 'I have to report at six o'clock sharp,' I told her quietly. 'The baby's been good today, and I don't anticipate her waking up while I'm gone, but I've left a bottle of milk in the fridge for her if she's hungry,' I explained. 'And I'll be home around midnight as usual.'

Annika had proved to be a good baby. She'd been sleeping twelve hours straight for a whole week now, which was amazing for a new baby, so I had been told. But just in case, I always left food and clean napkins out for her, so that Mrs Penny could deal with whatever she needed.

Mrs Penny nodded and then smiled. 'I would love the little darling to wake up, then I could have a nice cuddle,' she quipped, looking quite regretful that Annika was sleeping peacefully.

I couldn't help smiling at this, thinking about the round of feeding and changing that Annika had needed in the last four weeks. 'Ah, thanks, Mrs Penny. I'm so grateful for you helping out with Annika, and I don't know what I'd do without you,' I told her truthfully.

'It's a pleasure, my dear,' she replied with a tilt of her head.

Mrs Penny doted on Annika, which meant I could continue with my ARP duties. She was a caring landlady, who had also turned out to be a great support to both the baby and me.

When I had first arrived at the lodging house, I'd wondered if Mrs Penny would order me to leave Norfolk Square once she knew I was pregnant. I would understand if she took this decision, but I wanted to stay in Brighton.

In the end, I told her I was expecting a baby soon after my arrival, and that I was also unmarried. Then I asked her point blank if she preferred me to leave Norfolk Square lodging house and return to Lewes.

She had looked thoughtful. 'Do you love the father?' she'd asked, after a moment's silence.

'I do love him,' I admitted. 'But it's been complicated.'

She had glanced down at my slightly rounded stomach and then back up at me. 'It always is, but that aside, I like having you here and I don't want you to leave. But other people may not be so forgiving,' she added.

I understood that this was true. I knew others would be quick to judge me for having a baby out of wedlock. I was used to being judged, but my worry had been how to protect my unborn baby from the stigma of illegitimacy.

'I'll give you a bit of advice which might help both you and the baby,' Mrs Penny had continued sympathetically. 'You might want to tell other people you're a war widow,' she said, lifting her eyebrows.

I agreed this was a good idea, and decided to take Mrs Penny's advice. Knowing that my pregnancy would be showing soon, I changed my name from Miss Cunningham to Mrs Cunningham. And when I joined the Women's Voluntary Service to train as an ARP warden, I told them my husband was missing in action.

Now, wearing my peaked hat and uniform of dark blue trousers and battledress jacket, I crept out of the bedroom, leaving the door ajar so that Mrs Penny could hear Annika if she woke up.

'I'm off now. Will you be alright with Annika?' I asked from the doorway of the front parlour. Mrs Penny swung her legs off the footstool and said the same thing she always did before I went out to do my training.

'Of course, dear, you go off and do your duty,' she replied, getting to her feet and looking pleased that once again I was leaving her in charge of the baby.

I gave Mrs Penny a hug and thanked her profusely. 'I'll see you later then,' I told her, before grabbing my serge coat and gas mask on the way out, and closing the front door behind me.

Hurrying out into the bitterly cold night, I began walking in the direction of my warden post. As I strode along the blacked-out streets towards Montpelier Road, I pulled my coat tighter around me and held my torch close to the ground.

In the darkness I could hear the soft sound of the waves coming into shore, and could smell the sea air, while I tried not to think about Frankie and how much I longed to see him.

Drawing level with number sixty-four Montpelier Road – a two up and two down shored up by sandbags – I looked up at the large sign screwed onto the brickwork stating: *Your local Warden Post, Information Concerning ARP & Civil Defence Matters.*

Mr Bartholomew had already spotted me through the window, and was making his way towards the front door. As he lumbered towards me and I waited for him to let me in, I thought about how the raids in Brighton had been far and few between since I'd completed my training.

Certainly, there had been nothing as bad as the one Ruby and Harriet had got caught up in that terrible day when poor Harriet was killed, outside Hannington's department store a whole year ago. When I thought about that night, and the report that Hitler's intention was to make The Royal Pavilion his headquarters, it sent ice cold shivers up my spine.

'Good evening to you, Mrs Cunningham,' Mr Bartholomew said, giving me a toothy grin as he opened the door for me. 'Nothing much happening tonight, by the looks of it,' he said jovially. 'Come on in then, my dear.'

Mr Bartholomew was dressed smartly as always, with a clean white shirt and a tie on his vast body, as if he were going to work in a managerial role instead of running an ARP post. A retired teacher, he told me how he deeply regretted not being able to join up, but that he loved helping with the Civil Defence Service.

I nodded back at him and glanced up into the night sky. It was full of stars twinkling amongst the blackness, and I hoped that tonight would be free of Hitler's bombs.

'Fingers crossed there will be no raids tonight then,' I told him, as I followed him through the narrow hallway.

Stepping onto the brown linoleum floor of the front parlour, I saw that, as usual, Mr Wright was already here, ready and waiting to be told what to do. There was no sign of the two spinster ladies, a Miss Taylor and Miss Davies, who always arrived slightly late.

'Good evening,' I greeted Mr Wright, who was

perched on the edge of the settee, and he nodded solemnly back at me. A skinny, quiet, unassuming man, Mr Wright was also retired, and had been a factory worker. I got the feeling he had signed up to the ARP to get out of the house and avoid a nagging wife.

Sitting down on the settee, I waited for Mr Bartholomew to return. He'd disappeared into the back room, which was reserved for the ARP only, and which also served as the tea-making room.

The clatter of the cups as he went about this ritual happened every night I was on duty. Four of us would arrive to be briefed by Mr Bartholomew, on what the night's duties would be, and then congregate in the back parlour to have tea.

'Pretty bad that attack on Pearl Harbour, wasn't it?'

Mr Wright's voice interrupted my thoughts and made me jump. He wasn't normally one for talking much, and had never directly addressed me before.

'It was truly horrific, Mr Wright,' I agreed, remembering yesterday's news reports which told of the Japanese attacking the U.S. naval base near Honolulu in Hawaii.

The attack had taken the Americans by surprise and was devastating in its impact, destroying twenty naval vessels, over three hundred airplanes, and killing more than two thousand people. This morning's news had been all about how President Franklin D. Roosevelt had now declared war on Japan.

Before we could discuss this further, Mr Bartholomew appeared back in the room. 'Tea's up,' he said, just as a loud knock came at the front door. 'You two go through to the back room,' he ordered, 'and I'll let the ladies in.'

Once we were all settled around the table in the back parlour, Mr Bartholomew began his instructions. These instructions were always the same, because he was a complete stickler for following the rules.

'You all know what to look for,' he said, looking at us all in turn.

Miss Taylor and Miss Davies nodded their heads solemnly at Mr Bartholomew and we all followed suit.

'Start with any breaches of the blackout, and then check the shelters. Don't forget to look for people wandering about, and of course anyone in need of assistance,' Mr Bartholomew continued.

'If there's a raid on, get everyone under cover quickly. Mr Wright has the list of who is where tonight,' he glanced towards Mr Wright, who agreed that this was indeed the case.

'Later on, hopefully we can all get some sleep, with turns being taken to watch the street. All except Scarlett, of course, who can't stay later than midnight, as we all know.'

Mr Bartholomew had installed camp beds for the other three wardens in the front room. And they took it in turns to stay over, so that they could watch over the street from the window.

'And how is the little one, Mrs Cunningham?' Mr Bartholomew now turned to me and smiled, showing a wide gap in his front teeth.

'Annika is doing very well, thank you,' I told him to a murmur of appreciation across the table, and I wondered if they would be quite so keen on asking about the baby if they knew the truth about her birth.

Mr Bartholomew drank the last of his tea and stood up. 'Right now, I think we're all ready. Grab your hats, and don't forget your gas masks on the way out, everyone.'

With a clatter of chairs, everyone reached for their black steel helmets, which hung from nails on the wall behind us, and then we made our way towards the door and out into the blackness of the night.

Chapter Twenty-Nine

Ruby's eyes shone as she gazed down at her new baby boy. The child had dark eyes and hair, and olive coloured skin. And from how Ruby had described her lover Reilly Brownlow, it seemed the baby was the image of his handsome father.

Ruby was resting up at home in her small, terraced house in Kemptown, after giving birth a few days before. I had been with her during her labour, which – unlike mine – had been long and hard. Thankfully, eventually, the baby had been born healthy, making his presence known in the world by screaming for England. However, now he looked rested and happy as he lay peacefully in Ruby's arms.

'He's beautiful, Ruby. Have you got a name for him yet?' I probed. With our two babies born so close in age, we hoped they would grow up together and become firm friends.

Ruby looked up at me with a soft gaze, and a smile quirked at her lips. 'Not yet, but I like the name Noah. What do you think – does it suit him?' she asked uneasily. 'I think it's a name that Reilly would have liked, too,' she added, with a frown between her brows.

I swallowed the lump in my throat, feeling Ruby's pain. 'Noah suits him just fine,' I returned. 'If you like that name, then Noah it is!'

Ruby nodded at me and smiled down at the baby. 'Hello, Noah,' she said, trying out the name just as he opened his eyes and looked up at her.

'I'm really sorry, Ruby,' I said, placing a hand on her arm. 'But I'm going to have to go now,' I told her regretfully. 'Mrs Penny can only look after Annika for a short time today. Have you heard from Dick, or about when he'll be home on leave again?'

A dark cloud passed over Ruby's face at my words. 'Oh, Scarlett, I wish I never had to see him again,' she said with a heavy sigh, pulling the baby in closer.

Dick had been home for a few weeks leave the month before Noah had been born, and Ruby had found she had to tiptoe around him to keep him happy. She was full of worry that he would take out his temper on her and her unborn child. Thankfully, he had spent most of his time in The Fortune of War pub, getting drunk.

Ruby's contented look had now been replaced by the look of fear she always wore when Dick was around, or when his name was mentioned.

'Hopefully, he won't be allowed leave for a while now,' I suggested, trying to reassure her. 'Try to take one day at a time,' I soothed. But in truth, I was worried about Ruby and Noah; they both needed to escape from the evil Dick, but how this was to be done wasn't yet clear.

Ruby nodded thoughtfully and then her face brightened. 'Enough of my troubles. Have you written to Frankie yet?' she asked, passing the baby from one arm to another.

The thought that soon I'd see my precious Frankie again filled me with yearning, and made me impatient to hold him in my arms again. Every night I dreamt we were reunited, and in the end I'd realised that I had to find a way to get past the guilt I still felt over Eric.

'I did write to him, even though it's taken a long time – I've finally gone and blinking well done it!' I was hardly able to contain my excitement. The feeling of elation was mixed with apprehension, as doubts about whether he still loved me plagued me daily.

'That's marvellous news!' Ruby gushed. 'I'm so happy for you, but… how do you feel about Eric now?'

I looked down at my hands and let out a long sigh. 'I will always be grateful to Eric for what he did for me, Ruby,' I told her truthfully. 'But having Annika made me realise I had to forgive myself for my part in his death, and move on. And Frankie should know he has a daughter.'

'You both deserve some happiness,' Ruby said with a tilt of her head. 'So you've told him about Annika?'

I shook my head. 'I haven't told Frankie about his daughter yet. I want to tell him when he comes home, and I'm hoping now that I've written to him, that will be quite soon,' I said uneasily. 'Especially as he should have nearly finished his training now.'

I could see Ruby was trying to be brave, but I knew her too well, and the envy she was trying to hide in those dark eyes of hers was blatantly obvious to me.

I placed a hand on her arm. 'Oh, Ruby, honestly, I just wish things had turned out differently for you…' Tears were pricking the back of my eyes at the sadness my friend was carrying.

Ruby lifted her chin and set her jaw. 'Please don't feel sorry for me, Scarlett,' she said with a determined air. 'I have little Noah to look after now, and don't forget you need to tell Frankie how you really feel about him, when he does eventually get home on leave.'

'Oh, I did that all right, Ruby! But we can't rule out that I may be too late, and that he might have moved on since I last saw him.'

Would Frankie push me away after the way I had treated him? I worried. Having finally told him the truth about my feelings, I was waiting with bated breath for him to reject me. But whatever the outcome, I needed to be truthful with Frankie before it was too late.

Something, though, had held me back from telling him about the baby. Deep down, I understood that I needed Frankie to love me for myself, and not to marry me only to give his daughter a name. If he didn't love me any more, I would survive, and somehow bring up Annika alone, however tough that would be.

Ruby's voice interrupted my thoughts. 'Honestly, Scarlett, I don't think there's much likelihood of Frankie not being *still* madly in love with you,' she said, widening her eyes. 'You've not heard back from him yet?' she asked as she rocked Noah from side to side.

'Not yet, and if I'm being truthful here, I still feel awful about what happened to Eric. But as I told you before, the moment I set eyes on Frankie, I knew he was *the one* for me.'

Ruby nodded her understanding. 'No need to explain anything to me,' she said, shifting on the bed, before placing Noah over her shoulder to bring up his wind. 'We all need to take what happiness we can in this life, especially in these uncertain times. Don't you forget that, Scarlett. And I truly believe that you and Frankie are made for each other.'

Ruby was right. There was no other way to live now, but to take every opportunity at happiness that arose.

'Thank you, Ruby,' I said. 'Now, I really have to go back to my own little angel,' I told her, full of hope that Frankie would soon reply favourably to my letter.

Chapter Thirty

Frankie

Frankie had got his wings and completed his final training at the operational training unit in Quebec when he received Scarlett's letter.

Unfortunately, by the time it arrived, he had already cancelled his Christmas leave home, which had been scheduled for December. And he had been given a date for his posting to RAF Exeter Airfield.

He read:

> *Dearest Frankie,*
>
> *I love you. Please forgive me for pushing you away when you came to tell me about Eric, but at the time the guilt was too much for me to bear. I loved Eric, you see, but not as I love you now. I loved him for looking after me, for treating me like a person and not an object, and for being there when I needed him most.*
>
> *When I looked back on my younger self, I was a very confused young lady. What I thought I wanted from life and what I needed were in fact two different things.*
>
> *I told myself I wanted a man to give me everything I had never had as a child. I needed someone wealthy,*

to spoil me with all the beautiful things that money could buy. But as soon as I met you, I realised that I had been gravely mistaken. What I really needed, Frankie, was love, and whether that love came with money or with poverty really didn't matter.

With you, I've found that love, and also found passion. The love I have for you is so strong that nothing can break it – even my guilt over Eric has not torn it apart. It took me a while to realise this, and I'm sorry, but if there is the slightest chance you still feel the same way about me, then I will count myself lucky. But if you don't, then that's all right, too. Either way, I'll thank God to have known you, my darling.

On his return to the training base, Frankie had put everything into working hard to secure his wings. Despite Eric's love of ships and being in the Navy during the First World War, Frankie had always wanted to fly a plane.

His hard work paid off and helped ward off disturbing thoughts of his father's untimely death and Scarlett's painful rejection. Heartbroken over the way Scarlett had pushed him away, he had been left confused. He could have sworn she felt the same way he did, but had to accept he must have been mistaken and that it was his father she had truly loved, not Frankie.

In order to go on with his training, he'd had to find a way to focus on flying and forget about what had happened between them. So when he'd been offered leave at Christmas time, to be taken before his posting to Exeter Airfield, he had quickly refused it.

'I'd rather stay here at the base,' he'd explained

to his sergeant, who was surprised; nobody was daft enough to refuse leave home.

But Frankie had his reasons. For a start, what did he have to go home for? He couldn't bear to see the accusation in his mother's eyes, or to be rejected by Scarlett again. And being alone over Christmas at the airbase seemed preferable.

It was hard to believe he would never see Eric again, and he supposed it wouldn't be until after the war had ended that he would truly understand his father wasn't coming back. Frankie had not even begun to think about the business his father left behind; his father's death meant he was now the new owner of Johnson and Johnson Shipbuilding company.

When Scarlett's letter arrived, Frankie experienced several different emotions. Regret that he'd turned down his leave and so he would not be reunited with her until his next leave home – whenever that would be; sadness, because he didn't know when he'd see her again; and excitement, that she had finally said she loved him.

***

Today was Frankie's first solo mission from RAF Exeter Airfield. The operation had been planned after the Civilian Observer Core had spotted Hitler and his bombs on his latest mission of destruction.

Tonight, they were to intercept the Luftwaffe who were currently mounting night-time attacks against Britain. These attacks were in retaliation for recent RAF bombing raids on Lubeck and Rostock, and were directed at less defended places such as York, Norwich, Bath, and Canterbury.

Flying a Spitfire Super-marine was a dream come true for Frankie, and he tried to focus on that, even though he was nervous, excited, and full of dread all at the same time. As he started up the engine, its fiery roar drove everything else from Frankie's mind except this important mission and the will to survive whatever happened.

Once he'd eased himself into the cockpit, secured his helmet and goggles, and adjusted his seat, he was ready for take off. With the Lancaster bombers and Spitfires all starting up their engines at once, the noise was deafening, and Frankie straightened his spine and braced himself for what might lie ahead.

In those brief few moments while he waited for the signal, wise words from his more seasoned colleagues spun in his head.

'No-one talks about the fear here, lad,' they'd told him. 'It's every man for himself once you're up in the air, so don't forget that, and look out for number one.'

Frankie's heart lurched, and he suddenly wondered exactly why he'd thought this was a good idea. But then he understood the meaning of his fellow pilots' words. They were saying that if the fear were let loose, it would have a paralysing effect on the men. And this must never happen if Great Britain was to have any chance of defeating Hitler and winning this terrible war.

However this unwritten rule was carried out, the men were totally different once they were back in the barracks after these dangerous missions. In that safe place, they drank ale, patted each other on the back, and congratulated those who had made it back. And together they felt sadness for those men – their friends and colleagues – who had been lost in the darkness of

189

the battle of the skies.

Frankie touched the joystick of the plane affectionately. 'Come along, Scarlett, don't let me down today,' he said, letting out a long sigh. He'd named this beautiful Spitfire after the feisty, brave woman he loved back home, and just speaking her name comforted him as he waited for the signal to go.

Thoughts of Scarlett helped Frankie overcome his fear of being shot down, captured, or – even worse – burnt alive while trapped in the cockpit. These scenarios played out in his mind daily, but seemed worse today as he prepared for his first ever mission in the dark skies above.

Frankie was determined not to give in to the fear. If the other men could do it, so could he. Instead, he bowed his head and prayed that whatever fate had in store for him, he would survive, so that he could live to see the real Scarlett again.

As the signal went up at last to start the mission, Frankie's heart began to race. During his training he'd been taught several things to memorise, which he'd been told had been learned from the experience of WW1.

These included the following: if you had the height, you controlled the battle; if you came out of the sun, the enemy could not see you; and if you held your fire until you were very close, then you seldom missed.

Frankie hoped these three nuggets of information would stand him in good stead when he went into battle, and he felt reassured that he had a chance of surviving if he followed these guidelines. As his plane climbed the skies, along with the Lancaster bombers and the other Spitfires, there was no time to think any more.

Before long, the enemy came into sight. Within moments, the sound of gunfire and bombs being dropped filled the air, and his squadron were picking the Germans off one by one. Frankie quickly spotted a Messerschmitt ahead, and began a dogfight in the air, swooping and diving towards the plane and then circling it.

This was the first time he'd done this for real, and it was harder to negotiate in the dark. But the advice came back to him about waiting until the last moment before shooting it down, because there was more chance of success this way.

Frankie put everything into his effort, somehow holding his nerve, and then shot at the very last second. Then he watched as the plane plunged to the ground in a plume of black smoke.

Despite the night sky, he had got so close to the other plane that he had seen the outline of the pilot's stricken face. That terrible image would be with him for a long time, but Frankie understood now more than ever that this war meant you had to kill or be killed.

The hours ticked by in a frenzy of activity, as they all aimed and shot at the enemy planes. The Messerschmitts proved to be easy pickings as they succumbed to their losses and crashed to the ground far below.

The new De-Havilland Mosquito, which was a recent addition to the airfield, was proving to be a great help in these battles. The 'Mossies', as they were nicknamed, made a very efficient companion to the Lancaster bombers and the Spitfire Supermarines, and Hitler's men stood little chance against them.

'Well done, old chaps, another successful mission!' The squadron commander's voice sounded triumphant as they all turned around to head back to base.

Frankie breathed a sigh of relief that his first mission was over, and it was a good feeling to know they had defeated the enemy. The Luftwaffe was simply no match for Great Britain's capable air defences.

As he flew his plane back to Exeter, Frankie thought about the letter he had sent back to Scarlett. Despite her declaration of love, there was nothing else for it but to tell her the truth – that he loved her, too, but that he had cancelled his leave home before her letter had arrived.

On my next leave home, my love, we will be together, he had written. And while he waited for a reply from Scarlett, he prayed to God this would be the case.

As he landed the plane back on the airfield, Frankie looked forward to a pint with Jimmy in the mess, where they could congratulate each other on their first flight in battle – and on defeating the enemy.

Chapter Thirty-One

Scarlett

While I was feeding Annika the next morning, Mrs Penny delivered a letter to me. I immediately saw it was from RAF Exeter Airfield, and knew it must be from Frankie. My fingers shook, and I could barely open the envelope for the rapid beating of my heart.

Frankie's first line of correspondence told me that my letter to him had arrived too late, and because he had believed I had no feelings for him, he had turned down the leave he had over Christmas.

His letter read:

I was unable to face coming home, Scarlett, and with my father gone it would have been difficult being with my mother, who continues to grieve for him. I'm still feeling guilty about him finding us together the way he did, and also after what happened between us last time I saw you. I truly believed you didn't love me and had never loved me. This thought tore me apart, my darling, and so I decided I'd rather stay at the training base until my posting was imminent.

I'm so sorry, as this means I have no idea when I will see you again, my love. Especially as I've now been posted to RAF Exeter Airfield. But please, Scarlett, understand this, I still love you with all my heart and have never stopped loving you.

Frankie went on to say that as soon as he could secure more leave, he would be coming home to see me. My heart lifted at his words of everlasting love, and I could only hope that he would be offered leave again soon, so that we could be reunited, and he could be introduced to his new baby daughter.

Chapter Thirty-Two

March 1942

I knocked on Ruby's front door and waited impatiently for her to answer, as unease prickled slowly up my spine. A moment later, she opened the door to me with a worried frown on her face.

The nightmare had come to me in the middle of the night, and I had woken with sweat beading my brow and my heart racing, knowing that I had to see Ruby and warn her about the dream.

'What's the matter, Scarlett?' she asked urgently, shooting a quick glance towards the baby, who was in his basket in the corner of the room.

Ruby knew me well and must have seen the concern on my face, so I came straight to the point. 'I've seen something, Ruby,' I told her, walking quickly past her into the small front parlour. 'Something that concerns you.'

'It's not to do with Noah, is it?' she returned, her frown deepening.

'Oh, Ruby, it's nothing to do with the child,' I reassured her, but what I had to say was not good news and would come as a shock.

'It's two-fold, really, so I'll tell you the bad news

first,' I said, trying not to sound too dramatic and alarm her further. 'You'd better sit down for this one, though.'

Ruby rubbed a hand across her forehead and lowered herself onto the settee. 'The bad news first?' she echoed, her face turning pale.

'The thing is, Ruby. You know that what I'm about to tell you may not happen, don't you?' I lifted my eyebrows at her, and she nodded slowly without taking her eyes off me, as Noah's cries echoed around the room.

'It's to do with your parents,' I told her as I paced the room, wondering how to break it to her without too much upset. In the end, there was nothing else for it but to tell the truth.

'I dreamt there was a train crash,' I began, feeling a headache forming across my forehead. 'Your mother and father boarded the train, and as it gathered speed, it... smashed into the back of another train.'

I gazed down at my hands as the image of the train in pieces, strewn across the tracks alongside the bloodied bodies of the dead, came back to me. I looked slowly up at Ruby.

When she continued to stare back at me, I added: 'I know you never got on with them, but... honestly, Ruby. It was *such* a horrible death.'

She shook her head as if she couldn't believe my words, then walked across the room to Noah, who was still whimpering, and lifted him up from his basket.

'You're sure it was them you saw getting on the train?' she asked, as she rocked the baby on her hip, while glancing towards the wireless on the sideboard.

Doubts crowded my head, and I wondered if perhaps I shouldn't have told Ruby about the dream.

After all, she was estranged from her parents, and sometimes the events I witnessed didn't happen. I had no idea why this was, but it was the way of things, and I felt bad that I might have worried Ruby needlessly.

'I didn't mean to upset you, Ruby,' I told her, full of regret now that I'd been so impulsive. 'It might have been best if I'd kept this to myself.'

Ruby stopped jiggling Noah, who looked up at her with a questioning gaze. 'I'm glad you told me, Scarlett, because I could warn them, couldn't I?' she asked, before laying Noah back down again.

This was a grey area when it came to my predictions. I'd tried warning people in the past about what I'd seen, and been on the receiving end of sarcasm and disbelief. That was the real reason I never told anyone about my gift, or usually kept what I saw to myself.

'You could try and warn them, but I'm not sure they'd believe you,' I told her truthfully.

Ruby looked deep in thought, as if she were considering this, then she gazed across at me steadily. 'What was the other thing you were going to tell me, Scarlett?' she asked, returning to the settee where she sat down next to me. 'You said there were two things you had seen.'

Taking a deep breath, I tried to prepare Ruby, and once again regretted saying anything. But it was too late now; I could only hope I wasn't about to break her heart all over again.

'Please don't get your hopes up, Ruby,' I began tentatively. 'But... I have the sense that Reilly might still be alive.' I was trying to choose my words carefully, but I watched the spark of hope in Ruby's eyes before her face drained of colour.

'Oh my God, Scarlett! I can't breathe...' she said

hoarsely, putting a shaky hand across her mouth and staring at me with wide, frightened eyes.

'Calm down, Ruby,' I told her, and shifted closer to her on the settee and touched her arm. 'Remember, this might come to nothing,' I warned her uneasily.

'But... are you really telling me that Reilly isn't dead?' she whispered, her eyes filling with tears. 'Scarlett! I need to know, I really do!'

'I'm sorry to give you such a shock, Ruby. But I have to be honest here. I'm really not sure. At the moment, it's only a sense, that somewhere and somehow, he is alive and well. I had my doubts about telling you this, of course I did, but if there's hope – however small – I wanted you to know.'

Ruby swallowed hard and then stared into the middle distance. 'Oh, Scarlett. If only you're right. If only... that were true.'

Then to my dismay, she put her head in her hands and began to cry – great noisy sobs which echoed around the room. The heavy weight of guilt was on my chest again as I took her in my arms and tried to comfort her.

What had I done? It seemed at that moment that I'd only added to Ruby's woes, as the sound of Noah's whimpering from the corner of the room filled the air.

'I'm sorry,' I told her. 'I shouldn't have told you about the dream; it was too upsetting for you.'

As Ruby tried to compose herself, I scooped Noah out of his basket. 'It's alright, little chap,' I told him, and he immediately stopped crying and regarded me with those big dark eyes of his.

Ruby scrubbed a hand across her face and held her arms out for her son. 'It's fine. Honestly, you did the right thing in telling me about Reilly.' She gave me a wobbly smile and cuddled Noah in close. 'Although, how on earth I'm supposed to find him if he did survive the war, I really don't know,' she said, rubbing a hand gently on Noah's back.

After that difficult conversation, the subject of Ruby's parents and Reilly was put to one side, and we discussed the effects of rationing in the town and the long queues outside the shops to buy food.

'The American GIs are arriving all over the place,' Ruby reflected, and I knew she was trying hard to focus on other news that was going on around us.

When it was time for me to leave, I tried to reassure her. 'Please don't worry about what I've told you today. I know that's hard... but you know where I am if you need me.'

Ruby thanked me, and as she saw me to the door, I was hopeful that Reilly *was* still alive, because Ruby and little Noah deserved some good news.

Later that evening, when Mrs Penny told me I had a phone call from Ruby, my heart was racing at what she was about to tell me.

'After you'd gone this morning, Scarlett, there was an announcement on the radio,' Ruby told me sombrely, her words trailing off down the phone line. 'There was a train crash...'

Chapter Thirty-Three

Frankie

It was midnight, and Frankie felt breathless with excitement as he and the rest of his squadron waited for the phone call which would be the signal to scramble. Tonight's mission was the bombing of the city of Stuttgart, in the south-western region of Germany.

Finally, the call came through from the control room, the order went up, and, along with the others, Frankie raced towards his Spitfire. The adrenalin was coursing through his veins as usual, along with the anticipation of what lay ahead.

Amid the usual scene of planes starting up and propellers whirling, Frankie jumped into the cockpit, fastened his flying helmet, and put on his mouthpiece.

It was pitch dark as the sound of the engines all taking off at the same time roared through the air, and soon the night sky was filled with planes. Jimmy was flying behind Frankie in his own Spitfire, and he lifted his hand to his friend as they soared into the air.

This was their good luck signal to each other whenever they took to the skies, and Frankie smiled and waved back at his friend, praying – as he always did on take-off – that they would both survive the mission.

As the nose of the plane lifted off the ground, Frankie focussed on what was ahead, and shut his mind off to what had gone before. And soon they were flying in formation in the night sky, the Spitfires flanking the bigger Lancaster bombers. Frankie's heart beat faster as he negotiated the plane and listened carefully to the Squadron Commander's instructions.

When Stuttgart came into view, the bombing began, and the air was filled with the sound of the Lancaster bombers dropping their cargo. The night sky was lit up like a firework display, as Frankie and the other pilots raced across the sky like lightning, targeting any enemy gunfire and Luftwaffe planes as they appeared.

When he was in the middle of a bombing raid, Frankie could only focus on the frenzied activity in the air. It was what he loved about flying, and it drove everything else from his mind, including guilt over his father and thoughts of his beloved Scarlett.

During these raids, his heart raced, and the blood pumped through his veins at a rate of knots. It was only afterwards, when each and every mission was over, that his body and his mind returned to normal.

'Well done, again, chaps, that was another successful mission. It's back to base now!'

The Squadron Commander's voice came loud and clear through the earpiece, and they all turned their planes around and began heading back. Frankie heaved a sigh of relief at the thought of catching up with Jimmy, and drinking a few, well earned pints with his friend.

The journey back to the barracks was always more relaxed, and they glided through the air just as dawn was breaking. Frankie felt a deep sense of satisfaction and accomplishment as he flew over France, and with the light just beginning to break through the clouds, his thoughts as always turned to Scarlett.

If Frankie hadn't fallen for her the way he did, and if Eric hadn't caught them together, his father would not have joined up. As a result, Eric would not have been killed at the battle of Tobruk; Frankie was certain of that. Instead, Eric would still be running his depleted shipping business, making guns for the government – even though he wasn't happy about it – and visiting Scarlett in any spare time.

Eric might have been disillusioned with the way business was heading at Johnson and Johnson, with the War Office's request and the Americans building the liberty ships, but Frankie knew his father would have towed the line, as he always did, and done as he was asked.

Now, though, Eric was lying dead somewhere in Tobruk, with no proper burial, and no place for the family to grieve his passing. Frankie shook his head to dislodge the dark and dismal thoughts, just as two things happened in quick and dramatic succession.

He suddenly became aware that his plane was deathly quiet, and that the noise of the engine had completely gone. Left in its place was a deafening silence, and an ice-cold shiver ran up Frankie's spine as he stared intently at the fuel gauge, which – horror of horrors – was showing as empty.

Maybe there was a fuel leak? Frankie thought anxiously. *But if that were the case, why hadn't the instruments alerted him to this, and what the hell was going on?*

The plane quickly began drifting sideways, and Frankie's unease turned to panic. His breath caught in his throat and his mind raced in all directions, while the plane dipped towards the earth and began its shuddering descent towards the ground far below.

Frankie realised he had mere seconds to get out of the plane before it crashed. *Focus, Frankie!* he told himself, as he forced his frozen limbs into action and attempted to unstrap himself from the cockpit. His hands shook uncontrollably, and his heart was racing so hard it was painful. Was he about to have a heart attack before he could escape from the plane?

'If you want to see Scarlett again, you have to get out of this plane now!' he yelled into the air, knowing that if he didn't manage to get out in time, he would be killed on impact with the ground.

Using all his strength, Frankie managed to undo the strap. By now the plane was heaving heavily from side to side, smashing his upper body into the side of the cockpit. Panic threatened to immobilise him as he suddenly realised his legs and lower body were completely trapped in the seat.

As the plane gathered speed and began plunging towards the ground, Frankie briefly thought about all the German pilots he'd shot down, and how they must have felt in those last seconds before death. *This wouldn't do.* Forcing his mind back to Scarlett, Frankie had one last go at escaping from the seat and, thank God, managed to free his legs.

While the plane continued to race towards the ground, Frankie scrambled out of the cockpit as fast as he could. The freezing cold of the early morning air hit his face, as he realised he was plunging dangerously towards the earth; within minutes, this could all be over.

Frankie dug deep within himself, and forced his mind to focus once again. Then, using every ounce of strength he had left, he grabbed hold of the ripcord and pulled hard. Just in time, and with merely seconds to spare, the parachute was released.

Taking a deep, shuddering breath into his painful lungs, Frankie's body jolted in the air… then he began floating towards the ground below, and into enemy territory.

Chapter Thirty-Four

It was dawn, and the first light of the day was beginning to peep through the overhead clouds as Frankie's parachute bobbed downwards, and then landed with a hard thump onto the earth below.

The ground was soft where it had been turned over recently, and Frankie saw it had been dug out into long, deeply rutted rows. It was hard to see anything else in the half darkness, but whatever was being grown under the protective covering had been squashed flat under the weight of his body hitting the ground.

Gathering his wits about him, Frankie scrambled quickly to his feet, while praying that his descent from the stricken Spitfire; had not been seen by the enemy.

With his heart thumping wildly in his chest, he quickly checked himself over for injuries, and thankfully found nothing that seemed serious. His ribs were quite painful, but that was because he'd landed on his side; hopefully he would be fine once he got his body moving.

Half-expecting a German soldier to appear in front of him at any moment, Frankie swiftly untied his harness. He had to force his agitated fingers to work, as they were frozen with cold, and it was difficult to get them to move. At last, he dropped his harness onto the ground in a heap, stood upright to straighten out his aching back, and took in his surroundings.

The silhouette of a farmhouse came into view through the dim light, and Frankie was about to run towards it when he remembered the parachute. It was still lying on the ground next to his discarded harness, and would be the first thing the enemy would find. Leaving it in the field would be a dead giveaway of his whereabouts, so he swiftly gathered up the slippery silk fabric and rolled it messily into a massive, round ball.

With the material trailing uselessly behind him, and clutching the harness, he headed towards the farmhouse, closing his mind off to where the Spitfire might have landed, and strode on.

Stopping a few feet from the front door of the house, a sharp pain shot through his chest and across his ribs, taking his breath away and making him double up in agony. He must have been injured after all, but there was no time to examine himself now; he had to find somewhere to hide and be quick about it.

Frankie clutched at his ribs and took a long, deep breath, and the pain eased a little. As he tried to decide which way to go and where to hide, he noticed the curtains of the house were still closed. It was still very early, and silence hung heavily in the air around him.

Glancing to his left and then to his right, while still clutching the rolled-up parachute, hope flared inside him as he noticed there was a hay barn to the side of the property. It would make an excellent place to hide until he could assess whether the people here were friend or foe, he told himself.

With his heart in his mouth, he made his way swiftly towards the barn. But as he neared the door, the sound of a dog barking from inside the house behind him, broke the silence.

Frankie's legs were shaking from falling out of the plane, and the pain in his ribs intensified, as he pushed hard on the large, heavy door of the barn and peered inside. Several pairs of eyes turned in his direction and glinted at him in the darkness, and he wondered what farm animals he had disturbed. More than likely they would be pigs, or perhaps sheep; at least, he hoped there was nothing more dangerous than that in the barn.

Frankie had only taken a few steps inside when two aggressive looking geese appeared out of the darkness and honked loudly in his direction, before running back to the corner of the outbuilding. Luckily, there were no guard dogs here, but there was definitely one in the house, which was continuing to bark loudly.

As Frankie's eyes became accustomed to the half-darkness, he surveyed what he could see of the animals, including several sheep and a pig. 'I come in peace,' he told them solemnly, while still holding the troublesome parachute.

The sound of a goat bleating drew his eyes to Frankie's right, and he saw the offending animal staring at him accusingly, near a large stack of hay. A large pig was fast asleep, lying sprawled next to the goat.

With the dog still barking in the house, Frankie was sure that any moment now the farmer would appear, so he didn't have long to get out of sight and hide.

When he was reassured that there was nothing that would attack him in the barn (hopefully the geese would only continue to honk angrily), he quickly looked around for a place to hide. In front of him was a solid wooden ladder leading up to a hayloft.

Without hesitating, Frankie quickly climbed the ladder, hearing it creak loudly under his weight as he went, dragging the damned parachute and harness behind him.

When he reached the top of the ladder, he looked around at the loose hay on the floor, then pushed the silk material into a corner of the room, making sure it was well hidden. Below him, the animals had settled down again; the geese had at last lost interest in him and had stopped their honking.

Breathing a sigh of relief, Frankie collapsed onto the floor alongside the parachute, and hid under the hay, in case anyone should walk into the barn below. His eyes were drooping with exhaustion, but he fought to stay awake as every instinct told him he had to remain alert.

Burrowing deeper into the corner of the hayloft, Frankie made himself as comfortable as he possibly could. But just then, the sound of footsteps approaching the barn reached his ears, and the dog's barking was getting nearer, too. Frankie's throat was parched, his ribs were excruciatingly painful, and his stomach grumbled loudly with hunger, but he tried hard to lie still.

The barking became louder at the sound of the barn door being swung open, and the heavy footsteps of the farmer echoed loudly around the building. Frankie held his breath as the footsteps neared the bottom of the steps.

Cocking his ears, Frankie listened intently. He could tell the farmer was hesitating at the bottom of the ladder, and then he heard the man addressing the dog.

'What's the matter, old boy?' the farmer said in French. 'Is there someone up here? Is that what you're barking about? Shall we go up and find out?'

Frankie was glad he had paid attention to his French lessons at school, as it meant he understood exactly what the man was saying. Right at that moment, though, it made no difference, as he had nowhere to run.

The dog barked loudly in response then, to his horror, Frankie heard the creak of the ladder as the farmer began climbing up it, getting steadily closer to the place where he was hidden in the hayloft.

Chapter Thirty-Five

Frankie sat very still, sensing the farmer was very near to him now. Then the man's footsteps stopped just a few feet away from his hiding place in the corner of the barn.

Frankie's heart was racing so hard he thought it might explode, as he listened to the dog continuing to bark loudly from its position at the bottom of the ladder.

Suddenly, and without warning, the covering of hay was ripped away from Frankie and he was left exposed, with the farmer towering over him and glaring down at him angrily.

'*Qu'est-ce que vous faites*?' the man demanded in a gruff sounding voice, as he lifted a shotgun and aimed it straight at Frankie's head.

Scrambling quickly to his feet, Frankie put his hands up in surrender, trying desperately to remember the French word for 'friend'. But his mind had gone completely blank.

The farmer kept the shotgun aimed at him, then pushed him roughly towards the stepladder, and gestured for him to climb down. Frankie briefly glanced back towards the hidden parachute with a pang of regret that he was leaving behind the last vestiges of his journey here. The safety of Great Britain was far behind him now, as he was marched unceremoniously towards the farmhouse, the farmer walking behind him with the gun in his back, and the dog snapping at his heels.

Outside, it was much lighter now, and the sun was emerging from the clouds. Frankie's mind was running in circles wondering how he could convince the farmer that he wasn't the enemy, but with limited French it was going to be hard.

Squinting at the brightness overhead, Frankie kept his hands up in the air just in case the farmer was in any doubt about his intentions. As they came abreast of the farmhouse, he read the word '*La Milleterie*' carved out on a wooden sign to the side of the door.

The farmer muttered something then rushed ahead of him, pushed open the door, and shoved him roughly into the darkened room beyond. As Frankie stumbled inside and came to an abrupt halt, he saw a woman sitting at a wooden table, preparing vegetables. She looked up startled as the two men came in, then stood up abruptly and shot a concerned look from Frankie to the farmer.

The man spoke to her in French, but they talked so quickly that Frankie struggled to understand what was being said. As he tried to concentrate on the words, there was a lull in the conversation and they both stared across at him intently. Frankie spread his hands out in front of himself and gave the couple a beseeching look, and the farmer lowered the shotgun.

'My name is Frankie Johnson and I'm an English RAF pilot,' he explained slowly in pidgin French, desperately hoping they could understand him. 'Please don't shoot me,' he pleaded with the farmer, who was now holding the gun by his side.

Even though he wore his RAF uniform, the couple were staring at him as if they didn't believe him, so Frankie tried to think of some other way to prove who he was. Rummaging in his back pocket, he pulled out his RAF ID card, and held it out to them.

The woman's expression softened as she stared down at the card bearing his photograph, then she nodded slowly at him. Glancing quickly at her husband, who gave her an understanding nod, she indicated that Frankie should sit down on a nearby chair.

Feeling completely and utterly exhausted, Frankie replaced the card in his pocket and lowered himself onto the chair. But as he sat down, a sharp pain shot across his chest, making him catch his breath and clutch at his injured ribs.

The couple looked at him in concern, then conversed between themselves before sitting down opposite him. Frankie was pleased to see that the farmer had put the gun away and was looking less angry now; they both seemed to be waiting for him to speak.

Frankie's tired mind spun around the words he needed in French to somehow explain to this couple that he wasn't a threat. As he had told them what his name was, and even showed them his ID card, he tried asking what their names were, but they continued to stare back at him blankly.

'It's best if you don't know our names,' the farmer eventually replied solemnly, in broken English. 'We want you to know that we would help you, but… at the moment, this is impossible.'

He looked out of the window and indicated to the left of the farmhouse, then he hesitated for a moment and met Frankie's eyes. 'Our neighbours were arrested by the Germans only yesterday, so we cannot risk keeping you here – not even for one night. It would be much too dangerous,' he said with a shrug.

Frankie was glad they were now conversing in English, but was alarmed to hear this bad news. He had hoped to find someone at the farmhouse to help him, not people who were going to set him loose in enemy territory. Without help, he had no idea where to go or what to do.

'I'm sorry to hear that. What happened to your neighbours?' he asked, leaning forwards in the chair. 'Were they harbouring an escapee, is that why they were arrested?' he heard the panic in his own voice, but he couldn't help himself.

The farmer nodded sadly, then explained that their neighbours had been hiding an American pilot from the Gestapo. 'The pilot had been shot down near here and was injured quite badly, which meant he couldn't be moved onto a safe house for a few days,' he said sombrely.

The man glanced across at his wife, then back at Frankie. 'Unfortunately, a local villager heard about this development,' the farmer said, his face reddening. 'The villager thought it was his place to inform the enemy what was going on, and that's exactly what he did. The Germans came and arrested the neighbours who were harbouring the pilot, and they took the airman away the next day.'

Frankie could see how frightened the couple were, and what a dilemma they were in with him turning up on their doorstep. He realised he had to move on quickly and leave them in peace before the village spies saw him, too.

'I don't want to put you both in danger, so if you

213

could just point me in the right direction?' Frankie told them, ignoring the fear rising in his chest.

He rose from the chair and tried to ignore the pain in his ribs, but to his surprise the couple shook their heads vigorously at this suggestion.

'You must not leave yet!' the farmer told him urgently. 'Under cover of darkness is best, and you must change your clothes first. We will burn your parachute and ID card. Did you leave the parachute where you landed?' he asked with a concerned frown.

As the men talked, the farmer's wife made Frankie a cup of tea and offered him a piece of bread. He took it gratefully, only realising how hungry he was when he began to eat.

'Then I will leave this evening,' he told the farmer between mouthfuls. 'My parachute and harness are hidden underneath the hay in the loft,' he added, nodding towards the barn.

The farmer said he would go and retrieve the evidence now, and quickly disappeared out of the door, leaving Frankie alone with the man's wife. For want of something to say to her, he asked the woman what they farmed there. He was curious to know what soft crops he had landed on in the field, and why they were set out in rows and covered up.

'We farm millet and white asparagus here,' the woman explained. Then, seeing his expression of surprise, she added, 'You may be wondering about the cover on the crops. The asparagus has to be covered up until it's harvested, to keep it from changing colour,' she told him. 'My family have been here for generations,' she added proudly, with a lift of her chin.

When the farmer walked back through the door, he told Frankie, 'I'll burn the parachute on a bonfire later, and get you another set of clothes.'

***

It was late afternoon, and Frankie was wide awake, lying on a bed in an upstairs room at the farmhouse. He was exhausted but unable to sleep, as he waited nervously for it to get completely dark before he could leave the farm, as the farmer had suggested.

The pain in his ribs had intensified in the last few hours, and was becoming really bad. But Frankie had no choice but to ignore it. He knew he could not be taken to a hospital; the risk of capture was too great.

Earlier in the day, the smoke had risen high into the air as his parachute, harness, and RAF uniform were burnt to a cinder, and the last link with home went up in smoke.

Frankie must have eventually drifted off to sleep, because the next thing he knew he was being shaken awake by the farmer. He came to with a jolt to see that his room was now in total darkness.

'It is nine o'clock and time to leave!' the farmer told him urgently. He looked very agitated as he held the bedroom door open wide for Frankie. 'Hurry now!' he added quickly.

Once they were downstairs, Frankie swiftly put on a jacket the farmer had given him over the top of the trousers and shirt the man had also found for him to wear. The clothes were a little big, but with the addition of a belt for the trousers, and by tucking in the shirt, Frankie had managed to make the clothes look like they fitted him.

The farmer's wife gave Frankie a rucksack with water and bread inside, then stood wringing her hands as the farmer ushered him quickly towards the door. Frankie wished he knew their names, but he understood why they didn't want to divulge this information to him.

Frankie turned towards them on the threshold of the door and hesitated, reluctant to leave the safety of the farmhouse. The couple's actions in the circumstances were very brave; to harbour him even for a few hours was courageous, after what had happened to their neighbours.

'Thank you so much, both of you,' he said, wanting to hug them for the kindness they had shown him.

The woman nodded sadly at Frankie and tried to smile, but the farmer was straight-faced, betraying no emotion as he gave Frankie directions to a safe house in the village.

'It's a mile up the road,' he told him, then he revealed what Frankie needed to say on arrival at the safe house. 'I cannot write the address down,' the farmer explained solemnly. 'You will have to memorise it. But it is an easily recognised house, because the outside is painted pink.'

After he'd told Frankie what the address was, he added, 'When you arrive, knock four times and give the person who answers the door the code name 'helpers'.' Then he gently pushed Frankie out of the farmhouse door.

'But... how do I find the village?' Frankie asked, suddenly worried sick he would forget the address and the code name before he had even gone ten paces up the road.

The farmer gave him a weak smile and told him it was simple, then he stood next to Frankie at the open doorway and pointed up towards the road.

'Walk out of our farm gate, across the road, and into the woods. Then follow the path ahead until you come to the village of Cuon. This is the fastest and safest route to follow,' the farmer added, patting him firmly on the back.

Frankie thanked the farmer and asked how he would see his way to the village in the woods, as it was nine o'clock and already it was pitch dark outside.

The man looked towards his wife and then back at Frankie. 'Do not worry, a small torch has been included in the bag for you. But for your own safety, don't use it unless you have to. It will draw attention to your whereabouts.'

As the door closed on Frankie, he felt very alone and had the sudden urge to run back into the farmhouse and tell the couple he couldn't do this by himself. But he knew that he had no option. The farmer and his wife were at risk if he stayed here, and he had no desire to put them in further danger.

With no choice in the matter, Frankie walked through the farm gate, across the road, and into the dark, dense woods. As he headed for the safe house the farmer had told him about, he prayed that he wouldn't be seen and captured by the enemy before he reached the village of Cuon.

Chapter Thirty-Six

Frankie was soon lost in the woods, despite following the main trail and the farmer's instructions. He was disorientated, and he could feel the pain in his ribs worsening as he tried to find his way.

Constantly aware that he was in a German-occupied village, he kept expecting an enemy soldier to leap out, aim a gun at him, and shoot him dead at any given moment. It was nerve-racking in the extreme, and he could feel his legs shaking beneath him as he stumbled through the undergrowth towards the village.

He tried not to use the torch, as the farmer had suggested, but this left him stumbling around in the pitch darkness of the forest, without any light at all.

Everywhere was deadly silent, apart from the rustling sound of an animal moving about in the undergrowth, or when Frankie stepped on a twig or broken branch. At these times, the noise echoed eerily through the trees, and his heart missed a beat.

Frankie constantly repeated to himself the address in Cuon, which the farmer had given him; trying to imprint it on his brain was the only way he wouldn't forget it. And the word 'helpers' kept spinning in his head.

He was terrified of forgetting this information, just as he'd forgotten French words he'd learnt years before, when he had been faced with the farmer in the barn.

What kind of people would be at this safe house? he wondered. He hoped they wouldn't point a gun at him the way the farmer had done. The man had only been acting in self-defence, after what had happened to the couple's neighbours, but still, Frankie had found it very unsettling.

At last, after using the torch sparingly, Frankie could see the end of the trail in sight, and what looked like the dark outline of the village beyond. As he found himself in an open space, instead of hemmed in by the trees, he breathed a sigh of relief at being out of the dense, wooded area.

The farmer had instructed him to turn left here, and explained that the safe house was two roads down on the left. Again, Frankie recited the address in his head, then began walking purposefully down the quiet street ahead of him.

Glancing around him constantly and keeping his head low, Frankie was expecting to see German soldiers on the street corners. And although the pavements seemed to be deserted, he reminded himself that he needed to stay alert.

Quickening his step, Frankie passed a crowded bar, but resisted the urge to peer in through the window as the sound of raucous laughter from inside echoed along the street. The bar seemed to be packed full of German soldiers, and as Frankie caught sight of the swastikas on their uniforms, the breath caught in his throat and he rushed past.

At last, he located the address of the safe house, and stopped in front of the pink painted house the farmer had described, hesitating uneasily at the door. The sound of a drunken soldier in the distance, however, forced him to act, and he quickly knocked four times as he'd been instructed to do.

Frankie held his breath. It seemed like an age until he heard footsteps approaching the door, only to be opened by a young girl of about fifteen years of age. He stared at the girl, who had dark eyes, and long hair tied back in a high ponytail.

'Bonjour, monsieur,' she said, looking at him steadily.

Frankie pulled himself together. 'Bonjour, mademoiselle,' he returned, playing for time as he tried to bring the password back out of the depths of his memory, while aware that the sound of the soldier's drunken song was getting closer.

Then it came back to him. 'I've been told to say the word "helpers",' Frankie whispered urgently, speaking in pidgin French. He felt extremely vulnerable standing on the doorstep and being scrutinised by this young French girl.

But immediately her expression changed, and a look of relief crossed her face as she opened the door wider, stepped aside, and invited him into the house. Frankie heaved a sigh of relief to be off the streets, but doubts crowded his head as he remembered the farmer's words about Hitler's spies being everywhere.

The girl quickly led him through a dark hallway into a small sitting room, where a middle-aged woman sat in an armchair sewing. As they entered the room, the woman looked up, and the girl explained that Frankie had been sent from the farmer at *La Milleterie*.

Standing up, the woman put down her sewing, and smiled at Frankie. 'Please come in. We are pleased to meet you, monsieur,' she told him. Then, hardly stopping for breath, she asked, 'Are you *anglais*?'

When Frankie explained that he was an RAF pilot, the woman gave an understanding nod and then began conversing in English.

'I don't know if you've been told this, but we do not disclose our real names, so I am simply known as Manon,' she told him. 'That way is safest for everyone.' She indicated the young girl who was hovering nearby. 'This is my daughter, who is known as Josephine.'

'I understand, and I'm pleased to meet you, Manon. You, too, Josephine,' Frankie said, looking at the girl. 'I'm sorry to arrive at your home so late,' he said, before glancing down at his watch to see it was half past ten.

'Our pilots arrive at all times of the day and night,' Manon reassured him, 'so do not worry. There are some things that can only be done under cover of darkness.'

Frankie was overwhelmingly grateful to Manon and her family, even though he'd only been here a few minutes. 'Thank you for accepting me into your home,' he told them both, knowing the great risks these people must be taking to help him.

She quirked her head at him, and nodded her understanding. 'What is your name, monsieur?' she asked, lifting her eyebrows.

Frankie thought quickly. The farmer had not told him what he should say to this question, but he realised he could not tell Manon his real name; that would be dangerous. So he said the first male French name that came into his head.

'You can call me Hubert,' he told them both, understanding that he would now have to remember this name for future reference.

'Hello, Hubert. My husband is out at the moment,

but he will be returning shortly,' Manon told him. 'Take a seat, and I will explain everything to you,' she continued, indicating an armchair in the corner of the room. 'Josephine, please bring us some refreshments,' she instructed the girl.

Frankie watched Josephine leave the room as he sat down in the dimly lit lounge, feeling a bit more at ease in Manon's company.

'Firstly, we will give you the address of another safe house,' Manon began. 'This next one will be in a nearby town called Saumur, and you will have to use a bicycle to get there.'

Frankie tensed at the thought of finding another safe house, since he'd only just arrived at this one, but he straightened his back and listened carefully to Manon.

'My husband goes by the name of Louis,' Manon continued. 'He will sort out a false identity for you. You'll also need a story ready in case you are stopped on the journey, you understand? This is so that you can explain why you are travelling to south western France.'

She glanced across at the window and then back at him. 'It's unfortunate, but you can't stay here long, as it's far too risky,' she told him, with a worried frown on her face.

Frankie understood why, after what the farmer had told him. 'How far away is Saumur?' he asked, praying it wouldn't be a long journey. He'd hoped he could stay here with these good people for at least a few days and rest up. His ribs had become even more painful.

The door opened and Josephine came back into the room with a tray of tea and fruitcake. She handed Frankie his cup and a slice of cake, and while they ate and drank, Manon's husband arrived home.

'Louis, this is Hubert. He's just arrived from La Milleterie,' she informed her husband.

'Bonjour, monsieur,' Louis said, shaking hands with Frankie. Then he changed to speaking in English when Manon explained that Hubert was an English RAF pilot.

After Louis had been updated on Frankie's situation, he showed him upstairs to Josephine's bedroom. 'You can hide in here,' he told Frankie, opening a tiny trapdoor which, when closed, looked exactly like the rest of the wooden panelling along the wall in the room.

Frankie crouched down to go inside the trapdoor, but found himself clutching at his painful side, which caused him to stumble into the small space. Once inside, he found himself in a room about six feet square, with a camp bed pushed up against the wall and a small wooden chair next to it.

'Are you injured?' Louis asked, looking at him with concern as he followed Frankie into the tiny, hidden room.

Frankie understood there was nothing for it but to work through the pain in his ribs. 'Thank you, but I will be fine,' he replied.

When Louis gave him a disbelieving look, Frankie went on, 'I hurt my ribs on one side when I fell out of the Spitfire plane. But I fell onto an asparagus field, so it was a soft landing,' he grinned, trying to make a joke of it and preferring not to focus on his injury.

Louis nodded his understanding as they both sat down; Frankie was on the camp bed, and Louis on the chair.

'I know I can't stay here long, but when should I move on?' Frankie asked, unable to keep the anxiety from his voice, and eager to know the next move.

Louis pursed his lips, as if he were thinking about the question. 'This is a petite village, Hubert, and the Germans are bored here,' he said with a shake of his head. 'They have lots of time to find those of us who are helping the Allies. As soon as I have concocted a story for you – meaning you'll have something to tell the Germans if they happen to stop you – it'll be time for you move on.'

Frankie was relieved; it sounded as if he would be able to stay here at least a short while. One whole night would be better than nothing, and certainly longer than he had been able to stay with the farmer at La Milleterie.

'Now, you must get some rest, Hubert,' Louis said, interrupting his thoughts. The man stood up and stooped low to get through the small, panelled doorway.

'What about the false papers I'll need to show the Germans?' Frankie asked, leaning back on the pillow, which felt incredibly soft beneath his head, and letting out a long sigh.

'I'm sorry I can't give you those, Hubert, but our friends in Saumur will help you out with them, so don't worry.'

After Louis had gone, Frankie wondered how long it would take for him to sort out a credible story. And despite being extremely tired, he found it hard to sleep.

His mind ran in circles all night, thinking about the next part of his journey, and whether he would reach the second safe house without incident. He was fully aware that the family harbouring him was taking huge risks, for which they could be executed, and he was completely in awe of their bravery.

Eventually, though, Frankie slept. But he awoke with a start in the middle of the night, and the darkest of thoughts churned over in his mind as he shook with fear at what lay ahead. As he lay on the camp bed trying to calm his racing mind, he tried to imagine his reunion with Scarlett on his return to Blighty.

As Frankie visualised her beautiful turquoise eyes and blonde hair, he found some respite from the clawing worry over his dangerous situation here in occupied France, and managed enough peace of mind to sleep once again.

Chapter Thirty-Seven

Camille handed the tray of food up to Frankie from the loft ladder. But instead of closing the hatch and disappearing again, as she usually did, this time she climbed up into the attic space.

'I have brought your breakfast,' she said unnecessarily, because she had done this every morning at seven o'clock since he had arrived at the safe house in Saumur.

Camille was the young Frenchwoman who had opened the door to Frankie four weeks earlier – the day he had arrived by bicycle from Manon and Louis's house in the village of Cuon.

When Louis had given him the address of this second safe house, and the code name he needed for whoever opened the door to him, this time Frankie found he'd had no trouble memorising the information. Maybe this was because he soon realised that if he forgot what he was told, his cover would be blown to the Nazis.

Even so, it was still a nerve-racking experience arriving at the address and knocking on the door. Before he had left Cuon, Louis had told him about the many spies amongst the villagers – local people who worked for the Germans – and how there was no way of knowing who these people were.

Frankie's heart had raced as Camille had introduced

him to Bastille, her husband, and they had welcomed him into their home. He hadn't known Louis long, but long enough to understand the man would not knowingly have sent him into a house of spies. However, the worry was still there, niggling away at the back of his mind.

'What is your name?' Camille had asked, once he was inside their house.

'My name is Hubert Baudin,' Frankie had replied.

The false name had come easily to him once he knew that was how the game had to be played. He was ready to tell them the story that Louis had concocted for him, in case they asked, that he was a Belgium seaman home on leave from Bordeaux, and was travelling to see his elderly mother.

However, Camille and Bastille didn't ask him any more questions; it seemed the code name was enough for them. And he understood that the story was really in case he was stopped by the German soldiers and quizzed about why he was in the area.

As they'd chatted, Bastille had assured Frankie he would soon be sorting out his identity papers so that he could move on yet again.

As Frankie thanked Camille for the tray of food, he was ravenous as usual. He often wondered if it might be something to do with being hidden away, or being confined in this dark, little attic space, which made him extra-hungry all the time.

Perching on the small wooden chair next to Frankie's bed, she cocked her head to one side. 'How are you today, Hubert?' she asked.

Frankie smiled weakly at her kindly face, and pondered for the umpteenth time how people like her slept at night, knowing that torture and certain death awaited them if they were found out.

'I'm fine, thank you,' he returned in French, though he wasn't fine at all. He was tired and exhausted from another bad night's sleep.

To his dismay, Frankie had started dreaming that he would never see Scarlett again, and the thought made him panic. Last night had been another night of tossing and turning, and his head ached daily from the battle he was waging with himself.

He had also been worrying about when exactly he would move onto the next house. And even when he did manage to fall asleep, he worried that he would wake up with a German soldier pointing a gun at his head.

He had been here a week, sleeping alone in the attic, when the other two pilots showed up. And now, as several weeks had gone by, he was aware it had been a month since his arrival at Camille and Bastille's house.

'Hubert, you are somewhere else today,' she joked, while positioning her chair so that she was facing not only Frankie, but the other two escapees – Claude and Armand. They were sitting on their camp beds on the other side of the attic.

'I have some good news for you today,' Camille continued, her dark eyes lighting up. 'As you know, it has not been safe to move you all yet, so we've had to wait it out. But our founder will be arriving today, to brief you on the next leg of your journey. The journey you will be undertaking very soon.'

Camille looked pleased with herself, and Frankie understood it must be a huge relief for her and Bastille to be able to pass their dangerous cargo over to someone else. The thought of leaving here made him excited and panic stricken, at the same time.

Frankie took a deep breath and tried to hide how he was feeling, and instead focussed on who exactly was arriving today. 'Do you mean the founder of this resistance line, Camille?' he asked.

'Let me explain, Monsieur Hubert,' Camille replied. 'This group is called The Comet Line,' she said, and then she paused as if remembering something else. 'It was named that, because when an aircraft was seen coming down, the people would say, "I have seen a comet.",' she explained with a wry smile.

'The Comet Line was started in Brussels by a small group of volunteers, but its founder was a young Belgian called Andree de Jongh, who is known as Dedee.'

Camille pulled her shoulders back and lifted her chin. 'This person is truly remarkable, as you will all soon find out,' she told them with a note of pride in her voice.

Frankie had to speak up. In his opinion, this Dedee whoever she may be, was not alone in her bravery. 'Anyone who harbours the Allies, the way you and Bastille do, is truly courageous,' he said, looking directly at Camille.

She gave him a thoughtful look. 'Thank you for that, Hubert,' she said seriously. 'We all do what we can in these difficult circumstances.'

'Of course, but we're all very grateful for your help, Camille, otherwise where would we be?' Frankie said, indicating the other two escapees in the attic with him. 'In the hands of the Nazis, no doubt.'

Camille stood up and dipped her head to avoid hitting the attic beams. 'Quite likely, but we do it because we don't want *them* to win,' she said over her shoulder, as she walked towards the attic ladder.

Frankie felt an ache in the back of his throat. Even though he'd longed to hear they would be moving on from this house, suddenly he didn't want to go. He felt protected here in this cramped attic. 'When do we leave?' he asked, dreading the answer.

Camille paused on the top rung of the ladder. 'That has not been decided yet, Hubert, but I *can* tell you that you'll be travelling by train most of the way to Bayonne,' she explained. 'But none of you can leave until Dedee has briefed you on how to act without arousing suspicion with the German army on your long journey ahead.'

An ice-cold shiver ran up Frankie's spine. He had assumed they would be hidden in a goods lorry, or something else equally furtive, on the route towards south western France.

'Why are we travelling by train to Bayonne?' he asked, fear gripping him at the thought of being on public show in a possibly crowded train carriage full of soldiers. 'Surely that will not be safe, in the circumstances?' he added, unable to keep the concern out of his voice.

Camille shot him a sympathetic look. 'Do not worry, monsieur,' she told him firmly, 'Dedee will train you well. And please remember, it is imperative that you listen to everything you are told. If you do not, then the consequences for both you and for us, as helpers, would be unthinkable.'

When she had gone back downstairs, after telling them she would let them know when Dedee arrived, Frankie exchanged an anxious look with Claude and Armand. No-one spoke, but the fear showed plainly on all of their faces.

Frankie lay back on his bed and placed his hands

behind his head. He wondered how one person would be able to look after all three of them on the trip south, which would surely be a long and dangerous journey.

He glanced across at the breakfast tray Camille had just brought them, knowing he was no longer hungry; his stomach was hollow, but he had just lost his appetite.

Chapter Thirty-Eight

Scarlett

From the moment I woke up this morning, a feeling of gloom had settled in my bones. I couldn't eat any breakfast, and was unable to shake off the bad feeling all day.

I'd dreamt about Frankie, and that he was on a train. In the dream, I saw uncertainty and danger up ahead of him, and every time I tried to reach him, he turned away and moved out of my reach. These conflicting thoughts spun in my head all night long, making me feel drained of energy the next day.

Now, with Annika lying in her cot looking up at me with that beautiful expression which was so like Frankie's, my heart turned over. And despite the tiredness, my mood lifted a little. The baby was seven months old now, and as I cuddled her small body in close to mine, I tried not to think about the heaviness in my chest and the thumping ache across my forehead.

Later that day, after Annika had gone down for her morning nap, Mrs Penny appeared. 'You have a visitor, Scarlett,' she said. 'The lady said her name was Beverley, and I've put her in the front parlour where she's waiting for you now.'

'Thank you, Mrs Penny,' I replied, as a distant memory lingered on the edge of my mind. Somehow the name was familiar to me. Was Frankie's sister called Beverley?

Making sure the door to my room was left open so that I could hear Annika if she woke up, I quickly followed Mrs Penny downstairs. And as I walked into the communal parlour, my visitor stood up to greet me.

'Good morning, are you Scarlett Cunningham?' the woman asked, while holding out her hand to me. 'I'm sorry for the intrusion. My name's Beverley Johnson and I'm Frankie's sister,' she confirmed with a slight lift of her eyebrows.

My heart lurched as I shook her hand. Frankie had once described his mother to me, and now those words came rushing back to me: '*Round and plain, but she has a kindly face.*' Beverley was a younger version of Frankie's mother. After confirming that I was indeed Scarlett Cunningham, my next worry was why Beverley was here?

'Please take a seat,' I indicated the settee. 'Is Frankie all right?' I asked urgently, full of fear for his safety as last night's dream came flooding back to me. Was his sister here to tell me the worst news imaginable?

'I'll get straight to the point, Miss Cunningham,' Beverly said after she'd made herself comfortable. 'My brother Frankie is missing in action.' She gazed across at me steadily as she spoke. 'I'm sorry to be the bearer of bad news,' she added shakily.

My hand flew to my chest and the breath caught in my throat. 'Bloody hell! Oh I'm sorry for my language but...' I stared back at Beverley with my heart thumping, willing her to tell me Frankie was still alive.

'Do you have any information about what happened to him?'

Beverley's shoulders slumped, and she looked up at me with sad eyes. 'Frankie's plane came down over France. Other than that, we don't know any more,' she said dismally. 'We can only hope he's survived and found someone to help him.' Her voice shook slightly as she spoke, betraying her emotions. 'It's the best we can hope for, Miss Cunningham,' she added solemnly.

'Please call me Scarlett,' I said, while searching inside myself for a glimmer of hope that Frankie would survive this ordeal. Instead, all I found was heartache, and fear that I would never see him again.

The air between us was filled with a morbid kind of grief as I looked across at Beverley. 'Where there is life, there is hope,' I said, trying to find courage for both of us, but instead I could feel hot tears burning the back of my eyes.

Surely I would know if Frankie were dead, wouldn't I? I questioned myself. For the first time since finding myself with this strange gift of second sight so many years ago, I wished it could tell me what Frankie's fate was right now.

The gift had always been a curse, and it was often a burden to me knowing when bad things were going to happen to others. But right now, when I longed to see Frankie's dangerous path in France, it was failing me miserably.

I rubbed my forehead with the back of my hand and tried to soothe my headache away. Where was Frankie, and what had happened to him after his plane came down in occupied France? Had the enemy captured him, or was he safe?

Our collective sorrow over Frankie hung heavily in

the air between us. 'How did you know where to find me?' I asked, suddenly aware that she would not have had my address.

The frown was deep on Beverley's forehead as she took in a long, deep breath. 'That was easy, Scarlett. Frankie gave me your address before he left for RAF training school.' Tears filled her eyes as she spoke.

'He told me to let you know if anything happened to him. Frankie was very specific in his instructions, even saying I had to come and see you in person.' She sniffed, and then pulled out a handkerchief and began wiping the tears from her cheeks. 'For him to say that… means you meant a lot to him,' she murmured into the hankie.

Hearing this made my painful heart ache, and I stared down at my hand, imagining a band of gold on my wedding finger. If this war hadn't happened, could I have been happy with Frankie? The answer came back that I would have, because there was no doubt he was the love of my life.

As I looked up, I became aware that Beverley was staring at me in a strange way. 'What is it?' I asked, feeling hot under her scrutiny.

Beverley tilted her head to the side, as if studying me for the first time. 'I must admit, I was surprised when I saw you,' she said. 'You're a little older than I thought you'd be.' She replaced the handkerchief in her pocket, and sat up a little straighter.

Again, Frankie's words echoed in my head. 'The years between us don't matter, Scarlett,' he'd said, taking me in his arms. And now I understood he was right, because nothing else mattered except us being together.

'We were not lovers,' I lied easily, lifting my

chin, and thinking in some misguided way that I was sparing Beverley's feelings. Why was I trying to convince Frankie's sister that there was nothing between Frankie and myself, when she must know we were deeply in love?

Beverley gave a small, deep laugh, which lit up her face and made her look almost pretty. 'Whatever you say, Scarlett. Although I doubt that very much, after the way he spoke about you. And also what he said I should tell you, in the event of his…' She broke eye contact with me and stared into the middle distance.

My heart lurched painfully at her words. 'What message? What did Frankie say to tell me?' I asked falteringly, my voice shaking as I struggled to get the words out.

Beverley looked me straight in the eye and didn't blink. 'Frankie said I was to tell you that you are a very special lady…' she paused for a moment. 'He also said he loves you,' she added, with a frown etched between her brows.

I nodded my head sadly, and for a moment neither of us spoke. When I looked up, she was still gazing at me with sympathy on her face.

'Thank you,' I whispered, trying to swallow the hard lump in my throat. I was aware that I was thanking her not just for coming here today, but also for not judging me, as so many other people would.

Frankie had been right when he'd said his sister was like his mother, and I could see she was a kind and thoughtful person. 'I know he loves me, Beverley,' I told her now. 'But… it's been complicated.'

How could I tell Beverley that I had loved her father before Frankie? Not in the same way as I loved Frankie – with such passion, longing, and desperation. I'd loved Eric for saving me, and for helping me change my life.

But she didn't ask what I meant by 'complicated'; perhaps she already knew.

'When did you last see Frankie?' I asked, longing to know more than I feared this woman could tell me, and desperate for news of any kind. 'Do you know what happened when he went missing?'

Beverley shook her head. 'Frankie was due to come home at Christmas, but in the end his leave was cancelled,' she told me dismally. 'Mother and I were not told why this was,' she continued, before taking out her handkerchief again and blowing her nose.

I tried to fight the guilt that surged through me at Beverley's words. Frankie hadn't made it home, possibly for the last time, because of me. That had been hard on this woman and on her mother.

My letter to Frankie had arrived too late, as he'd already cancelled his leave, thinking that he had nothing to come home for. I tried to think of some way of expressing my gratitude to Beverley for visiting me today, while I battled with this deep and irreversible regret.

'Thank you for coming to see me today, Beverley,' I told her. My chest was as heavy as lead, but I made an effort to smile, realising that I liked this woman very much. She was my last and only link to Frankie, and I didn't want to lose contact with her.

She nodded thoughtfully. 'You're welcome, Scarlett,' she said. 'I can certainly see why Frankie would fall in love with you.' There was an envious expression on her plain features.

Beverley's watchful gaze was making me feel uncomfortable. I wanted to tell her that kindness meant more than how pretty you were, but I didn't want to sound patronising.

Besides, I couldn't deny that I'd used my good looks in the past to help me find my way in life, so my words would sound hollow – even to my own ears.

She scrubbed a hand across her face. 'Our father was killed in action recently, and I don't know how I'll bear it if Frankie dies as well,' she said, as if it were already a forgone conclusion.

'Frankie will survive. I'm sure of it,' I told her firmly, praying that I was right but knowing that this kind sister of his needed some hope in her heart. 'Why don't we stay in touch?' I added impulsively, trying to think of some way of easing her grief.

'We all need to keep busy while this war is going on. What do you do with your days, Beverley?' I asked, as I watched her fiddling with a loose button on her cardigan.

Beverley glanced up at me and shrugged. 'Nothing. I don't really have a purpose; I only wish I had,' she replied forlornly.

'Why don't you volunteer for something to help the war effort then?' I suggested.

Beverley's face lit up at my suggestion, but then her expression changed again. 'I'd love to, but I couldn't leave my mother. You see, since my father died, she has become more dependent on me,' she explained.

'Maybe both of you could do something worthwhile? You live in London, and there must be lots of help needed there,' I encouraged, aware of how many bombs were dropped on the capital every day, and how risky it must be living there.

She nodded thoughtfully. 'You could be right. It's got to be better than waiting to get bombed out all the time, and worrying about whether you're going to survive the night or not. It plays havoc with the nerves,' she said, smiling through her sadness.

'Exactly, write to me and let me know how you get on,' I suggested, 'or visit me again anytime. I'm either here or out on the streets of Brighton doing my ARP duties.' I didn't add that I'd also be looking after Frankie's baby daughter.

Beverley glanced down at her watch and then quickly stood up to go. 'I have a train to catch in half an hour,' she said regretfully. 'I'm sorry I must go now.'

Later, when Beverley had left, I stared out of the window at the passing traffic, thinking about Frankie lying mortally wounded somewhere in France. Was he suffering at the hands of the enemy right now? I bit down hard on my lower lip in an attempt to dispel the powerful images in my head, and to find the hope that he was still alive and safe somewhere.

Tonight, Mrs Penny was babysitting while I would be out doing my ARP duties later, because keeping busy was the only way to survive right now. As the shrill sound of Annika's cries filled the air, I put Beverley out of my mind and hurried back up the stairs to my baby.

As I lifted Annika from her cot, I was filled with a deep regret at the way I had pushed Frankie away and not told him I was expecting his child.

At least he had received my letter before his plane went missing. So, if he was still alive, he knew that I loved him. Hopefully, that would bring him comfort in whatever situation he had to face in occupied France.

Chapter Thirty-Nine

Frankie

Frankie had thought about Scarlett far into the night, and his body ached with fatigue this morning. If only her letter had come earlier, he would not have cancelled his leave in December, and they could have had some time together before his plane had come down over France.

In the middle of the night, Frankie told himself he would survive this ordeal and be re-united with Scarlett, but doubts and fear at what lay ahead had continued to crowd his head.

He had been awoken by Camille that morning, and she had gathered them together in a small room at the back of the house where she introduced Frankie and the other escapees to the resistance leader called Dedee.

As Dedee strode purposefully into the room to meet them, Frankie could hardly contain his surprise at her appearance. He had expected Dedee to be a woman, on account of her name, but he had *not* expected to see the delicate looking girl who stood before them. She had dark, fluffy hair and arched eyebrows, and was wearing a flowered dress and white ankle socks.

Placing her hands on her hips, Dedee lifted her chin and addressed them all. 'Bonjour, comrades,' she said in a heavily accented tone. 'I will very soon be escorting you all to south western France and on to safety.'

Camille had told them earlier that the young Belgian was twenty-four, but this girl looked barely eighteen, and she was so tiny she hardly took up any space in Camille and Bastille's small back room.

Everyone listened in awe as Dedee began describing the journey they would be undertaking. 'Make no mistake that this crossing will be hard,' she announced, while gazing at them steadily.

'We will cover over four hundred miles. It will involve at least one long ride on a German-patrolled train, stealthy border crossings, and a gruelling night-time trek over the Pyrenees.'

It was ingrained in them all, Frankie reminded himself, to think of war as men's work, to measure success by what could be overpowered. But as he watched her reveal the plan of escape, he understood that Dedee might be young looking – almost fragile in stature – but as soon as she spoke, her determination and bravery showed through.

Dedee's explanation of what must be done was said with complete authority. She did not mince her words, but told them plainly how it would be in Nazi-occupied France, and how facing the enemy meant keeping your wits about you at all times.

Camille had told them earlier how Dedee liked to make sure her escapees reached safety herself, whenever possible. And even though she could have sent one of her helpers to get them across the border, she had come herself. Now, watching Dedee put into words how difficult this journey would be, Frankie began to believe that this petite young woman would succeed in her mission to get them all to safety.

Dedee finished her speech and regarded them all with a furrowed brow. 'Do not be in any doubt that this will be dangerous,' she said. 'But bear in mind that I've done this many times before, so you may be reassured that I know *exactly* what I'm doing.'

There were a few questions put to Dedee by the other escapees, mainly how long any train journeys would be, and Frankie saw how anxious they all were about boarding a train. He felt exactly the same way, and to him that was the worst part of the upcoming journey.

When everyone had finished talking, Frankie asked a question which had been going around in his head. 'How was the Comet Line started?' He was curious to know how and why this young woman had become so embroiled in such a risky project.

Dedee smiled and lifted her chin. 'It is quite straightforward really, Hubert,' she explained. 'When the war started, I volunteered with the Belgian Red Cross, where I began nursing wounded Allied soldiers.'

'Then, after my country surrendered to the Nazis, British troops were evacuated and the battle shifted to the air,' she hesitated briefly. 'It was then I turned my attention to the men who had been shot out of the sky.'

'You were not happy with the nursing?' Frankie asked. 'Why do you take such terrible risks for strangers?' He was genuinely interested in why Dedee would swap nursing for this dangerous work.

She placed her hands on her hips, as if thinking carefully about this question. 'Nursing was fine wartime work, but in the end, not for me,' she replied, seeming lost in the moment before looking up at

242

Frankie. 'The work with the Comet Line is there to be done,' she said, simply giving a small shrug of her shoulders.

Frankie was impressed with the blasé way in which Dedee explained away the danger, and he could see that she thrived on the risks involved. There was something about her which reminded him of Scarlett; he wasn't sure what it was – perhaps her bravery, or her refusal to give up.

'We will be leaving tomorrow at first light,' Dedee continued. 'However, first I need to teach you how to behave naturally and to blend in seamlessly – both of which are very important on the journey. That way, you won't arouse suspicion and risk capture.'

Dedee went on to explain how they must remain calm at all times. Even if they thought a German soldier suspected them... even in those extreme circumstances, they must never show worry or panic.

'At all costs, you must act as if you travel on the train every day,' she stressed. 'You must have your paperwork to hand, as fumbling around for your identity papers will make the situation even more serious. I understand that you all have your papers now?' she looked at each of them in turn.

Everyone confirmed they had their identity papers ready, Frankie included; he had been handed them that very morning by Bastille. Dedee emphasised how they must remain vigilant at all times, and what to remember while travelling on the train. She particularly warned them of arousing suspicion when visiting the toilet, which could be dangerous.

'If you do not leave a coin for the attendant, you will get shouted at, and the Germans watch out for these very moments,' she said, knitting her brow. 'Anything at all that draws attention to you *will be* noticed, rest assured of that. The Germans are very crafty and have been trained to notice everything and anything out of the ordinary.'

Frankie was now even more nervous about what they were about to do, but he understood he had no choice. He could not stay indefinitely at Camille and Bastille's little house, because eventually the Nazis would learn of his presence and he would be arrested, along with them.

During the whole of his nineteen years, Frankie had never really been frightened of anything. But right now, he was scared to death about venturing outside of this house of safety and travelling halfway across occupied France with Dedee and the other escapees.

Forcing his mind to focus on what Dedee was saying, he listened intently as she spent hours going over how they must act in different scenarios. He made sure he memorised what she said, and this helped him to take his mind off the ever-present fear.

'You will be travelling on two different trains to eventually arrive at St-Jean-de-Luz station, which will take around fourteen hours,' she explained.

'On arrival at the station, there will be bicycles – enough for us all – hidden in a nearby house. We will then make our way to the village of Anglet, which is between St-Jean-de-Luz and Bayonne.

'There, we will stay with a couple whose codes names are Tante Go and L'Oncle, who live with their two grown-up children; they also help in the resistance. Tante Go is a very important part of the Comet Line, and is the driving force of a courageous family. She is in charge of operations in the Spanish frontier zone.'

There was a hush across the room as they all digested

this information, and again Frankie wondered how these 'helpers' slept at night whilst taking such huge risks. *How brave it was of Tante Go and L'Oncle to let their children help with the resistance*, he thought.

'After a few days at Tante Go and L'Oncle's home, you will travel to another safe house to await the right conditions to begin the journey across the Pyrenees,' Dedee explained, pacing the room. Then she stopped and regarded them. 'A Basque guide by the name of Florentino, who knows the area like the back of his hand, will be helping you across the mountains.'

'Is that where you will be leaving us?' Claude asked Dedee with a break in his voice.

She shook her head vigorously. 'Rest assured, I shall not leave you until we are all safely across the French/Spanish border and I have handed you over to a British Diplomat in San Sebastian,' she said with a determined air. 'The British Diplomat will then take you onto Madrid, and subsequently Gibraltar.'

Frankie was hugely impressed by how tough Dedee was when he heard that it was her intention to take them *all* the way to safety. She would not be leaving this final part of the journey to someone else. And as he thought about this bravery, he had an odd thought: *Would this young woman attempt the mission in her flowery cotton dress, or would she be disguised as someone else?*

Dedee's final words to them echoed exactly what they needed to remember on their dangerous mission. 'You must all show courage and physical strength, comrades, so that you can get through this ordeal,' she told them, setting her jaw. 'And when you are tired and lacking in these things, then you must dig deep and be brave, and most of all, think of your loved ones back home.'

By the end of the day, Frankie's head was buzzing with 'things he must remember' once they began their long journey, which was planned to begin the following morning.

But he made a promise to himself that when the going got rough, he would bring Scarlett to mind, and remember exactly how very much he loved her. He was sure that would give him the strength he needed to get through the ordeal ahead.

Chapter Forty

Scarlett

As I pulled on Annika's coat, I could hear Mrs Penny greeting Ruby downstairs from the open door of my bedroom. Glancing across at the clock on the wall, I saw it was already ten o'clock; Ruby and Noah had arrived bang on time.

When I awoke this morning, all I could think of was that Frankie was still missing, and it wasn't until after breakfast that I remembered I'd promised Ruby we could meet up today. We were taking the little ones to the green behind Norfolk Square for some fresh air.

However, I hardly slept last night for thinking about Frankie, and there was nothing but a black hole of worry hanging over me. Annika, who must have sensed my unease today and was usually such a good baby, kept bursting into fits of tears.

After carrying Annika downstairs, I walked outside and squinted against the bright sunlight of the day, before putting her into the pram which was parked beside the front door. Ruby and Noah had been waiting patiently for us outside, and they joined us now as we began the short walk to the green.

'It's a lovely day,' Ruby observed, stopping to adjust

Noah's little sun hat before indicating the cloudless blue sky above. 'Don't you agree, Scarlett?' she said, giving me a quizzical look.

I nodded heavily, but for me, the beautiful day was tainted with dark thoughts of what Frankie was enduring under that same blue sky. And I fought against the dread threatening to engulf me as we arrived at the parkland.

When we'd settled the babies on a blanket on the ground and they were playing happily, Ruby sat down next to me on the bench and gave me a puzzled frown.

'Scarlett, what's happened?' she asked urgently. 'You look awful.' She touched my arm gently as she spoke.

The breath caught in my throat at the sympathy on her face, and I found it hard to get my voice to work. Covering my face with my hands, I fought against the tears, worried that Annika or Noah would get upset at the sight of my sadness.

Ruby waited patiently for me to gather myself, and then at last I was able to speak. 'I had a visit from Frankie's sister yesterday,' I began falteringly, still not wanting to believe this terrible situation myself. 'Frankie's gone missing, after his plane came down over France.'

There. I had said it aloud. I had spoken the words which had been spinning in my head endlessly, since Beverley's visit to me yesterday.

'Oh, Scarlett, I'm sorry to hear that. Have you any idea what's happened to him? I mean, you haven't seen anything… have you, about what his fate might be?'

The sound of Noah yelling out in frustration rang through the air, and Ruby quickly leaned over and gave him the rattle that he couldn't quite reach on the blanket.

'I don't know anything, Ruby,' I answered with a heavy sigh, as she settled herself down next to me again. 'My sixth sense is failing miserably right now, and I'm finding it really hard to have any *blinking* hope of a good outcome here.'

Ruby gazed at me with concern on her face. 'I'm sure everything will be all right,' she said in a gentle tone. 'I understand it doesn't seem that way at the moment, but where there's life there's hope.'

I shook my head and gave her a weak smile, remembering how I'd said that very thing to Beverley the day before. But how could everything possibly be all right, when my poor Frankie was either dead or had been captured by the enemy?

'Scarlett, please listen to me,' Ruby leaned towards me. 'I haven't given up hope yet about Reilly, have I? And if I did…' She moved her head slightly. 'You would tell me not to lose faith, so that means you mustn't give up hope that Frankie will survive,' she said, setting her jaw.

I understood that Ruby was referring to what I'd told her about Reilly, and how I'd had a sense that he was still alive. So far, though, that feeling had no substance, and a part of me regretted giving her false hope.

'I still believe what you told me is true, Scarlett,' she continued. 'That somewhere out there, Reilly is still alive. I will *never* give up hope, and if I'm truthful here, that's pushing me into finding the strength to leave Dick. That one day I will be reunited with Reilly again.'

There were no words of reassurance from me on

this, only guilt on my part for planting the idea in her head that Reilly had somehow survived. I regretted with all my heart that she was hoping for a miracle now when it might never happen.

'I'm sorry,' I whispered, and I dipped my head towards my chin and tried to swallow back my sorrow.

'Don't be sorry, Scarlett. I know how you feel, of course I do. But you're not alone, remember that,' Ruby said, before leaning over the babies to check they were all right as Annika began crying.

I watched her for a moment as she sat down on the blanket next to Annika and soothed the baby's brow, knowing how lucky I was to have a friend like Ruby.

'Thank you,' I said, understanding that without her, my life would be much harder. And our eyes met as she gave me a reassuring nod. 'How are things with you now?' I probed when Annika was settled again.

For several months, Ruby had been hiding the knowledge of her parents' death from Dick. We both knew he wouldn't hesitate to steal her inheritance if he knew, and that would leave her with no means of escaping his bullying ways.

'Dick's due home next week,' she told me, her face darkening. 'As usual, I'll be on tenterhooks until he goes back to Southampton again.' She stared across at Noah for a moment, as if thinking of ways to protect her son from her husband.

'I can't thank you enough for helping me with the sale of mum and dad's house, Scarlett,' Ruby said, looking back at me. 'Hopefully, it'll go through in the next few weeks without a hitch,' she tilted her head doubtfully. 'And before Dick finds out about it.'

'There's no reason why Dick should find out about the house sale, is there?' I tried to put paid to her fears, wondering if Ruby was perhaps dwelling too much on what might never happen. 'After all, the money will be safely in *my* bank account until you need it, just as we planned.'

She gave an understanding nod. 'True enough, but I wish I could leave him right now, Scarlett,' she admitted. 'Every time he comes home on leave, I get so frightened – for myself and for little Noah. The violence is never far away with him, and sometimes I can see him itching to set it free.'

She stared dismally across at Noah, who was happily passing a toy to Annika and giggling in his cute baby way. 'It's getting harder to keep Noah quiet around Dick now that he's older.'

Ruby had told me in the past how her husband's temper was often out of control when he was home on leave, especially if he'd been drinking. And I struggled to find the words to reassure her that everything would be fine; until she escaped from Dick, the risk would constantly be there.

Leaning forward, I gave her a reassuring hug. 'You need to be brave and patient just a bit longer,' I told her firmly. 'Once the house is sold, we need to find you and Noah somewhere to live. It'll be a place where Dick won't be able find you – a village in a quiet, rural area would be best, so that you can hide away.'

Ruby nodded at me and we sat in silence, lost in our own thoughts, until it was time to leave. 'Are you on ARP duty later, Scarlett?' she asked, as we placed the babies back into their prams, folded up the ground blanket, and put away their toys.

'I blinking well am, and looking forward to it, too. Honestly, Ruby…' I straightened up and stretched out my back where it was aching from sitting on the bench.

'It's such a good distraction from everything that's going on right now. And I'm lucky that Mrs Penny likes to look after Annika for me. She's a real treasure.'

Ruby knitted her brow. 'How lovely. I envy you. I'd like to still be working in the pub,' she reflected sadly.

Dick had forbidden Ruby to work in The Fortune of War pub once they were married, because he liked to control her in every way, and she had no choice but to comply with his wishes.

Later, as we said goodbye on the doorstep of number fourteen Norfolk Square, Ruby gave me a steady look. 'Take care of yourself, Scarlett,' she said tenderly. 'You've had a shock, and I know what that's like. When I heard about Reilly, I couldn't function properly for days.

'And you mustn't lose hope about Frankie,' she persisted, straightening her shoulders. 'Never give up thinking about him surviving, whatever you do,' she added over her shoulder, and she began pushing Noah in his pram towards the two up, two down home she shared with Dick McCarthy in Kemptown.

Back in my room, I fed Annika her lunch before putting her down for a nap and told myself that Ruby was right. I must keep my body and spirit strong, in case – or when – Frankie returned to me one day.

From somewhere deep inside, I hoped and prayed with all my heart that this would happen. The alternative was unbearable, because I didn't know how to face my life, or be strong for Annika, without my beloved Frankie by my side.

Chapter Forty-One

Frankie

Frankie had spent most of the night hoping he would remember all Dedee's instructions and advice, and that he would be strong enough for the long journey ahead of them.

It was barely light when they all gathered in Camille and Bastille's front parlour, looking tired and nervous, and Frankie prayed that every one of them would survive their long and treacherous crossing.

Through the gloom, Frankie smiled to himself when Dedee appeared, dressed in a simple blouse and skirt with flat shoes. His theory that she might undertake this dangerous journey in disguise had proved fundamentally wrong. He tried to push to the back of his mind that his life and the lives of Claude and Armand now depended on this wisp of a girl.

Once she had checked they were ready to leave, and made sure they all had their papers in order, they all thanked Camille and Bastille for their hospitality.

'Please remember everything I told you yesterday,' Dedee said, turning to Frankie, Armand, and Claude. 'As I explained yesterday, we will now walk to Saumur station, which will take us no more than about

253

twenty minutes.'

They all acknowledged her words, and waited nervously for the moment to come when they would leave the safe house. 'I will walk ahead of you, but from a distance, so that you can follow me safely. Once we reach the station, you must quickly purchase your train ticket and then meet me on the platform.'

Dedee straightened her back and looked at them one at a time. 'Do not forget that we don't know each other. Is that understood?'

They all nodded their understanding, and Frankie put his hand in his pocket and touched the French francs Camille had given him for the journey. Nerves fluttered through him and made him feel nauseous; his breakfast of bread and jam was lying heavily in his stomach.

Dedee went first, just as she told them she would, and then a minute later Armand and Claude followed her out of the door. While Frankie waited his turn, he again thanked Camille and Bastille, who both offered him an encouraging smile. Then at last, he stepped out of their front door, into the unknown and dangerous world beyond.

Frankie's limbs shook and his heart beat faster as he emerged from the safe house after so long being hidden in the attic. Stepping out into the street, he tried to ignore his nerves as he stared up the road and caught sight of Dedee in the distance. She was walking quickly towards the station, followed by Armand and Claude who were a little ahead of him.

Making quick strides, he followed the two men, but was careful to keep some distance between them. As Dedee disappeared around a corner, he quickened his step, heaving a sigh of relief that so far there had been no sign of the German army.

The walk seemed to take longer than twenty minutes, but eventually they all arrived at Saumur train station. The platform was quiet and, as expected, a few German soldiers were standing around watching everyone as they waited for their trains to arrive. There was an air of tension in the air as the soldiers paced up and down the platform, while at the same time watching everyone intently.

Thankfully, the ticket-buying had gone without incident, and Frankie saw Armand, Claude, and Dedee standing slightly apart from each other on the platform. He felt jittery and on edge, and tried to help this attack of nerves by glancing across at Dedee from time to time.

This young woman has been successful many times in saving Allied airmen from the enemy, he repeated in his head, while taking a deep breath. Hopefully, this time would be no different from those successful missions, and they would all arrive in Bayonne without incident.

As the train pulled into the platform, all four of them quickly boarded. Dedee had said that even though they were not supposed to know each other, they all needed to sit as close as possible so that she could watch out for them on the long train journey. It would also be helpful when they had to alight from the train and change platforms, just in case any of them forgot which station was theirs. They had all tried to memorise the train stops they needed, because Dedee's information could not be written down.

As Frankie stepped into the train carriage, he remembered that this journey would take about two hours before they had to change. Thankfully, so far the soldiers didn't seem to be taking any notice of him and the other two airmen, but he knew he couldn't get complacent.

When Dedee stood up a few hours later, as they approached St Pierre-des-Corps station, they all followed her out onto the platform at a safe distance. And Frankie heaved a sigh of relief that the first train journey was over.

The next one was equally uneventful. This time, the carriage was half empty, and as Claude and Armand sat opposite him, Frankie had been tempted to chat to them. But he reminded himself to stick to the rules, which were there to protect them, and his heart missed a beat when he glanced across at Dedee to see her sitting next to a German soldier.

She had told them they would have to try and endure the eight-hour journey without any food or drink. That way, they would be unlikely to have to use the toilet facilities, and would not draw attention to themselves.

But Frankie was so thirsty that his throat was closing up, and his stomach was grumbling loudly with hunger, despite having had breakfast, but he gritted his teeth and heeded Dedee's advice.

Eventually, the train pulled into Saint-Jean station. Even though this next one was the final train journey, Frankie understood he must not yet relax. This journey would take a further two-and-a-half hours, and as he boarded the train, he saw immediately that this time it would be harder.

There was a different feel to the atmosphere on this train. There was something in the air – a feeling of trepidation so strong that Frankie could almost touch it. He tried to work out what it was as he glanced around him. Perhaps it was because there were more

German soldiers boarding, and he tried to quell the unease building inside which was making him feel rigid with fear.

Chapter Forty-Two

The train to Bayonne was busy and packed with people of all ages, and it had proved difficult for Frankie to sit near to Dedee and the other two men. At least he had been lucky enough to get into the same carriage as them, which helped to ease his mind a little.

For now, his raging hunger seemed to have gone away, and as Frankie settled into his seat by the window, he told himself that at the end of this journey, they would be able to eat and drink.

He glanced across at Dedee, to see that she was seated next to Claude and opposite Armand. They were near to the door that led out into the corridor. This was where Frankie dearly wished to be, but all those seats were taken so he had to remain where he was for now.

Forcing breath into his body, Frankie pushed away his bad feeling about this journey, reminding himself that there was nothing to suggest things wouldn't go as they had on the two previous trains.

However, there were definitely more German soldiers on this train, which made him feel anxious, and Frankie tried to practise looking relaxed by gazing out of the window and watching the passing landscape.

They were about halfway to their destination of Bayonne, and Frankie was beginning to think their journey would go without a hitch, when things took a turn for the worse.

He had been feeling very drowsy, after another night of fitful sleep, and the feeling of hunger combined with the movement of the train resulted in his eyelids beginning to droop.

Suddenly, with a jolt, Frankie was wide awake. There was a sharp unrelenting pain in his already aching ribs, and as his eyes flew open, he came face-to-face with a German soldier.

The man was leaning over him and angrily jabbing his machine gun into Frankie's chest. The pain was excruciating, as though he were being stabbed. And worse still, the soldier began shouting loudly at him in German. Frankie was drowsy, and he struggled to recollect where he was and what the hell was happening to him.

His throat had completely dried up, and no words would come out of his mouth. It was only later that Frankie realised this had been a blessing. In that moment, while he was in that sleep-deprived, befuddled state, he could easily have said the wrong thing and put them all in a desperately dangerous situation.

The realisation that he was on a packed train in an enemy occupied country suddenly hit home, and he quickly yanked himself up in his seat and faced the soldier. His heart missed a beat as the man shouted at him again, and seemed to be getting angrier by the minute.

Frankie didn't understand the language and couldn't comprehend what he had done to make the soldier so angry. Then he heard a rustling of paper beside him, and caught a glimpse of the person sitting next to him out of the corner of his eye.

Frankie dare not look towards his neighbour or ask the soldier what he wanted, for fear of being shot right there and then. But in that split second, he understood exactly what he needed to do to appease the man.

The soldier was obviously furious that Frankie was dozing on the train when he'd asked to see his paperwork. Dedee's words immediately echoed in Frankie's head, warning him that he must have his papers to hand when they were needed, in order to avoid trouble.

He stared up at the soldier who jabbed him again, sending a shooting pain through Frankie's whole body and taking his breath away. With a huge effort, he tried not to show how much the gun was hurting an already injured part of his body, and quickly managed to pull the relevant papers from his pocket.

The papers were immediately snatched from him as the soldier lowered the gun, and quickly read them. However, the documents did not appease the man for long. After flinging them back at Frankie, this time instead of jabbing him with the gun, the soldier aimed it directly at his head.

A quiet hush fell over the carriage, and Frankie could not breathe. Slowly, he closed his eyes, expecting the soldier to do his worst; as he waited for the end to come, he hoped it would be quick. His chest was heavy with regret that he had almost made it to Bayonne and another safe house before disaster had struck.

Just then, a loud, clattering noise pierced the silence of the carriage, and all heads turned towards Dedee. Frankie watched her stand up abruptly from her seat.

She was staring intently down at her purse, which was lying open on the floor, with the coins scattered in all directions. The soldier turned and glared angrily across at her, his gun still aimed at Frankie's head.

'*Pardon, chacun*,' Dedee said, holding her hands up in despair and addressing the people in the carriage. She looked visibly distressed, as she bent down and began picking up the small change, while cursing rapidly under her breath.

For a split second, everyone looked at her, then down to the floor strewn with money. Then one by one they got up out of their seats and began to help her pick up the coins.

The carriage was immediately transformed from the tense atmosphere of a moment ago to a chaotic scene, as passengers tried to retrieve the coins and pass them across to Dedee. People were peering underneath and down the side of seats for the lost money, and the carriage was filled with their loud chatter. The soldier and his threat to Frankie had been temporarily forgotten.

Frankie watched the man lower his gun and scowl angrily at Dedee, before angrily shoving people out of the way and quickly disappearing through the door leading to the corridor of the train.

Frankie let out the breath he had been holding, and ran his hands shakily through his hair. Then he looked across at Dedee, and as they made eye contact, she nodded at him and smiled. Forcing his trembling legs to work, he stood up and began searching for coins on the floor, just like everyone else.

Thank God for Dedee. Frankie knew without a shadow of a doubt that he would more than likely be dead now if she hadn't created a diversion, which had saved his life.

The rest of the journey went without incident, and

less than an hour later, the train pulled into St-Jean-de-Luz station. Frankie stepped out onto the platform and breathed in the cool, fresh air. Then heeding Dedee's advice, he rounded a corner up ahead, so that the soldiers alighting from the train wouldn't see where he had gone, and waited patiently for the others.

Soon Armand, Claude, and Dedee had caught him up. She looked around them for a few seconds to make sure that the coast was clear, before explaining what their next course of action would be.

'It's about an hour's cycle ride to the safe house in Anglet from here,' she told them, while still keeping an eye on their surroundings. 'However, I can see that you all need sustenance before we attempt the journey. So, firstly we will find a small café in which to refresh ourselves. Then, as usual, I will lead the way and you must all follow. Before we go, are there any questions?'

'Do we sit together in the café, or pretend we don't know each other as we did on the train?' Frankie asked, wondering if they would be less conspicuous in this busy city.

'Once we are inside the café, the best thing to do is pair up,' Dedee said, looking at Armand and Claude. 'You two follow me and Hubert into the café at a safe distance, but don't sit with us, or make it look like you know us.'

Frankie was desperate to express how grateful he was to Dedee for what she had done on the train, but he could see there wasn't time to discuss it now. Instead, they split up, and he walked at a distance from her as she led the way into the city. He was relieved they were getting away from the station, which had been teeming with German soldiers.

As they came to a quiet back street, Frankie could

hold his tongue no longer, and he stopped and took hold of Dedee's arm. 'I must thank you,' he told her urgently. 'You saved my life on that train!'

He was filled with overwhelming gratitude at the thought that he might, with this woman's help, survive this ordeal and get home to see Scarlett again. But since getting off the train, he had been besieged with dark thoughts of what could have happened on the journey.

Dedee gave him a searching look. 'Be careful, Hubert,' she hissed, while glancing around her. 'We are not out of the woods yet. Houses have ears... and eyes,' she added, indicating the terraced houses nearby them.

Frankie let go of her arm and stepped back. 'Of course, I'm sorry,' he said, feeling a bit stupid to have mentioned it out in the open where they could be overheard.

Armand and Claude had almost caught them up, and Dedee moved away from Frankie and hurried on ahead. 'But please, have your papers on hand next time, and don't be asleep!' she berated him over her shoulder.

Frankie rushed after Dedee, keen to reassure her. 'Don't worry, I've learnt my lesson now. However tired I am, I will *not* fall asleep on a train,' he said, as he walked behind her and tried to keep his voice down.

Dedee stopped briefly again. 'Good for you, Hubert. As I said before, you have to be on your guard – always,' she said firmly.

Before she could go on ahead again, Frankie had to say what he'd been thinking. 'But Dedee... what if the soldier had shot you, instead of me, for dropping those coins?' he asked. His heart raced again at the very thought that he could have been responsible for

263

this young woman's death.

'It seems they don't need much of an excuse to use their guns,' Frankie continued shakily, when she said nothing. He knew that if Dedee had been killed, her loss would have been felt throughout the Comet Line, and would have had a much bigger impact than his.

Dedee's face reddened and her eyes blazed. 'Stop it, Hubert!' she said. 'Get rid of those doubts right now,' she reiterated. 'Something had to be done and I came to no harm – unlike you if I hadn't intervened. I know these German soldiers. They are cold and they are callous, but I also knew he was beside himself with anger, and a quick and timely diversion was all that was needed.'

Frankie was once again full of admiration for Dedee, who had only been thinking of him when she had taken the risk she did. He was grateful that her plan had worked, and the soldier had retreated from the dangerous situation and in the end had left him alone.

As they resumed their walk, with Dedee leading the way again, she told him another snippet of information which would stay with him for many years to come.

'A woman can't carry a gun or fly a bomber jet,' she told him wisely, 'but she can use her womanly wisdom in times of crisis.' Dedee shot him a knowing look.

Frankie smiled at Dedee and thought how Scarlett had used her womanly wisdom to find her way in life. Perhaps, if he made it back to Britain after this war, he would have a greater understanding of Scarlett and other women, and the struggles they faced in life.

Chapter Forty-Three

After they had refreshments in the café in Bayonne – sitting in pairs, as Dedee had instructed – Frankie felt the strength returned to his body. He was pleased to be able to stretch his aching limbs on the walk from the station, and in the café he had gulped down a cup of tea and wolfed down some bread and jam.

Luckily, it was quiet inside the cafe, and there were no German soldiers taking afternoon refreshment, which meant they could all relax a little at last. Dedee, though, never relaxed. Frankie noticed that her eyes constantly darted around them, even when there was nothing untoward going on, and he certainly felt safe with her around.

After they left the café, she led them – at a safe distance from one another – towards a derelict house on the outskirts of the town, and indicated that they follow her round to the back of the building.

Here, the bicycles Dedee had told them about were hidden in an old shed. She warned them that until they got away from the town, and were safely out in the countryside, they must still keep their distance from each other.

Cycling ahead, she led the way towards the village. And even though they all exhausted after the long train journey, there was no choice but to keep going. At last, Dedee indicated for them to stop up ahead, and Frankie assumed they were almost at their destination.

'The villa is down here,' she told them, pointing towards a narrow lane up ahead. 'Follow me,' she instructed, getting back on her bicycle.

After following Dedee down the lane, they came to a stop in front of a rather drab looking villa, which was hidden right at the end of the quiet lane. As they approached, Frankie saw that behind it lay the distant view of the mountains, and directly below the villa was the bay of St-Jean-de-Luz.

The journey by bicycle had taken them just over an hour, and Frankie's legs were now shaking with fatigue. He was worried he might collapse before making it inside the villa. However, he managed to get off the bicycle and, as instructed, left it around the side of the building. Then Dedee knocked lightly on the front door while they all waited on the doorstep.

The door was quickly opened, and a round-faced, slightly built woman stood on the threshold. She had short, auburn hair, a thick jumper on over a flowery dress, and fierce grey eyes. Dedee and the woman immediately embraced, as if they were long-lost friends.

'Dedee, it's so good to see you,' the woman said in French, then she looked around at the men in their tired, dishevelled states. 'Please, you must all come in,' she said, opening the door wider. 'Did the journey go well?' she asked Dedee over her shoulder, as she led everyone through the hallway of the house.

Dedee glanced across at Frankie and then back at the woman. 'There was only a minor incident on the train, involving one of our escapees, but nothing more,' she said, shrugging her shoulders as if it were of no consequence.

Nearly being shot dead was hardly a minor incident in Frankie's book, but he kept quiet. Perhaps it *was* a minor incident to Dedee; she must have seen near misses many times in the course of helping the RAF pilots across occupied France.

The older woman gave a little tilt of her head, as if she agreed with Dedee, and led them into a small front parlour. The room was sparsely furnished, and housed only a small settee and several armchairs. She invited them all to sit down after their long journey, and Dedee turned towards Frankie and the other two escapees.

'This is Tante-Go,' she said, introducing the woman to them. 'She will look after us tonight, or until it is safe to move onto the next house, which should hopefully be tomorrow.'

Again, Frankie was surprised that such a prominent figure in the resistance was another slight, young looking woman. He was beginning to realise that appearances were deceptive.

As they all settled down in the front parlour, a girl of around seventeen appeared, and Tante Go introduced her to the men. 'This is my daughter – helper number 1,' she told them, and then asked her to bring them refreshments.

Even though he had eaten at the café not long ago, Frankie was starting to feel hungry again, and he leaned back in his armchair and let out a long sigh, allowing his tiredness to wash over him. Just as at Camille and Bastille's house, he already felt safe in this tiny villa, hidden deep in the French countryside.

Helper number 1 soon returned to the room with a

tray laden with tea and fruitcake, and while they ate and drank, Tante Go explained what was to happen to the men over the next few days.

'You will all stay here tonight and rest,' she told them. 'Then tomorrow night, under cover of darkness, we will take you to a safe house near here, where you will wait until the conditions are favourable. When that happens, you will cycle to Urrugne, which is the start of the Pyrenees, and from there you will be escorted across the mountains by a Basque guide.'

'How long will it take us to get across the mountains?' Frankie asked. He had no idea of the length of the journey ahead, although he had heard how treacherous it was getting across the Pyrenees.

'The journey usually takes about two days and nights to get across,' Tante-Go answered with a shrug. 'So long as there are no problems,' she added, glancing across at Dedee who nodded.

'Please try not to worry,' Tante-Go told them. 'Our Basque guide is a man by the name of Florentino. I always ask for him, as he's the very best there is,' she added. 'Rest assured that you are in safe hands with Florentino, because he knows the mountains like the back of his hand. And at this very moment, he is ready and waiting for the weather to turn before he will give us the signal to move.'

Frankie understood they were still a long way before being out of danger, and it was going to be tough crossing the mountains, but he had faith that their valiant leader – and hopefully the excellent Basque guide Florentino – would get them across the Pyrenees safely.

Later at supper, Frankie and the other men were introduced to L'Oncle, who was Tante Go's husband.

She also introduced her son to the men. He was helper number 2, and was a slight boy of around eighteen. L'Oncle was a tall, dark haired man with a friendly smile, and his son was a miniature version of him.

Frankie quickly warmed to the whole family, and knew he would hold their kindness in his heart forever. He longed to ask Tante-Go and L'Oncle how they had become involved in the resistance, but he knew that the less he knew about the family, the better. In this situation, he had been told, secrecy was everything.

However, Armand, his tongue loosened by the wine that evening, was quick to ask the question Frankie had been mulling over. 'How did you find yourselves caught up in the resistance movement?' he asked across the dinner table. 'I mean... it's dangerous work.'

There was a silence as everyone stopped eating for a moment, and Tante Go frowned as she began to explain.

'When the Germans invaded Belgium, we quickly left and attempted to get to Britain. But of course, we were too late; the Spanish border was already closed,' she explained solemnly. 'Luckily, we found this house which was empty, and we were able to move in here.' She leaned back in her chair and let out a long sigh.

L'Oncle agreed. 'Lots of things work in our favour here,' he told them. 'My job as a translator and interpreter for the French with the German army, is one of them. I won't go into how that helps, but it just does,' he said, glancing across at his wife.

Afterwards, Frankie realised that although Armand's question had been answered, Tante Go and L'Oncle had still been evasive, telling them nothing about the resistance and how it worked. Instead, they had very cleverly focused on how they had come to be living in the villa deep in the French countryside.

Chapter Forty-Four

Everyone was clustered together in the cellar of a safe house in Anglet. They had just been moved here under cover of darkness, after spending the night with Tante Go, L'Oncle, and their two teenagers.

Frankie studied their Basque guide Florentino as he talked them through the hazardous journey they would soon be undertaking up the mountainside.

Tall and well built, with dark hair hidden under a black beret, Florentino exuded an air of confidence and determination. He showed not a hint of fear or doubt about what they were about to do. His confidence went a long way in reassuring Frankie, who felt secure in the knowledge that if anyone could get them across the border, fraught with danger, this man could.

The latest safe house was the home of a man named Gaylord. He lived alone, so helping the allied airmen was a way of alleviating his loneliness, he told them on their arrival.

'My wine cellar makes a good hiding place for escapees,' he explained with a knowing grin.

Gaylord didn't say very much, but mostly gazed at them all mutely from under his hooded eyes, while rubbing a gnarled hand through his dishevelled grey hair. He was a good host, though, and he made up for not talking much by making the men comfortable in the wine cellar.

As with all the others helping them in this dangerous mission, Frankie admired Gaylord's quiet courage, knowing what it would cost the man if he were caught harbouring fugitives.

That night, Frankie slept better than he had in months, and was so comfortable in Gaylord's home that he would happily have stayed there for the rest of the war. But Florentino told them that as soon as the weather changed, they would need to cycle to Urrugne, where their journey across the Pyrenees would begin.

Eventually, after two days and two nights spent with Gaylord, Florentino gathered them all together. 'The weather conditions are in our favour now,' he said, regarding them steadily as he spoke. 'And you must all be ready to leave here at midnight.'

Florentino looked so calm about the whole escape operation that Frankie wondered how he kept his nerve. Then he reminded himself that, like Dedee, this man had helped countless airmen across the border undetected, and had made this perilous journey many times before.

'The border between France and Spain is along the Bidassoa River,' Florentino continued. 'When we have reached that part of the journey, it is best done by wading across the river when it is shallow. But due to recent heavy rainfall, we will not be going this way now, as it will be too dangerous.'

Frankie heaved a sigh of relief that they wouldn't be going into the river, aware that his fear of water might have held him back.

'Instead of that route, we will be crossing the river by a suspension bridge near Endalaza, which is a much safer way at this time of the year. Are there any questions?' he asked, crossing his arms over his chest and looking at each of them in turn.

Frankie wanted to ask if they would make it safely across the border, but he held his tongue, understanding there were no guarantees. 'How long will it take to get to Endalaza?' he asked instead. 'Will we be able to get there in one day, or will it take longer?' he added, hoping the journey would take as little time as possible.

Florentino shook his head. 'Not in one day, Hubert. That is impossible.' He ran his fingers through his hair, making it stand up on end even more. 'Especially as we have to do the journey in the pitch dark of the night, and we'll need to catch up on sleep in one of the safe houses on the way. Mistakes happen when people are overtired,' he warned, widening his eyes as if to drive his point home.

They were all silent for a moment as they digested this information. 'How will we get across the suspension bridge undetected?' Frankie's heart was thumping harder at the thought of the crossing.

'Good question, Hubert. But first, I must warn you that the risk of being ambushed is worse nearer to the border, so please be on your guard at all times. 'There's an electrical plant by the suspension bridge in Endalaza, and the noise from this will be good cover for us as we get across the bridge undetected.' He spoke as if this would be an easy task, but his next words struck fear deeper into Frankie's heart.

'I have to warn you all that this will be tricky, because there's a guard hut by the suspension bridge which is continually manned by German soldiers. The water underneath the bridge is constantly being churned up by the electrical plant in action. But we have done this route before and been successful, so you have nothing to worry about.'

Florentino's firm assurances went some way to making Frankie feel less afraid, but the thought of crossing a bridge under the noses of German soldiers was terrifying.

'After we've crossed the suspension bridge, we'll walk along the railway track and through some tunnels along the way.' Florentino paced the room while he spoke, then he sat down and leaned his elbows on his knees. 'We'll more than likely have to spend more time in another safe house before reaching San Sebastian.'

'Is that where we will be met by a British Diplomat?' Armand asked, speaking up for the first time.

'It is indeed, Armand. You'll still have to be careful in San Sebastian, as there might not be German soldiers to worry about there, but there *are* Spanish police who will be on the lookout for escapees like you.'

Frankie knew the Spanish had declared themselves to be neutral in this war, but he was well aware that they were on the side of the Germans. General Franco, it seemed, thought his army was too depleted after the Spanish civil war to fight another war so soon, with either Great Britain or with Germany.

'The next part of our journey will be from San Sebastian to Bilbao, which will take about three hours on the train.' Florentino paused and looked directly across at Frankie. 'I heard about the incident on the train to Bayonne, Hubert, and I would advise no falling asleep this time please, monsieur?' He pushed back his dark head and laughed out loud.

Frankie's face flushed and, although he knew Florentino was trying to lighten the mood, he understood this was no laughing matter. He was still embarrassed about the way he had put everyone at such risk that day on the train.

'I promise to stay wide awake,' he told them, knowing that however tired he was from now on, he would not allow himself to make the same mistake twice.

Florentino shrugged and touched Frankie's arm. 'I know you will, monsieur,' he said good-naturedly. 'Moving on. Once we reach Bilbao, you will be taken by car to Madrid, which will be a long journey – about six hours in all. Reaching Gibraltar from there will be around two days, and at all times you must *still* be on your guard,' he warned them.

Frankie inhaled deeply. *God, it sounded like a journey-and-a-half*, he thought, as he listened to Florentino explaining how they would be flown back to Great Britain from Gibraltar. Then, after a brief rest, they would return to fighting Hitler in the skies.

The thought of home brought a hard lump to Frankie's throat and an image of his beautiful Scarlett into his mind. He could only hope and pray that they would all make it back to Gibraltar without incident, then onto that treasured flight home.

Chapter Forty-Five

It was midnight when Frankie and the others bade goodbye to Gaylord, to begin their cycle ride to Urrugne. And he wondered what perils lay in store for them all in the next few days.

An hour and a half later, they arrived at Urrugne, which was a small town at the bottom of the Pyrenees. After hiding their bicycles in a nearby safe house, Florentino gathered them all together.

'Our journey across the Pyrenees begins here,' he told them, glancing behind him to where the outline of the mountains could be seen in the darkness of the night, looming high into the sky.

Frankie's heart beat faster. This was it; this was the beginning of their route to freedom. He felt both excited and frightened at the same time.

'The rocky terrain will be hard to negotiate in the dark,' Florentino warned. 'Even so, the small torches you have been equipped with must only be used when absolutely necessary. And please keep close together at all times.'

Frankie's overriding fear was of becoming separated from the others and finding himself totally alone on the mountainside. Florentino had also warned of the risk of being ambushed, so they had to keep their eyes and ears peeled at all times for this happening on the route.

'The German military police are patrolling these mountains, as well as their specialist mountain troops who are deployed in the Pyrenees range itself,' Florentino said. 'So, we have to be on our guard at all times.'

'Florentino is right; we could be spotted at any time,' Dedee confirmed. 'It's all about moving slowly and steadily, and making no noise as we go about our journey. It will be difficult, but rest assured it can be done.' She looked across at Florentino and smiled. 'Together we will get you all to safety with no problems,' she added.

Florentino nodded his agreement, then gave a few final words to the escapees before they set off up the Pyrenees. 'Stick to the path, and don't lose sight of the person in front of you.'

***

Florentino and Dedee were up ahead of Frankie and the other two men, leading them in single file up the steep mountainside. They had been climbing for a few hours, during which Frankie kept losing his footing on the mountainside as he stumbled over loose rocks and boulders on the way.

Unable to see more than a foot in front of himself, in the pitch darkness, Frankie had his eyes glued to Armand, who was climbing up ahead of him. From behind, he could hear Claude struggling slowly up the steep incline.

The mountainside was tough terrain, and the trees were so dense that falling over their roots was a constant risk. As Frankie climbed higher, he struggled to catch his breath as the air became colder and thinner, and in some areas his feet slipped on wet mud from recent rainfall.

At least it was summer, and they were not climbing the mountain in the depths of winter, which would have been much worse. Florentino had explained to them that the Pyrenees were covered with snow in the colder months, but at this time of year there would only be snowfall at the very top.

Even so, Frankie was thankful for the heavy overcoat and woolly hat provided by the helpers. He was aware that without warm clothing, none of them would survive more than an hour in this cold and unforgiving environment.

Eventually, when Frankie's legs shook with fatigue, they arrived at a small log cabin, hidden deep amongst the trees. It was beginning to get light, which meant the enemy could easily see them now, and they all heaved a collective sigh of relief when the safe house came into view.

When Dedee retired to her bed in an adjoining room, the men chatted for a while, and Frankie took the opportunity to ask Florentino how he knew so much about the mountainside trails.

Their guide gave him a look, which said this was his favourite subject, and began to explain. 'During the Spanish civil war, I went into exile in France,' he told them proudly.

'Being a smuggler, I collaborated with small French resistance groups, taking photographs, and making plans. That's why I was chosen to help RAF pilots to escape into Spain.'

Frankie realised Florentino thrived on danger and taking risks, and as the conversation ended, the men thanked their guide for his help.

On that first night in the mountains, Frankie slept like the dead. He had been given a thin mattress on the floor alongside his fellow escapees, and his first instinct was to stay awake and be on his guard. But he had never felt so tired in his whole life, and realised that if he didn't sleep, he would be as weak as a kitten the next day when they carried on climbing the steep mountains.

Florentino eventually shook Frankie awake at eleven o'clock that night, after he had slept the whole day away. He could have slept for a week, and it wouldn't have been enough. When he woke up, he could barely remember his own name, let alone where he was or what he was doing in this most inhospitable of places.

After they had eaten, Florentino addressed them before they set off up the mountain again. 'We should arrive at Endalaza at about four in the morning,' he said. 'This is the ideal time to cross the suspension bridge, as the guards will be tired and, hopefully, they will drop off to sleep. If we run out of time and it begins to get light, we will stay in another log cabin or hut along the way, but hopefully we shouldn't need to do this.'

Frankie glanced across at Armand and Claude. They looked as tired as he felt, and they hadn't even reached this place called Endalaza yet. Despite the long sleep, Frankie was exhausted, but somehow, he knew he had to find the energy to keep going.

They set off, following the mountain routes so many escapees had walked before them. Again, they used the cover of darkness to avoid detection, and Frankie lost track of time as he battled with the hard terrain underfoot.

Hours later, Florentino stopped under the cover of some dense trees. The sound of the fast-flowing river was nearby, as they were told to listen carefully to his instructions.

As they gathered around their guide, Frankie's hands were clammy, despite the cold of the mountainside, as his fear of water gripped him. *Was this where it all went horribly wrong?* he wondered.

Chapter Forty-Six

'We are nearing Endalaza, where we have to cross the suspension bridge,' Florentino told the men in whispered tones, as they clustered around him under the trees. 'We only have about an hour's darkness left, so we need to move swiftly across it.'

Frankie looked into the distance where the outline of the bridge could be seen silhouetted against the mountains. He felt the hairs on the back of his neck stand on end as sweat beaded his brow.

As he waited for Florentino to give further instructions, he glanced across at Dedee in the darkness. Taking a deep breath, he tried to draw courage from their valiant leader, remembering all the other RAF pilots she had helped to safety in the past.

'Follow me and keep your heads down,' Florentino said firmly.

As before, in single file, he led Dedee and the men down a steep gorge, and Frankie could see they were moving silently towards a narrow road below. Suddenly, Florentino stopped up ahead and signalled for them to listen. Below their feet, the sound of the water had intensified, and Frankie tried to ignore the nausea building in his stomach.

At first, there was nothing to be seen in the darkness, just the sound of the water echoing around them. Then a white searchlight flashed across the river and shone on a rickety looking suspension bridge up ahead. The light also showed the guard post situated a little way ahead, between them and the bridge.

Frankie's heart was thrashing in his ears, but he told himself that Florentino and Dedee knew exactly what they were doing. It didn't help to alleviate the panic building rapidly inside, making his throat dry and his limbs feel weak.

This was a test of courage and of keeping calm under pressure, and the next few hours would push them all to the very limits of their endurance.

As they waited for the signal from Florentino, Frankie held his breath. He could see his guide's eyes focussed rigidly on the guard post, watching the criss-crossing of the searchlights across the river.

Slowly and silently, Florentino began to move towards the guardhouse, then he turned around and signalled for the rest of them to follow. As they drew nearer to the footbridge, the loud sound of snoring came from the guard post and echoed into the night air.

Frankie's gaze was riveted to the bridge. It was simply a sagging sling with rope sides and a wooden-slat floor, through which the roaring river below could be seen in between narrow strips of light. The bridge was swaying slightly in the wind, making an eerie creaking and whining noise.

Florentino abruptly turned back to them and said quietly, 'You each have sixty seconds to cross; that's how long it is between searchlights.'

The men stared silently back at him, each one looking scared to death at what lay ahead. Frankie longed to run back the way he had come and take his chance with the enemy. Instead, he steadied his nerves by planting his feet firmly on the ground, and waited to be told when to move.

The loud, humming drone of the nearby electric plant, and the water crashing and roaring below them as it splashed along the rock sides, was a good cover. But the searchlights and the rickety bridge were another thing altogether, and dread weighted Frankie's chest.

Suddenly he realised that Florentino was staring in his direction. 'You first, Hubert,' he ordered in hushed tones. 'You'll need to creep silently so as not to make the bridge sway too much,' he advised. 'And make sure you do the crossing in sixty seconds and no more.'

At that moment of extreme stress, Frankie's RAF training came back into his mind. Recruits were taught from the very start that fear was weak, and being fearful meant you lacked moral fibre. He felt ashamed of exactly how scared he was right now.

However, he had no choice but to do as he was told; there was no going back now. Taking a deep breath, he crouched down and began edging towards the bridge. Then, putting one foot tentatively onto the first wooden slat, he pushed down hard to test his weight.

He looked back at Florentino, who nodded encouragingly. The wooden slats had taken his weight, so he placed his other foot out in front of him. Now his whole body was on the bridge and he couldn't turn back even if he wanted to, so he forced himself to keep going.

The bridge was swaying from side to side, and he could hear the water being churned up by the nearby electric plant, as it roared noisily beneath him. Frankie clung onto the rope at the side of the bridge, and walked gingerly forwards, one step at a time, while still crouching low. He was aware that the searchlight might descend at any given moment and reveal him to the enemy.

Plagued with thoughts of ending up in the river and drowning, Frankie could barely see where he was going in the pitch darkness, but he could hear Florentino's hushed voice urging him on from the side.

Then it happened. Frankie had almost reached the other end of the bridge, when he stepped forward into thin air, and realised too late that one of the wooden slats was missing. Before he could act, his leg shot out from beneath him, and his whole body suddenly plunged towards the swirling water below.

For a split second, he dangled dangerously in mid-air, with his body trapped firmly by the slats of the bridge. His leg and half of his torso were now leaning sideways, perilously close to the water. Clamping his lips together, he tried not to make a sound while the snoring of the guard still echoed around him.

The bridge swung precariously around as he clung tightly to its sides, the pain in his chest and ribs was excruciating as he stared down into the dark, roaring water below.

Frankie was convinced he was going to die here alone in this cold river in the French mountains. He would never see Scarlett again, and the thought occurred to him that perhaps it was what he deserved after what he'd done to his father.

He had just resigned himself to his life ending in tragedy, when he heard Dedee's low whisper across the bridge.

'Hubert!' she told him urgently. 'Get up now and clamber back onto the bridge. You have only seconds left before the searchlights reveal us all to the enemy!' she hissed.

Immediately jolted back to reality, Frankie realising that if he stayed where he was, he would endanger his brave helpers and the other two escapees. Using all his strength, he hoisted his leg up to join the other one, and pushed the rest of his body into a sitting position. Then, as quickly as was humanly possible, he straightened up and put one foot out. This time, thank God, he found a slat that wasn't broken.

Taking one tentative step at a time, and being urged on by Dedee, Frankie clung to the sides of the bridge and eventually made it to the other side. Dropping to his knees, he lay on the ground, gasping for breath, just as the searchlight lit up the bridge in startling clarity. Shivering with cold and shock, and convinced he would feel the cold steel of a gun on his head at any moment, Frankie waited for Florentino and the others to join him.

At two-minute intervals, he watched each person creep silently across the bridge. They had all witnessed his near miss on the broken slat, so that section was treated with extra caution. Frankie kept his eyes focused on the others, hoping against hope they would all get across safely.

At last, when they were all safely across, Florentino told them they had to get past the electric plant next. And for the first time since arriving at the other side of the bridge, Frankie noticed there was a window to the plant just behind him.

This time, Florentino went first, and the others followed him, silently crawling beneath the window of the plant, then scrambling up the steep slope and into the darkness of a railway tunnel.

Once in the tunnel, Frankie was relieved to be able to straighten up again, and to find that the pain in his ribs had eased. Quickly, they all made their way through three separate railway tunnels which ran alongside the river, then they began heading back downstream.

When they emerged from the third tunnel, Florentino gathered them together again. 'The mountain gets very steep here, so be careful everyone,' he warned. 'It is also rocky, and you will have to cling onto these rocks as we go up, otherwise you will fall back down again.'

He looked across at the railway tunnel they had just come through, then back at Dedee and the men. 'We have to go this way to avoid the guard posts along the railway track,' he explained, lifting his eyebrows apologetically.

As they began the ascent of the steep hill, Frankie looked up to see that the mountain was almost vertical so the climb was going to be another huge struggle for them all. However, he had made it across that dangerous river intact, even though it had almost ended in disaster, so he reckoned he could conquer this mountain.

As Florentino began leading them all uphill, Frankie stopped and watched them for a second. Their bodies were silhouettes in the darkness as they began the climb by clinging onto the rocks, which jutted out of the mountainside.

Then, summoning every shred of strength he had left, and forcing his aching limbs to move, Frankie began climbing after them.

Chapter Forty-Seven

Frankie opened his eyes to the sound of Dedee calling his name. They had arrived at a tiny cabin, hidden away in the mountainside, just as dawn was breaking. And after a meagre breakfast, he had slept the time away from the moment his head hit the pillow.

He shivered as he remembered he had been dreaming about his walk across the suspension bridge, and it had not been a good ending. The dream had left him feeling uneasy.

Wincing in pain, he clutched at his ribs and sat up, throwing off the blanket and swinging his legs off the thin mattress. 'What time is it?' he asked Dedee, as she busied herself in the corner of the hut, getting food together for the journey ahead.

Frankie tried not to dwell on how his bones ached with tiredness, reminding himself that this was the final safe house before they moved onto Rentario and San Sebastian.

Dedee turned around to regard him steadily. 'It is ten o'clock, Hubert, and we must go very soon,' she replied.

Frankie stood up and straightened out his crumpled clothes, before realising they were alone in the cabin. 'Where are the others?' he asked, shivering as the cold of the night hit him.

Dedee put the food into her rucksack and pulled on her coat. 'They are waiting outside for us,' she told him. 'No-one wanted to wake you, because you were having nightmares last night and calling out in your sleep, but now we have to go.'

Frankie didn't ask what he had been shouting about; he knew it would be to do with the bridge episode. He scrambled into his coat, quickly put on his shoes, and followed her out of the door.

Everyone was outside waiting patiently for him. 'I'm sorry I overslept,' he told them, worrying that they might think him cowardly to be having bad dreams.

Florentino gave him an encouraging nod. 'We let you sleep, Hubert. Do not worry about it; we all need extra rest sometimes. And don't think you are the only one to be afraid,' he said, holding Frankie's gaze. 'Some of us may not show it, but the fear is always present in these dangerous situations.'

When Armand gave Frankie a smile and Claude patted him on the back, he began to feel better, as he listened carefully to Florentino's instructions for the rest of their journey.

'The forest is still uphill for a long distance yet, comrades, so you will need all your energy to get to the top,' he warned. 'It gets better as San Sebastian comes into view, but bear in mind that this last part of the journey is the most dangerous.'

'Why is this part the most dangerous?' Claude asked uncertainly.

'Because of the risk of being ambushed,' Florentino replied bluntly. 'As usual, we must all keep our wits about us along the way.'

Frankie tried to push to the back of his mind any thoughts of being ambushed, and concentrated instead on the thought that they would soon arrive at a safe destination.

The next few hours proved more torturous than anything that had gone before, and with every moment that passed, Frankie wondered how to physically put one foot in front of the other.

The mountain was so steep that it was difficult to find the energy to keep going, and the loose shale underfoot made slipping easy, particularly when they couldn't see more than a foot in front of them at all times.

Frankie saw that Armand and Claude were also struggling, but Florentino was taking the mountain climb in his stride – clearly used to the journey.

Dedee was behind Frankie, and when he stopped to catch his breath, she peered at him with a sympathetic expression. 'Do not worry, Hubert,' she reassured him. 'We will reach safety very soon – not long to go now.'

'Thank you, Dedee,' he said. 'You and Florentino are doing a great job for us.' Frankie attempted to smile through his fatigue.

Dedee set her jaw. 'We always succeed, Hubert, do not doubt that – ever,' she replied firmly. 'Soon the terrain will be all downhill, and then it will be so much easier, you will see,' she added with a quirk of her head.

As they resumed their journey, Frankie found Dedee's words comforting, and he seemed to find the renewed strength to keep going.

At last, ahead of them, Florentino stopped abruptly. 'We are almost there, comrades,' he told them, pointing over the hill. 'There is San Sebastian, where a British Consulate official will be waiting to meet you,' he said. 'They will escort you on the train to Bilbao, then you will be taken by car to Madrid and onto Gibraltar,' he added, then triumphantly punched the air.

They all heaved a collective sigh of relief, and Frankie would like to have cheered, but knew he dare not make a loud noise.

'Thank you to both of you,' he whispered to Dedee, while looking up at Florentino. He was concerned that there wouldn't be time for goodbyes or expressing gratitude when they reached San Sebastian. 'You are two very brave and courageous people,' he added, and Armand and Claude agreed.

'We are proud and privileged to be able help our allied airmen,' Dedee told them, and Florentino nodded. 'And we will continue to do so until the end of the war. But remember, comrades, you are not safe until you reach Gibraltar.'

As they began the descent down the other side of the mountain towards San Sebastian, Frankie thought about Scarlett, and hoped that his sister Beverley had been able to make contact with her.

Hopefully, by now she would understand just how much he loved her, and when he returned from the war and they were together again, he had no intention of hiding her away the way Eric had. Coming to terms with the guilt over his father was entirely another matter, and one that Frankie would have to face once all this was over.

As their small party descended the mountainside, Frankie and the others were at last able to see San Sebastian through the trees. The town was sleeping, its houses silhouetted in the darkness against the backdrop of the mountains. The only noise was the sound of the sea below as the waves washed onto the shore.

Dedee gathered them in close and lowered her voice. 'You must all remember that although the threat of German soldiers has gone here, you still have the Spanish to fear. They will arrest you without hesitation if they learn who you are,' she told them solemnly. 'We will pass you over to the British Diplomat shortly, but as before in France, you have to be vigilant and act as natural as you can when you are travelling on the train.'

They all nodded in agreement, then scrambled down through the undergrowth into San Sebastian. As the light broke through the clouds, Florentino led them silently through the deserted streets towards an automobile, where the driver had the engine running and was waiting for them to arrive.

The journey had been arduous and long, but they had to remember that they were not out of danger yet. However, finding themselves off the uneven ground of the mountainside and back on solid ground was a miracle in itself, and a huge relief to Frankie's aching feet.

Frankie reflected that he had nearly lost his life on the suspension bridge over the river, but he had made it, along with Armand and Claude. All the gruelling hard work had paid off.

Chapter Forty-Eight

Frankie tried to relax on the three-hour train ride to Bilbao, but it wasn't easy to sit still. He constantly wanted to stand up and stretch out his back, and his sore ribs were more painful when he couldn't move around.

Inside the carriage, it was stiflingly hot, and even though the small windows were open, there didn't seem to be any fresh air coming in.

Armand was sitting on one side of him in the carriage, and Claude the other. The British Diplomat, a stocky fair-haired Englishman whose name was Thomas Blackford, sat opposite, casually reading a newspaper.

They had only completed one hour of the journey out of the three that it would take to reach Bilbao, and time stretched endlessly ahead of Frankie. The slight rocking of the carriage, and the constant rhythmic sound of the train on the tracks, was making him sleepy. But he had learnt his lesson after dozing on the train to Bayonne and his encounter with the German soldier, so he couldn't risk there being any Spanish soldiers on the train.

When Dedee and Florentino had passed the three of them over to Thomas Blackford, it had been hard to say goodbye to their brave saviours.

'Take care of yourself, Hubert,' Dedee had said, giving him a quick hug, and Florentino had shaken his hand.

Frankie had watched them walk away, in awe of their bravery and the way they had looked after and protected the three airmen on their journey. He would never forget Dedee and Florentino. They, and the other brave helpers of the resistance movement, had restored his faith in human nature.

As the train arrived at the next station, Frankie took the opportunity to change seats and sit by the window, hoping this would give him more fresh air and stop him from dropping off to sleep. Just then, the carriage door opened, and a young woman with shoulder-length blonde hair, and wearing a red polka dot dress, walked in and sat down in the seat Frankie had just vacated.

Her striking appearance immediately reminded him of Scarlett, and his heart ached to see her again. If only Scarlett's letter with her declaration of love had arrived a few weeks earlier, they could have had some time together before he was posted to RAF Exeter. And if he had known in time how she felt about him, he would never have cancelled his leave last December.

But now was not the time for regrets. He had to get himself home safely and, if Scarlett agreed, they would get married before he had to return to the RAF and to flying again.

At last, to Frankie's relief, they arrived at Bilbao train station and followed Thomas towards an automobile parked outside. Now they faced a six-hour journey to Madrid, followed by a two-day journey to Gibraltar. But once there, they would only be a plane ride away from home.

Chapter Forty-Nine

When Frankie and his two companions finally arrived at RAF New Front Airfield in Gibraltar, they were exhausted, but overjoyed to be back on safe ground. Before boarding the plane to the UK, the commanding officer addressed them in the mess room to explain what would happen next.

'Welcome to Gibraltar, fellow pilots,' he told them. 'You'll be flying back to Exeter airbase first, but before you're allowed to go home and have some leave, you'll need to be checked over in the military hospital.'

Frankie was dismayed at this, but knew it was for the best. When he'd fallen out of the Spitfire and injured his chest and ribs on landing, he had known he would need medical attention at some stage.

And while negotiating the mountainside, the pain had been excruciating at times. Although the soreness in his chest had disappeared, his ribs had continued to be painful over the course of his long and treacherous journey across France.

Frankie remembered that Scarlett had said in her letter there was something else he needed to know, something important – and it would have to wait until he got home. Frankie had no idea what Scarlett wanted to tell him; after all, what could be more important than what she had already said? But he looked forward to finding out soon.

Now, as Frankie gazed out of the window to watch the B-17 plane begin its descent towards the RAF Exeter Airfield, he turned to Armand and Claude, who were sitting behind him, and let out a whoop of joy. And for the first time, he realised he didn't know the real names of his two fellow RAF pilots.

But he knew it didn't matter. Nothing mattered now except that he was back on home soil, and would soon be holding his beloved Scarlett in his arms once again.

Chapter Fifty

Scarlett

Recently, my every waking – and sleeping – thought had centred on Frankie. In my dreams, I could see Frankie up ahead of me, but he was always just out of my reach.

Mrs Penny was out shopping this morning, so I left Annika playing on the floor in the front parlour and answered the knock on the front door, to find Frankie's sister standing on the doorstep.

'Beverley, what's flaming happened?' I gabbled, the breath catching in my throat. 'Sorry for the swearing, but... have you heard anything from Frankie?' I was desperate for news, and my heart raced at the sight of her. Right now, nothing else mattered as much as news of my beloved.

'Frankie is safe!' she said quickly, her eyes filling with tears.

Those three wonderful words spun in my head. *My darling Frankie was alive. He had survived!* The world swayed beneath my feet, and I clutched the doorframe to stop myself from falling. 'Oh, Beverley, that's wonderful!' I gasped.

I was finding it hard to breathe, and Beverley

quickly took hold of my arms and steered me through the hallway, into the front parlour, where she pushed me gently into the armchair. Leaning back in the chair, I closed my eyes and took a deep shaky breath, willing the world to steady itself.

When I opened my eyes, Beverley had taken her coat off and was gazing intently across at Annika. I understood immediately that she knew who the child's father was.

Taking her eyes off the baby briefly, Beverley looked at me with concern. 'Take a moment, Scarlett,' she soothed.

'I think I'm all right now. Please tell me, what happened?' I asked, sitting up straighter now the dizziness had subsided a little.

She nodded slowly. 'Thankfully, when Frankie's plane came down on a farm in the Loire valley in France, the farmer and his wife were friendly. They told him about the first safe house, and then he was helped across France by the resistance. Isn't that marvellous news?'

I felt numb, and then as if the flood gates had opened, the tears poured unheeded down my face. Slumping forwards, I put my head in my hands and cried. Relief coursed through me that the months of waiting and wondering had finally come to an end.

'Mama...' The sound of Annika's distressed voice brought me up short, and I quickly sat up, took a deep shuddering breath, and looked across at my daughter. 'It's alright, darling,' I told her, dabbing at my eyes. 'Mama's fine.'

Annika's bottom lip wobbled, but once she saw I wasn't crying any more, she went back to playing with her favourite rag doll.

'Are you alright, Scarlett?' Beverley asked, concern furrowing her brow.

I sniffed into the handkerchief and looked up at her. 'How do you know all this?' I asked.

Beverley's eyes lit up. 'When Frankie arrived back at the military base in Exeter, he telephoned me with the good news,' she told me. 'And he asked me to pass the message on to you as soon as I could.'

My heart missed a beat. 'I've been beside myself with worry,' I told her. 'That's such wonderful news! Is he all right? I mean, was he injured while he was in France?'

'Only some broken ribs when he fell out of the plane,' she explained, 'but nothing too serious. Thank God.'

Beverley's eyes had once again strayed towards Annika, who held the rag doll up towards her. Leaning over towards the child, Beverley took the doll and pretended to cuddle it. I watched this tender scene, and my heart filled with gratitude to this kind woman.

'Thank you for coming all this way to let me know about Frankie,' I said.

Beverley gave Annika back her doll and met my gaze. 'You're welcome,' she said, looking slightly uneasy. 'Scarlett, how old is your baby? It's just that she looks so much like...' she hesitated, unable it seemed to finish her sentence.

'Looks like Frankie?' I finished the sentence for her. 'Annika *is* his child, Beverley,' I said, lifting my chin and laying my cards on the table.

'Frankie doesn't know about her yet, though,' I added quickly, before she could reply. 'I'm going to tell him as soon as I can. I mean... as soon as he's home again.' Beverley's expression went from mild shock to something else. *Was that pride on her face?* I wondered.

'Oh, Scarlett. That means I'm her aunt then?' she

said, stating the obvious and looking as if I'd just given her the crown jewels. 'That's absolutely wonderful!' she added, clapping her hands together with joy.

I couldn't help laughing at her reaction. 'Oh, Beverley, I didn't expect you to say that, but I'm *blinking well* glad you did.' I felt a warm glow in my chest at her words. 'Would you like to hold her?' I asked, and when she nodded, I lifted Annika up from the floor and placed the baby on her lap.

Annika didn't yell as she sometimes did when she was held by someone she didn't know, instead she gazed up at her aunt in a bemused way and gave her a toothy smile.

'Hello, little one,' Beverley whispered. 'I'm so pleased to meet you,' she added softly, looking totally smitten with her new niece.

'Annika likes you,' I said, observing the two of them gazing at one another.

After a moment or two of watching them bond, I asked Beverley the burning question. 'Do you know when Frankie will be home?' I was trying to still my racing heart at the thought of holding him in my arms again.

Beverley glanced across at me before replacing Annika on the floor with her toys. 'Frankie said he would be writing to you from Botley's Park military hospital in Chertsey, where he's being checked over,' she said. 'Hopefully, you should get a letter from him soon, telling you when he will be home.'

The intense longing to see Frankie had become like a physical pain in my chest, and now as I tried to envisage our reunion, it was difficult to be patient.

Beverley's face looked flushed a while later as she stood on the doorstep saying goodbye, and she leaned towards Annika and gave the baby a big kiss before she left.

'Can I come and see her again?' she asked tentatively, her gaze intent on Annika, who simply giggled and held out her chubby arms.

'Beverley, you two are related,' I told her, feeling a lump form in my throat. 'Ring me before you make the trip here, but you are most welcome at any time. And I really do mean that.'

Her eyes sparkled with happiness at my words. 'Thank you, Scarlett, and I promise I won't leave it too long before coming back to see you both.' She was rewarded with another toothy grin from Annika.

***

That evening, when Mrs Penny told me that Ruby was on the phone, I took the call in the communal hallway, and relayed the good news about Frankie to my friend.

'Oh, Ruby. He's safe,' I told her, still hardly able to believe it myself. 'Frankie's in a military hospital right now, but he'll be home soon,' I explained through tears of joy.

'That's great news, Scarlett. And what was Beverley's reaction when she met Annika?' Ruby asked tentatively down the telephone.

Dabbing at my eyes, I confessed how I'd come clean about the baby. 'When I told her she was Frankie's daughter, she loved Annika. Beverley really bonded with her. I just hope that Frankie loves her, too, when he meets her.'

'Scarlett, I'm sure Frankie will adore her,' Ruby reassured me down the phone, and I hoped she was right.

Chapter Fifty-One

Frankie's strong arms closed around me as his lips came down on mine. And as he deepened the kiss, my body was on fire with love for him.

A loud knock at the bedroom door jolted me from this dream-like state, and I pulled myself reluctantly out of his arms. 'I'll… just get that,' I gasped, trying to still my racing heart and tear myself away from the liquid desire in Frankie's hazel eyes.

Mrs Penny stood in the doorway looking slightly awkward, and I could hear Annika's cries coming from downstairs. I leaned closer towards her, concerned for my daughter.

'Is Annika all right?' I asked anxiously, before glancing back into the room where Frankie was now standing at the window gazing outside. 'Do you need me to come downstairs?'

Mrs Penny smiled kindly. 'Don't worry. You know how I love looking after her. Annika is fine. But I wanted to ask you if I could take her to the park? She's getting a bit restless and needs some fresh air.'

'Of course, that's fine,' I agreed. 'Her coat's hanging up in the hallway. It's a lovely day, so enjoy the sunshine.'

After Mrs Penny had gone downstairs, I closed the door to find Frankie standing behind me with a frown etched between his brows. 'Who's Annika?' he asked.

'Annika is my friend Ruby's child,' I said, telling myself I would explain the truth to him later. 'I was caring for her today while Ruby's at work, but then Mrs Penny offered to look after her because you were going to be here.'

Now was not the right time to introduce Frankie to his daughter, I reasoned with myself; we needed this time together first. My reluctance to tell him, though, was something I didn't care to examine right now.

'Now, where were we?' I said, as Frankie offered me a slow, sexy smile.

He stepped closer to me and stared into my face. 'Oh, Scarlett, I've missed you so much,' he said, his voice hoarse with desire. 'I don't know how I've survived all these months without you. I really don't. It's been so hard…'

I couldn't speak. The words had lodged in my throat as I reached out for Frankie. He had taken his jacket off, and as I went into his arms, I could feel the heat from his body through his shirt, making desire shoot through my veins.

My hands were trembling, and my pulse pounded in my ears as he pulled my dress up over my head, and coerced me towards the bed. As we tumbled onto the mattress together, the months of worry and waiting for this beautiful man to come home to me, had finally ended. For the first time ever, we could love each other freely.

'Oh God, Scarlett, you are so beautiful,' Frankie moaned softly, stroking my hair and gazing at me longingly. Then a shadow passed across his face. 'I'm sorry, Scarlett… about my father…' he said, without taking his eyes off my face.

'Me too, Frankie,' I soothed. 'But let's talk about Eric later.' We would have to address the guilt we both carried over his father at some stage, I knew that, but not now.

But as I pulled him gently towards me, I felt him wince in pain. 'What is it?' I asked, pulling back in alarm.

Frankie shook his head. 'Nothing really. My ribs are still a bit sore,' he admitted. 'Nothing to worry about; they will get better eventually.'

It was then I remembered he had been injured when he had fallen from his plane over France. 'I'll be careful,' I promised him.

He nodded wordlessly, and we came together in a haze of passion. As our lovemaking intensified and we became as one, I finally understood that he was the only man in the world for me. And that whatever happened when he returned to fight, whatever fate had in store for him in enemy-infested skies, we would always have these precious moments together.

A while later, as we lay in one another's arms reluctant to move, I heard Annika and Mrs Penny downstairs. It seemed they had returned from the park and were now in the front parlour.

Pulling the sheet around me, I sat up and looked down at Frankie. 'I love you,' I told him, and our lips came together once again, gentler now that the passion had been sated for a while.

When he smiled back at me, I swung my legs off the bed. 'Let's go downstairs for a cup of tea,' I suggested, with a fluttery feeling in my chest.

'Do we have to?' Frankie replied, a hurt look on his face. 'I'd say we have a lot more catching up to do,' he murmured, giving me another one of those slow lazy smiles of his.

Turning away from him, I began to dress, all the time avoiding his intense gaze. My heart raced as I realised I couldn't put this off any longer. The time had come to introduce Frankie to his daughter, but he still hadn't moved from the bed.

'We have loads of catching up to do, that's true, but I'm gasping for a cup of tea right now,' I told him light-heartedly, while fighting the urge to get back into bed with him and lose myself in his beautiful body.

It took all my willpower to walk away from Frankie, but I knew he would follow me downstairs. And sure enough, a while later he strolled into the front parlour where I was playing with Annika on my lap.

The sight of his tall, well-built frame filing the doorway almost made my heart stop, and Mrs Penny exchanged a meaningful look across the room with me. 'I have beds to change,' she announced, before striding briskly from the room.

Annika stopped playing with her doll and gazed up at Frankie, then her bottom lip trembled, and she burst into noisy tears. I pulled her little body in close to mine and she soon quietened down, but she still stared warily at Frankie.

He sat down on the settee and regarded us both, watching closely as Annika wriggled quickly out of my arms and bent down to retrieve a different doll which was lying on the floor by my feet.

As she plonked down on the floor and started playing with the doll, my mind was in turmoil, wondering how best to tell Frankie, but knowing there was only one way. Taking a deep breath, I stared across at him.

'Frankie...' I began, looking at the baby. 'Meet your

daughter Annika,' I said, before lifting my chin and filling my lungs with air.

He gaped at me. 'Oh my Lord, Scarlett,' he said, his eyes firmly on Annika now.

He stood up abruptly and crouched down beside the child, gazing at her as she played happily, then he lifted his head towards me with a questioning gaze. 'I can't believe it. Is she really mine?' He frowned slightly. 'I thought you said she was your friend's baby?'

'I'm sorry, Frankie, I lied to you earlier.' I smiled apologetically. 'I've been nervous about telling you,' I explained truthfully, 'and I thought we needed some time alone before I introduced you to her.'

Annika chose that exact moment to stop playing and crawl towards the door. 'Look at her, she's a feisty little minx,' I told him, getting to my feet to shut the door before she could disappear through it and get up to mischief.

Frankie's eyes were on me as I lifted a wriggling Annika up and placed her back down on the carpet with her toys. However, she arched her back in protest at this imposition of her freedom, and let out a loud yell of frustration.

When at last the room was quiet again and I'd found a biscuit for Annika to munch on, Frankie came over and sat beside me. 'How old is she?' he asked, staring tenderly across at his daughter.

I followed his gaze and took in Annika's blonde head of curls. 'She's nine months old, Frankie,' I replied, and I turned to look into that gorgeous face of his. 'Can't you see the likeness? Annika looks just like you.'

Frankie tilted his head thoughtfully. 'She has your turquoise eyes,' he said, shooting me a look of pure love before pulling me urgently into his arms. 'Oh, Scarlett, I wish you'd told me before.' His words were muffled against my clothes.

I had no excuse for not telling him. I could have mentioned Annika when I wrote to him at the training depot in Canada, declaring my love. But at that time I was worried that he would feel obliged to be with me once he knew we had a child together. And even though I longed for us to be a family, I had to be sure that he loved me for myself.

'It would have been nice to know about her,' Frankie continued regretfully. 'All that time, moving across France, the only thing that kept me going was you. If I'd known I also had a daughter...' his voice shook a little as he spoke.

I looked deep into his hazel eyes, took hold of his hand, and tried to choose my words carefully. 'I'm sorry, Frankie. I knew I was pregnant when you came to see me about Eric's death,' I told him truthfully. 'But I couldn't bring myself to tell you that you were going to become a father when your own father had just died.'

I tore my gaze from his and stared into the middle distance. 'It just didn't seem the right time.' I said sadly. 'And then your plane came down over France...' I couldn't finish the sentence remembering how Beverley had told me Frankie was missing and I had been left wondering if I'd ever see him again.

He stared at me longingly. 'If only you had known then just how much I was missing you, and how much I loved you,' he said simply. 'Perhaps then you wouldn't have had doubts about telling me about the baby.'

It was time for the truth, even though it hurt. 'It was

the guilt over Eric which stopped me admitting my true feelings for you, Frankie,' I confessed. 'I was in denial because I loved him, too. Not in the same way I loved you, but I *did* love him. And the way he found us together was heart-breaking.'

He nodded sadly. 'I understand... but from the moment I met you, I knew I was in love,' he replied. 'I couldn't admit it then, of course, because I was insanely jealous of my father.'

'It was the same for me, Frankie,' I whispered, my eyes searching his face. This was the truth, even though I didn't know it myself at the time.

Frankie shifted uneasily in his seat. 'Scarlett...' he began. 'I still feel guilty about my father, so how do I get over that?' he said, his voice cracking as he spoke.

I shrugged wearily, knowing that if we were to carry on our lives in this way, we somehow had to come to terms with what had happened to Eric. 'Frankie, please don't torture yourself this way,' I said, trying to find the right words.

'It was true we should not have come together the way we did, when I was still entangled with your father. But the thing is... you were my destiny. I truly believe this, because I had been dreaming of you for years before you *actually* walked into my life.'

'Really? But that's ridiculous,' Frankie blinked at me with disbelief on his face. 'You must be mistaken. How could that happen?'

I had thought about this long and hard while Frankie was missing, and had concluded that I would *not* tell him about my gift. Only one other person knew about that part of me – my friend Ruby – and that's the way I wanted it to stay.

I leaned in closer to Frankie. 'I really don't know,

but the point is that as soon as I saw you, I knew you were the one for me. This sounds kind of odd, I realise, but even if Eric hadn't been killed at Tobruk, I believe you and I would have still ended up together.'

Frankie held tightly to my hand for a moment. 'That does make me feel better about my father,' he said. 'And after all, we do have this little one to think of now.' He gazed across at Annika, who looked up at her father and gave him a beaming smile.

Chapter Fifty-Two

The familiar smell of incense and wood polish filled my nostrils as the wedding march rang through the air in St Peter's Church in Brighton. In the absence of a father to give me away, Ruby was beside me as I walked slowly down the aisle in my cream, floor-length dress.

When I reached the altar and stopped next to Frankie, I saw the look of nervous anticipation on his face, and I felt breathless with excitement.

This was a day I had longed for; the moment I didn't think would ever come. But here I was at last, getting married to the love of my life.

'Mama, Mama!'

The sound of Annika's voice echoed in the church, and I glanced behind me to where Mrs Penny was holding my beautiful daughter on her lap. I offered Annika a small smile, and she grinned and held out her pudgy little arms towards me.

Frankie touched my hand, sending a tingle of pleasure up my arm. He looked devastatingly handsome in his RAF uniform of smart blue-grey jacket and trousers. And as I turned back towards him and we exchanged a look of love, the minister began the ceremony.

'We are gathered here in the presence of God, family, and

friends, to unite Frank Johnson and Scarlett Cunningham in holy matrimony. Marriage is an honourable estate, and is therefore not to be entered into lightly, but reverently, advisedly, soberly, and with God's blessing.'

I listened to the words with joy in my heart, and after Frankie had said his vows, it was my turn. 'I, Scarlett Cunningham, take you, Frank Johnson, to be my lawfully wedded husband, to have and to hold from this day forward, for better, for worse, for richer, for poorer, in sickness and in health…'

As I recited my wedding vows, a worry niggled at the back of my mind. The thought of Frankie having to return to RAF Exeter Airfield was like a dark cloud hanging over me. Forcing my mind back to the present moment, I tried to forget thoughts of the future, and focus on the joyous event happening right now.

'You may now kiss the bride!' the vicar said enthusiastically a moment later, and there was a round of applause from our few wedding guests who were sitting in the pews.

Gazing into Frankie's face, I watched his mouth curve into a beatific smile, and my heart swelled with love for him. Everything I had gone through in the past, all the trials and tribulations I had lived through, had been worth it for this one precious moment.

If I were honest with myself, this is what I had been looking for all my life. All those years ago, material possessions had been my goal and all I wanted, but now I understood that what I *really* wanted was love.

'Well, Mrs Johnson, what do you say?' Frankie teased, pulling me into his arms and placing his warm lips onto mine.

My pulse raced as he deepened the kiss, and every nerve ending in my body came alive. For a brief moment, we lost ourselves in our own little world until a polite cough sounded behind us, reminding Frankie and me that we were not alone. Breathlessly, we pulled away from each other, and then turned to walk back down the aisle.

As we stepped outside the church into the late afternoon sunshine, I reflected on how strange it was that my sixth sense had disappeared since Frankie's return from France. I had no idea why this was. Maybe it would return to me one day, but if not, I would not miss it.

Lifting a hand up to shade my eyes from the sun, I spotted Ruby and little Noah standing amongst the small gathering of guests. She stepped towards me and lifted Noah up so that he could throw some confetti, then he giggled and wriggled in her arms.

'You okay, Ruby?' I asked my friend, unable to keep the silly grin off of my face.

'We're good thanks,' she said, pulling Noah further into her arms and giving him a little squeeze.

My heart twisted at the sadness and resignation reflected in Ruby's eyes. She had lost so much when Reilly died, but had still found it in her heart to be there for me. I knew she was genuinely happy that I'd found love with Frankie.

'Hopefully things will change soon,' I whispered. I was acutely aware that under that pretty hat, which was pulled low over Ruby's head, there were bruises – a parting gift from Dick McCarthy before he returned to the Royal Navy.

She looked quickly away and busied herself with Noah, but I could see she was unconvinced. Her reaction, though, made me all the more determined to find a way of getting her and Noah away from Dick

McCarthy before the end of the war.

A while later, after we had posed for photographs outside the church, Mrs Penny brought Annika over to stand with Frankie and myself.

'Congratulations to you both,' she said, hugging us tightly.

'Mama, I want you!' Annika yelled loudly, and I lifted my daughter into my arms and stroked her fair curls.

Later that day, after Annika was tucked up in her bed and Frankie and I were alone in Mrs Penny's front parlour, I found myself pouring my heart out to him.

'Oh, Frankie, I wish you didn't have to go back to RAF Exeter,' I whispered, the tears pricking the back of my eyes as he held me in his arms.

For once I had said what was in my heart, even though I understood that he had no choice in the matter; there was nothing either of us could do to stop the inevitable.

Frankie sat up straighter, and ran a hand through his dark hair. 'Me too, Scarlett,' he admitted, taking hold of my hand. 'I'd much rather stay here with you and Annika. You do know that, don't you?'

I could only nod in resignation. 'We have to be thankful that at least you won't be flying a Spitfire any more,' I reflected. I understood this was a bone of contention for Frankie, but for me it was a huge relief.

After a recent medical before a return to active service, the doctors had told Frankie that complications from his rib injury, sustained in France, meant he would not be flying any more for the foreseeable future. Instead, he would now be working on the ground at RAF Exeter airfield.

Frankie looked at me sadly. 'Flying is what I love

doing, though, Scarlett, and the thought of working in the office is not my idea of fun. But I can see it's for the best, or so the doctors say anyway,' he said.

He frowned slightly with concern. 'What about you and Annika?' he asked. 'Wouldn't it be better if you both returned to live in Lewes? You would get away from any threat of bombs here in Brighton, and it would be safer for you both.'

The idea had already crossed my mind, so Frankie's suggestion did not come as a complete surprise. I'd recently received a letter from the wife of the serving officer who was renting the house, informing me that she was moving out of my house in Lewes, and thanking me for allowing her to use it.

'I'll certainly consider it, Frankie,' I told him thoughtfully. I knew I would miss my ARP duties in Brighton, but was aware that it might be the safest option.

That, though, was a decision to be made at a later date. We had so little time before Frankie had to return to base, so we needed to make the most of our time together. And Frankie needed to get to know Annika better.

'Maybe we shouldn't think about the future right now,' I said, giving him a steady look. 'The week ahead will pass in a flash, and then Annika and I will be all alone once again. So let's enjoy it while we can.'

Chapter Fifty-Three

April 1945

'It's been a long time coming, and I hope in the future that you and Noah will be very happy here in Isfield,' I told Ruby, relieved that at last that she had managed to escape from Brighton and her bullying husband.

It was a warm afternoon in April, and on arrival in Isfield earlier that day, we had been enchanted to find the village full of apple blossom trees. The sun was shining down on us as we unloaded boxes from the removal van, bringing the promise of summer just around the corner.

Ruby touched my hand, and her gaze was soft, as we stood in the hallway of the large Victorian house. 'Thanks so much for all your help, Scarlett,' she said. 'I could never have done it without you,' she added with a hitch in her voice.

As the years had passed and the war progressed, Ruby and I had discussed when it would be best for her and Noah to move out of Brighton. Picking the right time was crucial, even though it had been hard for her to be patient.

With Dick away fighting, it was best for Ruby to move out of the family home before the war came to an end, and before he left the Royal Navy. Once he was back home for good, we both knew her chance to escape his controlling ways would be lost forever.

We had set a date to put this plan into action, and with the money from Ruby's inheritance – and behind Dick's back – she had purchased this beautiful Victorian detached property.

With four bedrooms, a front and back parlour, and a large kitchen, the house was far too big for just Ruby and Noah. But as time was running out, the deciding factor had been its location in a small village called Isfield, hidden deep in the Sussex countryside.

Once the purchase of the house was finalised, it was only a matter of picking the right time for Ruby and Noah to move in. From today, mother and son would be living here permanently, and no longer have to endure Dick's menacing presence.

Reports had been filtering through from the newspapers that the war was coming to an end, and Germany's surrender was imminent. The whole of the country was waiting with bated breath for this to happen.

Ruby walked over to the window and gazed out at Noah and Annika, now both three and a half years old, running madly around in the big front garden, shrieking with laughter.

'Are you all right?' I asked, aware that even though Ruby looked happier than I'd seen her in a long time, the worried frown was back on her face.

She turned to me and attempted to smile. 'Noah looks more like Reilly as each day goes by,' she observed, her eyes brimming with tears. 'Oh, Scarlett! If only Reilly were here with me right now,' she said, wiping away the tears. 'Sometimes I just can't bear it. I miss him *so much*.' She sobbed as she covered her face with her hands.

Guilt flooded through me at Ruby's words. 'I'm sorry, Ruby. I wish I hadn't told you that he might still be alive; it was blinking stupid of me.' I shook my head, annoyed at myself. 'I didn't mean to give you false hope, and as I told you at the time, it was more a sense that Reilly could be still alive than a certainty.'

She dabbed at her face with a handkerchief and then touched my arm lightly. 'I don't blame you, Scarlett, how could I? You told me because you thought it might help. And the thing is... I still feel as if he *is* alive. Every day, I feel sure that somewhere Reilly still lives,' she tilted her head regretfully. 'But maybe that's because I want him to be alive,' she added sadly.

With no words of comfort for Ruby, I could only hope that somehow Reilly had survived the war and hadn't been able to get home yet. After all, Frankie had been missing for months on end after his plane went down over France, and he had eventually returned to me.

However, it had been years since Ruby had heard that Reilly was missing, so it was hard to keep the hope going, even though my own feeling – like Ruby's – was that he was still alive.

I tried to choose my words carefully so as not to add to her torment. 'So many men have been lost during this war, and until it ends, we won't know how many have survived,' I reasoned.

Ruby nodded dismally before lifting her chin determinedly. 'You're right, Scarlett. For now I have to concentrate on looking after Noah, and getting him away from Dick was a step in the right direction,' she said, then added more brightly, 'At last I've done it,

I've escaped him. And I'll concentrate on making a good life for us both here in Isfield.'

'Too blinking right you will, Ruby. Remember, this is your chance to be away from that vicious bully you married, and his unpredictable temper. I'm sure you'll both be very happy here. Noah certainly looks excited playing in that garden,' I said, glancing towards the window.

Ruby nodded thoughtfully, looking a bit more like her old self. 'We must see each other often, too, mustn't we? At least once a week,' she said, before turning away to open a box full of kitchen crockery. 'Promise me we can meet up regularly?' she persisted, looking at me with wide eyes.

I strode over and gave her a big hug. 'Try and keep me away,' I replied, then held her at arm's length. 'Noah and Annika are so close, too, and they'll need to see each other often.'

Ruby stared longingly into the middle distance. 'Hopefully, Dick won't find me here...' she began. When she turned towards me, her eyes were full of fear, as if seeking reassurance.

'Why would he come after you?' I asked, hoping I was right. 'Knowing Dick, once he realises that you've left him, he'll move onto the next unfortunate woman who happens to fall for his charms.'

Ruby let out a long sigh and gave me a shaky smile as she turned to unpack the next box. 'You're absolutely right, Scarlett.'

A few weeks later, the RAF bombed Hitler's 'Eagle's Nest' in the Alps, in one of their final bombing raids before the end of the war.

Then, at the end of April came the news that had been eagerly anticipated by the nation – Hitler was dead, Germany had surrendered to the Allies, and the war was over. We had moved Ruby and Noah out of Brighton and away from Dick McCarthy just in time.

Chapter Fifty-Four

Spring 1947

'Oh my God, Scarlett, it was such a huge shock seeing him again last week, after all this time.' Ruby's eyes shone with happiness, and her voice was full of excitement as she explained about her reunion with Reilly.

We were drinking tea and sitting at the kitchen table in her large kitchen. It was late afternoon, and I'd travelled over on the bus from my home in Lewes so that Noah and Annika could play together and we could catch up.

'When I first saw Reilly, I wasn't even sure it was him at first,' Ruby explained. 'As you can imagine, he's changed quite a bit.' She knitted her brow as she spoke. 'It was only when he spoke to me that I knew it was him.'

The war had been over for two years now, and Ruby and Noah were happily settled in their large house in Isfield. It seemed to the world that Ruby had moved on and accepted that she would never see her beloved Reilly again, but the sadness was often reflected in her brown eyes, and I had always understood how much she missed him.

Now it seemed Reilly had returned, and the sense I'd had that he was still alive had finally come true. 'Good grief, Ruby,' I said, shocked that after all these years, Reilly had re-appeared in Ruby's life. 'What exactly happened then?'

Even though my second sight had been failing lately, a week ago I had dreamt this would happen. But I had thought it best not to tell Ruby about my dream, as there seemed no point in giving her what might be *even more* false hope.

She took a deep breath and leaned back in her chair. 'We were out for a walk, and Noah wanted to go on a train ride.' She smiled and glanced towards the garden where her son was busy climbing an apple tree, then she met my gaze. 'You know how much he loves trains,' she said wistfully. 'Train mad he is.'

I nodded thoughtfully, eager for her to get to the bit where she'd found Reilly. 'It's unlike you to venture out of the village, though. So what made you do it this time?'

Since Ruby had moved to Isfield, she had made sure that she and Noah stayed in the village, to avoid anyone who might know Dick seeing them.

'I know, I know…' Ruby looked down at her hands and bit down on her lower lip before continuing. 'Something made me take a chance on leaving the village; I don't know what it was. Maybe it was because Noah was desperate for a change of scene after the long winter, and it was a such lovely spring day.'

She widened her eyes at me. 'As you know, I wouldn't normally go anywhere near the coast, but that day I was feeling a bit reckless. Noah was restless, so on the spur of the moment we decided to take the train into Hastings.'

I shrugged. 'I guess you had to take a chance on leaving Isfield at sometime, although you should definitely avoid Brighton,' I warned. 'What happened when you got to Hastings?'

Ruby looked steadily back at me. 'When we got there, Noah ran ahead of me, as he'd spotted someone on the beach painting a picture.' She smiled at the memory. 'I'm convinced he'll be an artist one day. Anyway, I followed Noah towards the man, and when I got there, I found it was Reilly!'

'Unbelievable, Ruby. I can hardly believe it, and after all this time, too!'

'Exactly. I thought I was dreaming at first,' she admitted. 'I wasn't even sure it was Reilly at first. I mean... the man looked like him, but wasn't him, if you know what I mean?'

'I do know what you mean.' I realised that whatever had happened to Reilly during the war and afterwards would undoubtedly have aged him.

The sound of Annika shouting at Noah to come down out of the tree drew my eyes towards the window. Beside me, Ruby had gone quiet, and I braced myself to ask the important question.

I turned back to her and laid a gentle hand on her arm. 'Ruby, what happened to Reilly during the war, and afterwards, to keep him away from you?' I asked softly, and I watched her struggling to contain her emotions.

She told me shakily how Reilly had been sent to the battle of Crete, and when the enemy closed in, he had been put on a safe ship destined for Egypt. Unfortunately, the Germans had sunk the ship before it got very far from the shore, but Reilly and several others managed to swim to safety.

'Take your time,' I told her as she dabbed at her eyes with a hankie. I could see how upsetting the re-telling of Reilly's story was for her.

'I'm all right, Scarlett,' she told me falteringly, before continuing. 'Reilly told me that as soon he reached the shore, he was captured by the enemy and taken to a concentration camp in Italy. Soon after that he was moved to a camp in Berlin, and that was where he spent the duration of the war,' she said, staring dismally down at her empty hands.

For a moment we were both lost in our own thoughts. 'Poor Reilly, he must have suffered terribly,' I reflected, having read how awful the prison camps were. 'But I don't understand what happened after the war. I mean, it's been over for two years now, so why didn't he come and find you, Ruby?'

'That's easy. Reilly heard that I was married and had moved away. Don't forget, he had no idea about Noah,' she explained. 'He just thought I'd found someone else.'

Sadness filled me at poor Reilly's disappointment at finally getting home only to find that Ruby had married another man. 'Has he told you much of what happened to him during his time in the camp?' I asked tentatively.

She shook her head. 'Reilly hasn't said much yet. I got the sense that he's skimmed over the surface of what really went on during that awful time. But I can tell just by looking at him that he's a changed man.' She rubbed at a spot between her eyes and then let out a long sigh. 'At least he's back now, and together we can overcome all the other obstacles.'

'Thank God for that,' I said, feeling heat radiate through my chest at Ruby's good fortune. 'Is he going to come and live with you here?' I asked, remembering that Ruby was still wed to Dick, so she and Reilly would not be able to get married.

She raised her chin and gave me a determined look. 'Reilly is leaving his lodgings in Hastings and moving in here with us next week,' she told me. 'I'm a bit worried. You know what small villages are like for gossip,' she added.

'Maybe you need to get your story straight before Reilly moves in then?' I suggested, remembering how I had told the other ARP wardens that I was a widow when I was expecting Annika.

My heart went out to Ruby. All she wanted was to be with the father of her child, the man she thought she had lost, yet she could now be judged and even ostracised by people in the village for it.

'Don't worry, Scarlett, we've already thought of that. We will be telling the other villagers that Reilly had amnesia after a war injury,' she explained, 'and that prevented him from finding me when the war ended. So, now that he has recovered his memory, we have been reunited.'

'That's a good idea, but does that tie in with what you told them when you first arrived in Isfield?' I said, concerned that Ruby's white lies would be found out.

Ruby nodded. 'Yes, it fits in with my story about being a war widow after my husband went missing, presumed dead, during the war.'

'I'm so happy for you,' I told her. 'You of all people deserve happiness.'

Ruby looked back at me with tears of happiness in her eyes. 'Thank you, Scarlett, and for all your support over the years,' she said.

Just then Annika began crying, and we both rushed

out into the garden to find she had attempted to climb the apple tree and fallen down and scraped her knee.

As I comforted my daughter, I glanced across at Ruby's face, flushed with happiness. I hoped and prayed that she and Reilly would at last have the life they deserved, now that they had finally found each other again.

Chapter Fifty-Five

August 1951

Waking up in a cold sweat, I glanced across at the clock on the bedside table and saw it was already 7.30am. Unusually, I had slept past my normal waking time.

The dream had been vivid, and I wasn't used to this happening anymore. Needing the comfort of Frankie's arms, I instinctively reached across the bed towards him, but his side of the bed was cold and empty. He had already left for work at the shipyard. Swinging my legs out of bed, I went downstairs in search of a cup of tea.

'Get dressed for school, honey,' I told Annika as I passed her room on the way down.

She nodded distractedly at me, while playing with her dolls. At nine years old, she was growing up fast, and it was hard to believe how the years had flown by so quickly.

As I waited for the kettle to boil, I thought about what I had seen in the dream, and pondered what to tell Ruby. I closed my eyes and leaned against the kitchen worktop as the images came rushing back to me.

My heart began to race as I once again saw Dick

McCarthy. His face was contorted in anger, and he was pursuing Ruby through the hallway of her house, while young Noah ran away from the scene, leaving her to face Dick alone.

Ruby was cowering in the corner of the kitchen, and as Dick lurched towards her, I saw him rip the amethyst necklace from around her neck. The last image was the worst, though, and it sent ice cold shivers up my spine.

The worst thing was that I had no idea when this awful thing would happen, but I knew I had to warn Ruby. Breathless with fear, I walked into the hallway, lifted the telephone from its cradle, and began dialling Ruby's number. Suddenly a high-pitched scream filled the air.

I froze and dropped the telephone, and as it landed on the floor with a clatter, I looked up to see Annika tumbling head over heels down the stairs.

With my heart thumping in my ears, I rushed to my daughter's side. The breath caught in my throat as I stared down at Annika, who was lying completely still at the bottom of the stairs, with one leg stuck out at an odd angle, and looking as if she were dead.

Chapter Fifty-Six

December 1954

The tightness in my chest increased, and I shivered as an icy wind blew across the graveyard of St Margaret's Church in Isfield. My eyes were drawn across the landscape towards the old mill, which was just visible in the distance, and thoughts of the events, which had led up to this sad day.

As flurries of snow landed on my face and white droplets covered my black wool coat, I was jolted back to the present as the minister's words rang through the air.

'In the name of God, the merciful Father, we commit the body of Reilly Brownlow to the peace of the grave,' he said solemnly, with his head buried over his prayer book.

I leaned in closer to Frankie, who was holding onto Annika. And as he slipped his hand into mine, I tried to stem the tears, which were threatening.

Ruby was standing on the other side of me, with her gaze set on the wooden coffin below. She held a single red rose in one hand, and was clutching Noah close into her body with the other. The boy's dark head of hair and young face was also turned downwards, and tears dripped silently down his cheeks.

Stepping forwards, the vicar picked up a handful of earth and threw it down upon the coffin. 'From ashes to ashes and dust to dust…' he said. Then he looked across at Ruby and indicated that she could do the same.

She nodded her understanding and let go of Noah, stepped closer to the graveside, and threw the rose onto the lid of the coffin.

'Goodbye, my love,' she murmured softly, her voice breaking on the words. 'I'll never forget you…'

Then, as if she could hold it in no longer, Ruby covered her mouth with her hand and let out a heart-rending sob. My heart lurched at the terrible sound, and I stepped forwards to quickly steer her away from the edge of the grave, and back towards Noah.

As he put his hand in hers, Noah looked up at me with such sadness on his face that I had to fight the urge to take him in my arms. 'Your mama will be all right, Noah,' I reassured him, hoping I was right in this when she looked so broken. 'Frankie and I will look after you both, don't worry.'

Noah lifted his chin and nodded bravely at me, and my heart ached for this boy who had been through so much already in his young life. I could only hope that recent events would not have a lasting effect on him, and the guilt over his father's prison sentence for manslaughter wouldn't affect him too much.

Ruby had taken a while to recover from the injuries inflicted by Dick, but her worry over Reilly, after his arrest, had proved harder to overcome. And in the end, they had only had four short years together before the catastrophic and tragic events took place.

Reilly had only wanted to protect his son, but in the

end, he – and they – had paid a heavy price. Ruby had lost the love of her life for the second time, and young Noah the father he loved.

Dick McCarthy might well have got what he deserved, but it was Reilly who had paid the ultimate price that day in the mill. And there was no doubt that he had been a victim, not only of Dick's jealousy, but also of his experiences during his time in the POW camp in Berlin during WW2.

***

After the funeral service, everyone filtered back to Ruby's house, and together we passed out cups of tea and sandwiches, while I thought about the fateful day when Dick had eventually tracked Ruby down.

I constantly lived with the guilt that I hadn't been able to forewarn Ruby about Dick's visit, but when I told Frankie how I felt, he was adamant that I could not have done more.

'How could you have warned Ruby?' he told me. 'You didn't know Dick was going to find her in Isfield after all these years, or that he was going to attack her like that…'

Frankie had dipped his head and rubbed a hand across his forehead. 'Sick bastard,' he muttered, then looked up me. 'I mean, who would do that to a woman?'

It was then I remembered that I'd never told Frankie about my gift, and because it rarely happened to me anymore, I'd had no need to mention it in recent years.

'Dick McCarthy was a bloody nasty piece of work, that's for sure,' I'd replied. 'But thank God Ruby came through the attack in one piece.'

When I finally saw Ruby a few days after she'd been released from hospital, she was black and blue, but there were no lasting injuries. I'd visited her at home and explained about Annika's accident, and how my daughter had fallen down the stairs the day Dick had attacked Ruby, and suffered concussion and a broken leg.

'How did Dick know where to find you, Ruby?' I had asked, intrigued as to how he had discovered she was living in the tiny village of Isfield.

At first, she'd been reluctant to tell me, and just stared dismally down at her hands. 'Ruby?' I'd urged, experiencing a bad feeling in the pit of my stomach.

'Remember, Scarlett, Dick was not only violent, but he was also a liar and a cheat,' she told me finally, her face darkening. 'He said he'd overheard you talking to the barman in The Fortune of War pub,' she told me uneasily.

'What? Oh my God, Ruby,' I stammered. 'But I never saw Dick in the pub!' I said, while wracking my brains for when I'd had a sighting of him. 'I would have steered clear of him if I had,' I'd assured her, wringing my hands together.

Ruby didn't answer for a moment. Instead, she lightly rubbed a hand across her forehead where a dark bruise marked her head. I waited for her answer, afraid now that I had done something I would regret forever.

Lifting her gaze to mine, she had explained. 'Do you remember I told you how Dick used to sit in the corner booth of that pub, and hide? And how he used to watch me when I first met him?' she questioned. 'It's more than likely that's what he was doing when he overheard you talking in the pub. It's not your fault,

330

Scarlett. How could you have known he was there?'

The thought that Dick had heard me talking about Ruby's hidden location in Isfield, was truly mortifying, and just one more thing I found hard to accept in this devastating turn of events.

The cold weight of blame had already been heavy that day, even though I knew Frankie was right. I could not have stopped events unfolding, but if Annika hadn't fallen down the stairs, there was no doubt I would have been able to warn Ruby in time.

After the funeral, Frankie drove us back along the icy roads to Lewes, while I gazed out of the window at the passing landscape. It had finally stopped snowing now, and weak winter sunshine was slowly breaking through the white clouds overhead.

It seemed to me that this was a sign, that despite everything that had happened, Ruby and Noah would survive this latest tragedy. And with my help, they would come through the dark days ahead.

Epilogue

September 2005

'Scarlett, are you awake?'

I could hear the sound of Ruby's voice in the hospital room, and I desperately wanted to see my friend. There were things I had to say to her, but my eyelids refused to open. I searched my memory for what exactly was happening, and then remembered how I'd been brought into this hospital a few days earlier, after collapsing on my kitchen floor.

When at last I managed to prise my eyes open, Ruby's face swam into view, and I saw her peering closely at me from the side of the bed.

Somehow, I had been expecting to see a young Ruby – the one with glossy, dark hair, wide brown eyes, and clear smooth skin. The fifteen-year-old girl who turned up unexpectedly on my doorstep all those years ago; the girl who pretended she needed to borrow a cup of sugar, but who really needed a friend.

I have no idea why my mind was conjuring up these silly thoughts, because I knew Ruby was eighty-seven years old and no spring chicken, as my mama would have said. Ruby's glossy hair was now grey. And although her eyes were still a beautiful dark brown, her face was crinkled with lines – just like mine.

'Hello, Ruby...' My voice sounded raspy and dry in the silence of the sterile room, and my throat was parched. 'Could I have some water, please?' I whispered, and watched as she poured some into a cup from the jug at the side of my bed.

After I'd had a few sips of water and my throat felt better, I was suddenly impatient to move on to what Ruby needed to know before it was too late. 'Could you help me sit up, Ruby?' I asked.

Even though I was weak and could hardly breathe with the exertion of it all, she helped to prop me up on the pillows until I was at eye level with my lifelong friend. Ruby was watching me closely as she sat down on the side of my bed and waited, while I made a huge effort to keep my heavy eyes open.

'We need to talk,' I said, watching Ruby with her searching dark gaze on my face. 'I need to tell you how sorry I am,' I continued, wondering where to begin.

Ruby narrowed her eyes at me, then tentatively touched my arm. 'Scarlett, don't do this. What on earth are you sorry for?' she asked, shaking her head slightly in confusion.

'I'm sorry about what happened with Dick... and Reilly,' I told her breathlessly.

'None of that was your fault, Scarlett,' she countered, frowning. 'How could it have been?' She seemed puzzled by my apology. 'We've been over this many times before.'

In the many years since those terrible events, the feeling had persisted that I had somehow chosen Annika over Ruby that day. But the truth was that my precious child had needed urgent hospital attention right at the same moment that poor Ruby had needed me, too. And there had been no time to save them both.

I swallowed down the regret and tried hard to find the words to explain this to Ruby. 'The thing is… I've always wished I could have prevented Dick from attacking you,' I told her, knowing that terrible day had changed so many lives.

I shuddered and picked at a loose thread on the hospital blanket, as an image of nine-year-old Annika, lying at the bottom of the stairs, came into my head. I looked up to see Ruby staring down at my agitated fingers. 'If only I could have warned you, things would have been very different for you and Noah.'

'I have always wished that, too, Scarlett,' Ruby said, before putting her hand over mine and looking at me with a sad gaze. 'However, I know that if you'd been able to help, you would have done. Your mind was on Annika, who needed an ambulance urgently, and you had no choice. As parents, we do anything and everything we can to help our children. After all, look what Reilly did for Noah?'

I nodded, but my mind was still full of regret that we had not discussed this in the years since Reilly's funeral. Perhaps it had just been too painful. Ruby's voice interrupted my sombre thoughts.

'You've helped me and Noah enormously over the years,' she said. 'Just being around when I needed to talk, and listening to me, has been more than enough. Honestly, Scarlett, your support has been invaluable.'

She scrubbed a hand across her face as she spoke, then gave me a steady look. 'I don't know what I'm going to do without you, Scarlett,' she said, leaning forwards and giving me a gentle hug.

Ruby was right; I had done everything I could to support her and Noah in the intervening years, and we had remained close since the tragic day she'd learned of Reilly's passing. Then ten years ago, when my darling Frankie died and I had been broken with grief, I'd needed Ruby more than she needed me.

As we drew apart, I couldn't rid myself of the feeling that there was still so much I wanted to tell Ruby. But what else was there to say? I shook my head and tried to gather my thoughts, but they kept floating away from me, like a boat adrift on the open sea.

I became aware that Ruby was talking again. 'Scarlett, without you, my life would have been very different,' she said, setting her jaw. 'And for that, I'm grateful. Please know that you *have* made a difference.'

It was then I noticed Ruby was wearing the necklace. 'The amethyst is still so beautiful,' I told her, staring at the purple stone set in a surround of diamonds. I'd always had a fondness for the necklace, which I had been gifted in Calcutta so long ago.

'Do you remember, Ruby, that day you left home to live in at Hanningtons' store in Brighton, on the eve of WW2?' I asked her, seeing again the fifteen-year-old Ruby sitting in the front parlour of my house in Lewes.

Ruby was smiling now as we both remembered those early days, when the world was full of promise.

'Of course, Scarlett. How could I forget the day you gave me the necklace?' she said, then gave me a curious look. 'Tell me truthfully, Scarlett, did you really believe the necklace would protect me when I left home to move into Brighton?'

I thought hard for a moment. 'Well, I hoped it would protect you, Ruby. But despite what the man in Calcutta said, about the necklace having the power of protection, in the end it was just a necklace. A very beautiful one, it has to be said, but just a necklace all the same.'

Ruby gave an answering nod. 'We had grown fond of one another by then, Scarlett. And I understood that when war was declared, and I was moving away, you didn't want to lose me, the way you had lost your family to the Spanish Influenza,' she said.

I had to concede that was true, but there was one thing I'd never understood about the necklace. 'How come Jude sent the necklace back to you, along with the telegram, when Reilly went missing during the war? I thought you told me you gave it to Reilly to take with him, to keep him safe when he went off to fight?'

I'd never asked Ruby about this before, because she'd often found it too painful to talk about Reilly. But now was the time for the truth; it was all there was left.

'You're right, I did give it to Reilly,' she explained, 'and I thought he had taken it with him. But I learnt later that he didn't want to hurt my feelings by refusing to take it.'

Ruby stared into the middle distance as if remembering that day so long ago. 'He knew, you see... that he would have either lost it or had it taken away,' she said, and gave me a shaky smile.

'Reilly also knew how much I loved the necklace, and that you had given it to me. So, in the end, he told me he was taking it with him, but instead he gave it to Jude for safekeeping when he went off to fight.'

Ruby sighed. 'That was all such a long time ago, Scarlett, and I think it's time for me to go now.' She stood up and glanced towards the open doorway of the hospital room. 'It seems you have another visitor.'

I followed her gaze and saw a very special person

standing in the doorway. But even so, I was reluctant for Ruby to leave. I opened my mouth to ask her to stay, but no sound came out.

Ruby turned back and bent towards me before dropping a soft kiss on my forehead. 'Goodbye for now, my wonderful friend. I will always love you,' she whispered with tears in her eyes. Then she straightened up and walked purposefully out of the room.

Unable to speak for the lump which was lodged in my throat, I gazed longingly at Ruby's retreating back, sure in the knowledge that I would never see her again.

***

'Hello there, Grandma, how are you doing today?'

My grandson Jez stood next to my bed. His tall frame seemed to fill the hospital room, and he looked slightly awkward as he gazed at me with those familiar turquoise eyes.

'Hello, Jez. You never call me Grandma,' I joked, 'so why start now, this late in the day?' I longed to get up out of this bed and enfold him in my arms. Regret knotted my stomach that I couldn't manage this.

Jez was the favourite of my two grandsons. I'd never quite taken to his brother Pete in the same way, although I'd always tried to hide my feelings from Annika. What mother wanted to hear how one son was favoured over the other? And I wasn't proud of it.

With Jez, though, I had been drawn to him from the moment he was born. And it wasn't just that he looked similar to me, with those turquoise eyes of his; there was something else, something deeper. He thought the same way I did, and we were alike in so many ways. Jez had always called me Scarlett, and although neither of us knew why this was, it seemed right.

'It's good to see you, Scarlett,' he said now. 'I've missed our weekly tea and cake.' He gave a heavy sigh. 'I'm sorry, I meant to bring you some flowers, and I even picked some for you, but then I clean forgot to bring them with me.'

Jez had his own gardening business, and he had often popped into my house in Lewes when he was in the area, so that we could share a cuppa. 'I'm doing alright, Jez,' I lied, sinking back onto my pillows weakly.

He had always been a good boy, apart from a difficult time in his teens when he'd gone a bit wild and had needed a father's guiding hand. Annika's gentle giant of a husband, George, had died when Pete and Jez were little boys.

I had watched with dread as Jez reached his teenage years and began to go off the rails. But thankfully, after I'd explained the situation to Noah, he had stepped up to the challenge, and agreed to help the young Jez find his way in life.

Now, Jez eyed me warily before pulling up a chair and sitting down next to the bed. 'Are you alright, Scarlett?' he asked. 'You seem far away today.'

'I'm cool,' I said, using a word that Jez often used, which always made him smile. 'How's Annie?' I asked, changing from the tricky subject of me, and my deteriorating health, to the thorny issue of his wife.

Jez frowned and gazed down at his hands. 'Oh, Annie's alright, thanks,' he said, and then looked up at me. 'She sends her love and said she'll come with me next time I visit you.'

There wouldn't be a next time, and I could see from my grandson's expression that he knew it, too. Behind that façade of trying to act normally, Jez was struggling with my imminent demise.

I had no words of comfort for him right now but reassured myself that he would be fine without me. After all, he still had Annika, and his brother Pete. And I knew Ruby and Noah would look out for him, too.

Besides, I had no desire to see his wife Annie; she was a sweet girl, but she wasn't right for Jez, and I could see their marriage would soon end in divorce. The two of them had grown up together, and fallen into a relationship as soon as they were old enough. But already Annie was stifling Jez, and they hadn't been married long.

Jez needed someone more spirited and more suited to him. And I hoped he would find that other someone one day; someone who would make him happy enough to wipe away that constant frown on his face.

Just then, the nurse bustled in, took my temperature, and plumped up my pillows before bustling out again. After she'd gone, Jez gazed at me sadly and I understood he needed to tell me something. 'What is it?' I asked, hoping it wasn't something I couldn't answer.

'Are you sad to be going?' he whispered. 'I'll miss you so much,' he added, with a pained expression. 'What on earth will I do without you, Scarlett?' he said, echoing Ruby's words, as tears glistened at the corner of his eyes.

I swallowed the hard lump in my throat. Reaching forwards, I took Jez's hand in mine, and saw the irony of his youthful hand in my old and gnarled one. He was young and had his whole life ahead of him, with all the joy and pain that life brought with it.

'Oh, Jez, my dear grandson,' I said, looking straight

339

into his eyes. 'I've had a good life, and after all, what more could a person ask for? I'm ninety-six years old, and I've been lucky enough to live in my own home until the end. We have to look at the blessings in life, don't we?' I reasoned.

When he nodded solemnly, I was desperate to reassure him. 'You'll be fine. You've got plenty of people to look out for you; people who love you. And believe me, being loved is the most important thing in the world.'

Jez's chin trembled slightly. 'You're right, Scarlett,' he said shakily. 'We both have some very caring people in our lives,' he reflected, leaning back in his chair without taking his eyes off my face.

That was more like the Jez I knew and loved. 'We certainly do. We are both very lucky.' I was trying to smile, but felt as if I might burst into tears at any moment, and I didn't want to cry in front of Jez.

I bit down on my lower lip. 'Considering what my start in life was, I haven't done too badly,' I told him truthfully.

Jez gave me a knowing look and ran his fingers through his thick fair hair. 'Cool. I couldn't believe what you told me, you know, about the Spanish Influenza? I mean, losing everyone like that... how did you get through that and find your way in life?'

A warm glow filled my tired old body at his words, but the truth was far simpler than that. 'Determination not to be beaten, I think that was it, Jez,' I said, trying to recall what had spurred me on in those early days when it seemed the whole world was against me.

'And wanting to have a better life than what was mapped out for me.' That had definitely been a factor in how my life turned out. Because even if Ma and Da hadn't perished, I knew even at that early age, that I wanted my life to be different from theirs.

Jez still didn't quite understand. 'I know, but to be the sole survivor of your family, that must have been dreadful! You're really a true inspiration, Scarlett,' he insisted, looking at me affectionately.

My chest was heavy now, and my throat ached as I remembered my family. 'Thank you, but when it came to the Spanish Influenza I always felt as if I'd been saved for a reason... been given the chance of life when others hadn't. If that was true, I had to make the most of my time, and not waste a single moment.'

Jez smiled gently. 'Most people might have been broken by that, Scarlett, but not you,' he said proudly.

I thought about this for a moment. 'As I told Ruby once, what happened somehow made me stronger, more determined to have the things I wanted in life. Although what I thought I wanted and what I actually needed, were two very different things.'

Jez blinked at me in confusion. 'What do you mean by that?' he asked.

'I thought I wanted material things and that I didn't need love,' I told him, lost in another world as I remembered again how it had been. 'Love wouldn't bring me riches, or so I thought,' I said truthfully. 'But when I met your grandfather, it all became clear.'

I looked back at my grandson, who was hanging onto my every word. 'I understood then that what I was really looking for was love, and with Frankie, I had found it at last.'

Jez looked pensive and less burdened than when he had first walked through the door. 'I could see how much you loved each other, even after all those years of being together,' he said. 'I just wish... I mean

Annie's lovely and all, but…' His voice trailed off as he looked sadly down at his hands.

'There will be someone else out there for you, Jez, if Annie is not the right one,' I reassured him. And when Jez looked up at me, he seemed to understand. 'Just be patient, you'll know when it happens.'

Suddenly, the energy was draining from my body, and the world began to fade away. But as I sank back onto the pillows, I was desperate to cling on for dear life. I just needed a bit longer – a few more minutes with Jez.

'I think you should rest now, and I need to get back to work,' he said with a hitch in his voice. 'I'll bring Mum in to see you later,' Jez added unconvincingly. And I could see in those beautiful eyes of his that he knew, like I did, that I probably wouldn't be here later.

Jez bent towards me and gave me a hug, and I held tightly to him for a moment. Then he let me go, and I watched my grandson walk towards the door as I took in a shallow shuddering breath.

As he reached the doorway, Jez turned and gave me a wave. 'Goodbye, Scarlett, I love you,' he said shakily, then he disappeared down the corridor.

Letting out a long sigh, I regretted that I wouldn't get the chance to say goodbye to my darling Annika, Frankie's beautiful child, whom we had both loved and cherished, and who had always been a joy. But counting my blessings, as I'd just told my grandson to do, it had been a gift to see Jez and Ruby one last time – two of the most special people in my life.

I was thankful that I'd had a good life. There had been times when it had taken courage, and determination, to get to where I needed to be, and times when supporting Ruby over the years had been difficult.

But somehow, I had done all of those things and come through, and I was grateful for that as I lay wearily back on the soft pillows, closed my eyes, and slept.

If you've enjoyed this novel, do please leave a review – a few lines is all it takes. It's helpful to readers and makes authors very happy (me included)!

FREE COPY OF DELETED SCENES FROM
AMETHYST

Sign up to Susan's newsletter and claim your FREE book.

Deleted Scenes From Amethyst is an insight into India McCarthy's life before she steps into Ruby's house for the first time, in The Amethyst Necklace. It is exclusive content for my readers only, and a very special thank you for signing up to my newsletter.

Susan's newsletter is sent out only when there is something special to communicate – such as new book releases, special promotions and price reductions.

Go to the link below to be taken to the sign-up page. Your details will not be shared and you can unsubscribe at any time.

https://susangriffinauthor.com/subscribe-to-my-newsletter

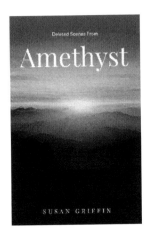

OTHER TITLES BY THIS AUTHOR
Bird in a Gilded Cage
The Amethyst Necklace
The Man in the Painting - coming soon.

About the Author

I live in East Sussex on the edge of the Ashdown Forest with my husband and a cat called Dave. I love writing romance with a mystery at its heart, and weaving secrets of the past with the present. I use my passion for history to research my novels, and am interested in how pioneering women in the past have managed to overcome adversity.

When I'm not writing I'm either singing with my local Rock Choir, or going for long walks in the nearby countryside.

Website:
https://susangriffinauthor.com/

Facebook:
https://www.facebook.com/susangriffinauthor

Acknowledgements

Research for Scarlett's Story led me to the resistance fighters in enemy occupied France during WW2, in particular Andree de Jongh (code named Dedee), whose bravery and courage made her a true heroine.

Andree founded The Comet Line during the war, and along with other brave resistance fighters saved countless Allied airmen. My research into Andree included reading the book 'Little Cyclone' by Airey Neave, which tells her story.

Other characters in the book based on real people are Tante Go and L'Oncle, their two children, and Florentino who was a real Basque Guide. All the resistance fighters risked everything to help others, and their courage and bravery was truly awe- inspiring.